AUTHORSHIP'S WAKE

AUTHORSHIP'S WAKE

Writing After the Death of the Author

Philip Sayers

BLOOMSBURY ACADEMIC
NEW YORK • LONDON • OXFORD • NEW DELHI • SYDNEY

BLOOMSBURY ACADEMIC
Bloomsbury Publishing Inc
1385 Broadway, New York, NY 10018, USA
50 Bedford Square, London, WC1B 3DP, UK

BLOOMSBURY, BLOOMSBURY ACADEMIC and the Diana logo
are trademarks of Bloomsbury Publishing Plc

First published in the United States of America 2021
This edition published 2022

Copyright © Philip Sayers, 2021

Cover image © Getty Images

For legal purposes the Acknowledgments on pp. 157–158 constitute
an extension of this copyright page.

All rights reserved. No part of this publication may be reproduced or transmitted in any form or by any means, electronic or mechanical, including photocopying, recording, or any information storage or retrieval system, without prior permission in writing from the publishers.

Bloomsbury Publishing Inc does not have any control over, or responsibility for, any third-party websites referred to or in this book. All internet addresses given in this book were correct at the time of going to press. The author and publisher regret any inconvenience caused if addresses have changed or sites have ceased to exist, but can accept no responsibility for any such changes.

Whilst every effort has been made to locate copyright holders the publishers would be grateful to hear from any person(s) not here acknowledged.

Library of Congress Cataloging-in-Publication Data
Names: Sayers, Philip, author.
Title: Authorship's wake : writing after the death of the author / Philip Sayers.
Description: New York : Bloomsbury Academic, 2020. | Includes
bibliographical references and index. |
Summary: "A book about writers and thinkers who were taught that the author is dead how their work consequently negotiates what it means to be an author"– Provided by publisher.
Identifiers: LCCN 2020031430 (print) | LCCN 2020031431 (ebook) | ISBN 9781501367670 (hardback) | ISBN 9781501372186 (paperback) | ISBN 9781501367687 (epub) | ISBN 9781501367694 (pdf)
Subjects: LCSH: Authorship–Philosophy. | Critical theory.
Classification: LCC PN175 .S29 2020 (print) | LCC PN175 (ebook) | DDC 808.02–dc23
LC record available at https://lccn.loc.gov/2020031430
LC ebook record available at https://lccn.loc.gov/2020031431

ISBN:	HB:	978-1-5013-6767-0
	PB:	978-1-5013-7218-6
	ePDF:	978-1-5013-6769-4
	eBook:	978-1-5013-6768-7

Typeset by Integra Software Solutions Pvt. Ltd.

To find out more about our authors and books visit www.bloomsbury.com
and sign up for our newsletters.

CONTENTS

INTRODUCTION: "WORDS STREAMING IN YOUR WAKE"   1
    1. Sole Authors   1
    2. Writing After   9
    3. Communication, Intention, Agency, Labor   15

Chapter 1
COMMUNICATION: MAGGIE NELSON AND THE LITERARY
TEXT AS LETTER   19
    1. Introduction   19
    2. Letters   21
       2.1. The Literary Text as Letter   21
       2.2. Epistolarity and *The Argonauts*   23
       2.3. The Risks of Letter-Writing   25
       2.4. Silence   27
    3. Communication, Nonsense, and Space   29
       3.1. "Whereof One Cannot Speak"   30
       3.2. Acknowledged Nonsense   34
       3.3. Space   36
       3.4. The Work of the Reader   39
    4. *The Argonauts* and the Ethics of Space   40
       4.1. Fragments   42
       4.2. Allusions and Family-Making   44

Chapter 2
INTENTION: THE INCONSISTENT ANTI-INTENTIONALISM OF
ZADIE SMITH AND JUDITH BUTLER   47
    1. Introduction   47
       1.1. Consulting the Oracle   47
       1.2. Intention and the Authorship Debates   49
    2. *On Beauty* and Anti-Intentionalism   52
       2.1. Zadie Smith and the Return to Authorial Intention   52
       2.2. *On Beauty* against the Critique of Intention   55
       2.3. *On Beauty* and Psychoanalysis   57
       2.4. *On Beauty* and Critique   60
    3. The Humanities Quandary   64
       3.1. Judith Butler and the Humanities Quandary   64
       3.2. Howard Belsey and the Humanities Quandary   68

	3.3. "In Effect If Not in Intent"	70
4.	Conclusion	75

Chapter 3
AGENCY: ROLAND BARTHES AND THE MEN WHO HOLD FORTH — 77

1.	Introduction	77
	1.1. "Mr. Very Important"	77
	1.2. "Men Explain Things to Me" in Context	79
2.	Autofiction versus the Man Who Holds Forth	83
	2.1. *I Love Dick*	83
	2.2. *How Should a Person Be?*	87
	2.3. *10:04*	90
	2.4. "What Is It to Hold Forth?"	92
3.	Roland Barthes, Man Who Holds Forth?	98
	3.1. The Charge of Apoliticism	98
	3.2. Barthes and Queer Politics	100
	3.3. Barthes and Post-1968 Orientalism	104
	3.4. Barthes and Feminism	107
	3.5. Barthes as Teacher and Author	111

Chapter 4
LABOR: DAVID FOSTER WALLACE, COWBOY OF INFORMATION — 117

1.	Introduction	117
	1.1. Bureaucratizing Writing	117
2.	Accountants, Writers, and Cowboys	122
	2.1. On Amy Hungerford Not Reading DFW	122
	2.2. Accountants	126
	2.3. Writers	129
	2.4. Cowboys	135
3.	Two Broad Arcs	143
	3.1. Neoliberalism and Information Work	143
	3.2. Low Theory	148

CONCLUSION: STUDY GROUPS — 153

Acknowledgments	157
Notes	159
Bibliography	196
Index	211

INTRODUCTION: "WORDS STREAMING IN YOUR WAKE"

1. Sole Authors

The fat sun stalls by the phone masts. Anti-climb paint turns sulphurous on school gates and lampposts. In Willesden people go barefoot, the streets turn European, there is a mania for eating outside. She keeps to the shade. Redheaded. On the radio: I am the sole author of the dictionary that defines me. A good line—write it out on the back of a magazine. In a hammock, in the garden of a basement flat. Fenced in, on all sides.

Four gardens along, in the estate, a grim girl on the third floor screams Anglo-Saxon at nobody. Juliet balcony, projecting for miles. It ain't like that. Nah it ain't like that. Don't you start. Fag in hand. Fleshy, lobster-red.

I am the sole

I am the sole author

Pencil leaves no mark on magazine pages. Somewhere she has read that the gloss gives you cancer.[1]

This is the beginning of Zadie Smith's 2012 novel *NW*. Leah Hanwell (the "she" of the passage) sits in a hammock on a hot afternoon in North West London and hears a phrase on the radio: "I am the sole author of the dictionary that defines me." She likes the phrase—"a good line"—and decides to "write it out on the back of a magazine."

"I am the sole author of the dictionary that defines me." I have authority, the status of authorship, and I am the only one to have it. What I am the author of is "the dictionary that defines me": I am defined by this dictionary, in the manner of an entry, but I am the one who is writing the definition. I am both author and authored—but I do not author myself directly; I do so through the dictionary, through language. Language is both what I "author" and what "defines me."

The phrase recurs throughout the short (a little over a page) chapter—or rather, its beginning recurs: "I am the sole. The sole. The sole."[2] Only once in Leah's attempts to "write it out" does she make it to "author," and when she does, it is to no effect: "Pencil leaves no mark on magazine pages." There is at least a double irony here: Leah aspires to be an "author," but the phrase she decides to write is not her own (it comes from the radio), and moreover she cannot seem to complete the act of writing—and it is the word "author" that is the stumbling block.

Also frustrating Leah's authorial ambitions is the distraction of the "grim girl on the third floor." Leah initially misreads her as screaming "at nobody" but later notices "a tiny device tucked in her ear": the Bluetooth headset signaling that she is addressing somebody after all.[3] In this conversation, the girl fights off a different misinterpretation, makes her own claim to authority: "It ain't like that." Both characters, then, are thwarted in their attempts to be "the sole author of the dictionary that defines" them.

In fact, *NW* as a whole is in some sense a novel about characters attempting, with mixed degrees of success, to be authors of the dictionaries that define them. The third and longest of the novel's five sections, for example, recounts the life history of Leah's childhood best friend Keisha Blake. The two women—one white (Leah), one Black (Keisha)—grow up in the same London council estate, but whereas Leah (as the first scene establishes) has trouble even writing the word "author," Keisha rewrites her life's trajectory, and even her identity, with apparent ease. Even as a small child, she thrills at the "unforgettable pulse of authorial omnipotence" she experiences when her predictions prove correct: "Maybe," she thinks, "the world really was hers for the making."[4] In university, she renames herself Natalie and gets—as Smith puts it in a chapter named "The sole author"—"crazy busy with self-invention."[5] She studies to be a lawyer and meets the man who will become her husband: Frank, who shares Natalie's insistence on seeing herself as an agent rather than a victim, as author rather than authored. There are in fact *two* chapters in the novel titled "The sole author," and Frank is the subject of the second.[6] By this point, the phrase has become a byword for a belief in individual social mobility, for a Thatcherite worldview that understands failure to be a question of personal responsibility rather than of institutions, structures, or luck. This is evident in the way that Natalie talks about Michelle Holland, one of three students from the working-class high school Natalie attended to gain entrance to the same prestigious university. When Michelle drops out halfway through her final year, it is this phrase—"I am the sole author"[7]—that comes to Natalie's mind, an indicator of her resolute belief in the power of individual self-fashioning. Under Natalie's worldview, the fact that Michelle's father is "in jail, [her] mother sectioned," is no excuse for dropping out: the responsibility is all on Michelle and what Natalie perceives as her failure to properly author herself.[8]

NW not only depicts the ways in which characters hang stubbornly to a fleeting sense of autonomy; it also demonstrates the destructive effects that such wishful thinking can have on other people. Natalie's belief that she is a "sole author" proves to be dangerous as well as delusional. At the novel's end, her marriage to Frank is in a state of uncertainty, after he discovers that she has been meeting strangers online for group sex. More insidiously, the novel's final scene gives us one more act of "authorial omnipotence." Responding to the murder of one man (named Felix) and to an encounter with another—their former schoolmate Nathan Bogle, now living on the streets and involved in various illegal activities—Natalie doubles down on her neoliberal I-am-the-sole-author vision of social mobility: "we worked harder ... We wanted to get out. People like Bogle—they didn't want it enough."[9] And she goes a step further: not only is Bogle guilty of not wanting success enough; he is also, she falsely concludes, responsible for the killing, which took place close to where she encountered him. "'I think I know what happened in Albert Road,' said Natalie Blake."[10] Just as she had been exhilarated as a child by the feeling that her acts of authorship could determine the world around her, so she decides here that the story of Felix's murder is hers for the telling. The novel ends with Natalie and Leah calling the police to report Bogle as a person of interest in the homicide. Bogle is the collateral damage of their desire to be the sole authors of the dictionaries that define them.

I begin with this summary of Smith's novel and the way it deploys the figure of the "sole author" for two reasons. First, *NW* clearly and concisely does what all of the texts I read in this study do: it makes a claim about what it means to be an author, in a manner that simultaneously alludes to and moves beyond the ways in which critical conversations about authorship have been framed over the past half century. "The sole author" in *NW* is not just a way for Smith to get at aesthetic and hermeneutic questions of the type raised most famously by Roland Barthes in "The Death of the Author"; it is also a figure through which her novel engages in deeply political questions: the lasting impact of Margaret Thatcher's neoliberal government; racial, gender, and class politics and the rhetoric of responsibility; the role of the state and of the individual in relation to crime, both violent and nonviolent. In the way that it posits a theory of what an author is and does *and* brings out the concrete stakes of such a theory, this textual example is therefore a microcosm of *Authorship's Wake* as a whole.

Second, the example of *NW* is a way for me to illustrate the book's key methodological commitment. In what follows, I want to highlight two different ways of reading Smith's concern with authorship—one a widespread and useful yet also importantly limiting approach, the other the approach that I adopt throughout the four chapters of *Authorship's Wake*.

The first way of reading this passage would go something like this: Zadie Smith (born 1975) is of the generation of writers who did undergraduate humanities degrees in Anglo-American universities at a time when critical theory—predominantly of the French poststructuralist variety—was in ascendance. At Cambridge University—as she recounts in her essay "Rereading Barthes and Nabokov"—she read Roland Barthes's "The Death of the Author" and found it empowering as a reader, but as she became an author herself her feelings about the authorial-death thesis became rather more mixed.[11] Accordingly, her fiction, with its numerous aspiring authors and its occasional semi-affectionate lambasting of the pretensions of critical theory (above all in 2005's *On Beauty*), can be understood as an extended response to theory's critique of the autonomous subject in general and of the author in particular. Under this reading, we can place Smith alongside other writers producing work after Barthes's famous essay who have—more or less explicitly—engaged with critical theory and the death of the author in their work.

Here we could think about the novelists (including Marguerite Duras, Margaret Atwood, and J. M. Coetzee) considered by Judith Ryan in the chapter of her *The Novel after Theory* (2012) that focuses on literary responses to Barthes.[12] Alternatively, we could consider Smith in relation to Dave Eggers and David Fincher: a writer and a filmmaker whose works—according to Benjamin Widiss in *Obscure Invitations: The Persistence of the Author in Twentieth-Century American Literature* (2011)—explicitly rehearse the authorial-death thesis and ultimately "refute Barthes' conclusions."[13] Looking at more recent work by theory-acquainted novelists like Teju Cole, Jennifer Egan, and Ben Lerner, Nicholas Dames argues in a 2012 article for *n+1* that by the beginning of the twenty-first century, "Theory had become—at least for students, ex-students, and academics—part of the furniture of their lives, in no need of defense and yet scarcely revolutionary."[14] For Dames, novels by Cole, Egan, and Lerner do not directly refute theory: rather, by presenting theory as dispensable intellectual furnishing within a realist novel—the very genre that theory deconstructed[15]—they indirectly testify to its fading relevance. In a 2015 article, Mitchum Huehls expands on the work of Ryan, Widiss, and Dames, offering an analysis of Salvador Plascencia, Ben Marcus, and Percival Everett as "authors of post-theory theory novels": novels that allude to theory, drawing on it as a resource for aesthetic innovation, yet keeping it at a certain distance.[16] For Huehls, theory *deconstructs*, whereas the post-theory theory novel—arriving at a moment after theory has "lost its cachet as the one true faith"[17]—"use[s] theory's concepts to build, rather than undermine, the world."[18]

Under a reading in the vein of Ryan, Widiss, Dames, or Huehls, *NW* comes into view as a novel defined by its relation to the project of critical theory, especially in its anti-authorial valences. From this perspective, we would read the phrase "I am the sole author of the dictionary that defines me" and, in its implication that the subject is defined by language even if they also wield language, we would see an echo of Barthes, who uses precisely the same metaphor—the dictionary—to illustrate his claim that "it is language which speaks, not the author."[19] For him, a writer's ideas are neither original nor outside of language: the "inner 'thing'" a writer seeks to express is "only a ready-formed dictionary," a set of significations that precedes and exceeds any one individual.[20] Smith's choice of words—"I am the sole author of the dictionary that defines me"—reads, then, as an allusion to Barthes's essay. And the way that she undermines Leah's authorial ambitions—having her continually fail to write out this overheard phrase—seems like an expansion of this allusion. Widiss would call this a "rehearsal"[21] of "The Death of the Author": it demonstrates Smith's theoretical smarts, her cultural capital, and situates her work in a longer history of novelistic engagement with ideas from other fields of intellectual production.[22]

But the consequence of reading *NW* as *alluding to* or *rehearsing* theoretical ideas is that the novel not only ends up being defined by its relation to theory, being reduced to a mere instance of an overarching theoretical concept; it also ends up being defined by its *separation from* theory. Under a reading like this, the novel is understood as a relatively autonomous form: it can absorb material from all sorts of sources outside of itself, but its boundaries remain stable. The novel writes back to theory—which is also to say that it is something other than theory. The theory novels that Judith Ryan reads "incorporate theory, they reflect on it, complicate it, and sometimes go beyond it," but they remain separate from it.[23]

The critical work I've cited provides an indispensable literary history of the novel's engagement with critical theory, but also a limited one. Here, then, I want to demonstrate the second of two possible approaches to reading *NW*'s concern with the sole author, the approach I take throughout this study. This method is premised on the following wager: that we would learn more from post-theory texts like *NW* if we laid aside the generic distinction between literature and theory. Instead of understanding *NW* as a novelistic rehearsal of or response to a set of theoretical ideas that originated in 1960s France and went on to influence Euro-American literary production in the decades that followed, why not read Smith and Barthes simply as participants in the same extended and transnational conversation about authorship? The difference between the previous approach and mine might at first glance seem relatively minor, but I would suggest that it accomplishes at least three things: it equips us to deal with the fact that (now more than ever) literature and theory are closely interwoven, it enables a move beyond the French poststructuralist version of the authorship debate, and in so doing it connects the figure of the author to a series of new and vital issues—political, cultural, and economic. Let us take these one by one.

First, then, laying aside the distinction between the literary and the theoretical recognizes a reality of postwar intellectual and literary production—that the writing of theory and criticism and the writing of poetry and fiction are increasingly intertwined. Institutionally speaking, this commingling is a function of what Mark McGurl calls, in his book of the same title, the Program Era: a periodic designation that demonstrates his argument that "the rise of the creative writing program stands as the most important event in postwar American literary history."[24] In the Program Era, both theory and literature are produced in close proximity to the same institution: the university (and in particular, the English department). They are taught in the same classrooms, to (and often by) the same people. While McGurl devotes relatively little time in his account to the resulting influence of one on the other, a glance at contemporary literary culture brings to light a plethora of cross-pollination—not only in the case of so-called theory novels like the ones Ryan and Dames discuss but also, perhaps more radically, in the case of texts that themselves confound the generic distinctions between the theoretical and the literary.[25] What such texts make visible—as an example, let's take Maggie Nelson's *The Argonauts* (2015), the subject of Chapter 1—is not just the fact that many contemporary writers are adept at integrating theoretical, narrative, poetic, essayistic, and other modes, but that the distinction between such modes was never really all that clear to begin with. Nietzsche, Benjamin, Fanon, Barthes, Du Bois, Irigaray: many of the writers who have come to be canonized under the heading of critical theory could just as profitably be read as makers of literature, or of other forms of writing. This indeed was the premise of a course that Nelson taught at CalArts under the title "Wild Theory": a course focused on "works which, for a variety of reasons, cannot be easily domesticated into a single discipline (i.e. philosophy, literary criticism, cultural criticism, creative nonfiction, and so on)."[26] Some of the titles this study considers—*The Argonauts*, Chris Kraus's *I Love Dick*, Roland Barthes's Collège de France lectures and seminars—might fit best under the heading of "wild theory." Others seem to skew more clearly toward the literary (Zadie Smith's novels, David Foster Wallace's *The Pale King*), and still others toward a relatively straightforward version of critical theory (Judith Butler's *Precarious Life*). Ultimately, though, I am interested in working toward a "more unified postwar canon" that does justice to the fact that—both institutionally and aesthetically—the theoretical and the literary are difficult to disentangle from one another.[27]

The second benefit to an approach that lays aside generic affiliation is that, put simply, the version of the authorship conversation we are used to has run its course. Expanding the range of participants—breaking the monopoly that critical theory and literary criticism have held over the debate—is a way not so much to revive a flagging conversation as the opposite: to show that, even as the academy has grown understandably fatigued with its particular version of the authorship debate, there has been an intellectually exciting conversation about authorship going on all along; it's just that it has been going on in texts not deemed to have sufficient scholarly authority to be part of the debate. From within the constraints of the scholarly version of that conversation, as any number of commentators on authorship have felt obliged to note, it is difficult to escape the centrality of two short essays, each half a century old: Barthes's "The Death of the Author" and Foucault's "What Is an Author?"[28] More recent scholarship on authorship has tended either to cement the significance of these two essays or to veer away from theory altogether and toward legal studies, book history, and other more historically oriented fields.[29] My approach here is closer to the former than to the latter—it is resolutely theoretical rather than historical in its intellectual loyalties—but it nevertheless tries to reorient the critical conversation so that the same two articles by Barthes and Foucault no longer occupy such a field-defining role.

In the case of each of these essays, I have taken contrasting approaches. On the one hand, *Authorship's Wake* ignores Foucault more or less altogether:

he appears as an interlocutor in Chapter 4's discussion of neoliberalism, but "What Is an Author?" remains entirely absent. At the other extreme, Barthes is everywhere in the chapters that follow. "The Death of the Author" has already made its presence felt in these opening pages, and it will continue to be a key reference point, but part of the argument that emerges from the aggregate of the following chapters is that "The Death of the Author" represents only a fraction of Barthes's contribution to the authorship conversation. It has become de rigueur in recaps of the authorship debates to point out the difference between "The Death of the Author" (published in 1967) and several of the texts that Barthes wrote in the 1970s (including *Sade Fourier Loyola* and *The Pleasure of the Text*), in which he seems far more sympathetic to the figure whose death he had declared and far less hostile to the intermingling of criticism and biography.[30] Here, however, my focus is on the triptych of volumes published in English by Columbia University Press between 2005 and 2013, based on the lecture courses and seminars he taught at the Collège de France between 1977 and his death in 1980: *How to Live Together*, *The Neutral*, and *The Preparation of the Novel*. These texts not only contextualize "The Death of the Author" as a particular moment within the overall trajectory of Barthes's thinking; they also provide a far more developed, mature, and (to use that most Barthesean of adjectives) nuanced theory of authorship, one that moves away from the questions that animated "The Death of the Author" (voice, textuality, originality) and toward new avenues (labor, power, psychoanalysis, affect).[31]

My interest in Barthes stems in part also from the fact that, as I mentioned above, his writing (especially in the final few years of his life) hovers on the boundary between the theoretical and the literary. By 1978 he is (or at least claims to be) writing a novel (the preparation of which he discusses in his final two years of teaching), but Barthes is also at this point working on *Camera Lucida* and *Mourning Diary*: texts that, like the writing of Maggie Nelson (for whom Barthes—as I discuss in Chapter 1—is a major influence), mix the personal and the theoretical in ways that put pressure on the distinction between scholarly and literary writing. My decision to include Barthes so prominently in this study therefore has as much to do with his stature as a (literary) author as with his stature as a (theoretical) critic. Implicit in this reasoning, moreover, is the argument that it is important to let authors have a say in the matter of their supposed death. The work of Ryan and Widiss, for instance, does this to an extent: in both of their monographs, novelists are given a chance to rebut the argument that their voice and intentions are irrelevant or never existed in the first place. But it seems to remain difficult to escape the shadow of the New Critical insistence that literature and criticism are two autonomous forms, that literature can be the object of criticism but never the subject doing the critique: the theory novels that Ryan discusses, for example, may well resist or complicate the claim that the author is dead, but *The Novel after Theory* tends to position these texts as footnotes to a conversation about authorship in which "The Death of the Author" remains immutably central.³² As far as I am concerned, such rigidity not only discards one of the key commitments of French theory—that everything can be read as text and therefore as a valid source of knowledge; it also does a deep disservice to the authorship conversation: as long as debate remains centered on the same two critical essays, we will be answering the same questions to diminishing returns, while shunting off to the sidelines the fact that there are many writers—especially in the last decade—whose work proves that the conversation about what it means to be an author is more vital than ever.

By listening to new voices such as Zadie Smith (and reframing existing voices such as Barthes), it becomes possible to ask new questions and thereby to make a new case for why authorship is worth talking about in the twenty-first century. This brings me to the third aspect of the case for a transgeneric and transnational approach: working with a more unified canon that includes a transatlantic campus novel and the teaching notes of a French theorist under the same roof makes visible the fact that authorship is at the center of a whole range of urgent issues across a variety of realms: aesthetic, hermeneutic, ethical, political, economic. Let me illustrate this argument via the example of *NW*. I suggested that if we follow a reading of *NW* in the vein of Ryan or Widiss, Smith's novel comes into focus as a rehearsal of a theoretical argument about authorship framed in relation to questions of textuality and originality. This is certainly part of the picture but, as I've suggested, the way in which Smith returns throughout the novel to the figure of the "sole author" ought to clue us into the fact that authorship, in *NW*, is the starting point for a far broader analysis of neoliberalism, social mobility, and race in twenty-first-century London. Like many critics, I would understand *NW* as a profoundly political novel.³³ Crucially, though, I would argue that it is Smith's engagement with *authorship* that forms the basis for her novel's political import. Rather than seeing *NW* as a novel that responds (as in Ryan's readings of Atwood or Coetzee) to the Barthesean version of the critique of the author, I read it as a text about authorship primarily in a political sense, a text as much about authority as about authorship more narrowly understood. Under this reading, *NW* is a book about two women who attempt, with mixed degrees of success, to be the sole authors of their lives, and it is a novel about who gets shut out—often violently—of the life narratives they write for themselves. As Smith herself puts it in a piece for *The Guardian*'s book club, *NW* gets at the fact that happy endings are "never universal. Someone is always left behind. And in the London I grew up in—as it is today—that someone is more often than not a young black man" (like Bogle, whom Natalie reports to the police).³⁴ To claim the status of "sole author" in *NW* not only entails a set of Thatcherite neoliberal ideas about the sovereignty of the individual (and, in Thatcher's famous terms, the belief that there is no such thing as society); it is also an act with concrete and violent consequences, consequences that tend to be distributed along lines—of age, race, and gender—determined by specific histories of exclusion and oppression.³⁵

Authorship's Wake is invested throughout in precisely this kind of reading—a kind of reading that locates authorship at the center of a whole range of specific issues, extending far beyond the chiefly aesthetic and hermeneutic stakes of "The Death of the Author." In the chapters that follow, these issues run from the smallest of scales (Chapter 1: a mother's negotiation of the ethical pitfalls of writing a letter to her son) to the largest (Chapter 4: shifts in the forms of property and labor in postwar America), addressing along the way a number of ongoing cultural conversations (Chapter 2: free speech and hate speech on university campuses; Chapter 3: "mansplaining" and the gendered divisions that determine whose voice is authoritative). I argue, therefore, that the authorship debate—which has for the last half century been centered around essays by Barthes and Foucault—is not a relic of the 1980s apex of high theory's reception in the Anglo-American university. In fact, over the last two decades it has entered a new and vital phase, precisely because of the fact that it now includes a whole range of new participants, across lines of nation, language, and genre. This study provides a platform for those participants and in so doing makes the case that in contemporary cultural production—literary, theoretical, or somewhere in between—the author is a more essential figure than ever.

2. Writing After

I have aligned this study's approach firmly on the side of the theoretical rather than the historical version of the critical conversation about authorship— broadly speaking, with the version that takes Barthes's dissection of authorial voice and polysemic textuality rather than Foucault's legally oriented genealogy of the author function as its starting point. Nevertheless, the premise of the project not only narrows in on a specific intellectual-historical moment—as the subtitle puts it, my canon is a body of "Writing after the Death of the Author"— but it also entails a specific way of thinking about history itself. What precisely does it mean to write *after* something—and, more specifically, to write *after the death* of something? What does it mean to write in authorship's wake? This is the question that the remainder of the introduction will address.

There is no shortage of ideas to draw on when posing the question of *afterness*. In any number of specific contexts, and through a wide array of intellectual genealogies, humanities scholarship—and theoretically oriented humanities scholarship in particular—has not only been answering questions that begin "what comes after ... ?"; it has also devoted a great deal of energy to interrogating what is at stake when we ask these kinds of questions. What kind of understanding of time and progress is operating in a question of this sort? What ideological purpose might such a chronology serve? And which alternative temporalities thereby remain unarticulated or unthought? For instance, postcolonial studies could be understood as a discipline founded on the interrogation of the assumption implicit in its name: that the colonial is something that one can be "post": in a widely echoed move, Ato Quayson insists on the necessity of "disentangl[ing] the term 'postcolonial' from its implicit dimension of chronological supersession, that aspect of its prefix which suggests that the colonial stage has been surpassed and left behind."[36] The continued presence of decolonization activism—in contexts ranging from the rethinking of university curricula to Palestinian liberation movements—testifies to the fact that colonization, in its settler and non-settler varieties, is anything but a thing of the past and that to think otherwise is precisely to perpetuate colonial ideology. In another context entirely, much work in queer theory, from Lee Edelman's polemic *No Future*, through the melancholic strains of José Esteban Muñoz's *Cruising Utopia* and Heather Love's *Feeling Backward*, to Elizabeth Freeman's critique of "chrononormativity" in *Time Binds*,[37] has been oriented toward a critique of the way that heteronormativity reproduces itself via a specific construction of temporal succession and futurity. Queer temporalities, for these scholars, can therefore provide resources for those of us invested in ways of thinking and being outside of the rhythms of what Edelman calls "reproductive futurism."[38]

Postcolonial studies and queer theory are by no means outliers in this respect. Trauma studies, informed by psychoanalysis, troubles normative chronology by focusing on deferrals and repetitions. Black Studies does so by making visible "the afterlife of slavery"[39] in the "haunting" of Black North American experience[40] and the "anarchronic improvisation" of the Black radical aesthetic tradition.[41] And Anthropocene scholarship such as Jedediah Purdy's *After Nature* does so via an argument that mirrors postcolonial studies: if for Quayson we have never been postcolonial (because colonialism continues to structure present-day lived experience), for Purdy we have *always* been "post-natural": the idea of nature as an entity that "stands apart from human beings" never really existed in the first place.[42] For postcolonial and Anthropocene scholars alike, what appears new and unprecedented in fact has considerable continuity with what came before. From foundational figures like Hegel, Marx, and Freud, through twentieth-century giants (to take two: Walter Benjamin, in "Theses on the Philosophy of History"; Jacques Derrida, in *Specters of Marx*), all the way to contemporary scholars like Elizabeth Freeman and Fred Moten, critical theory has provided the humanities with a staggering conceptual array of alternatives to a linear, successive understanding of temporality.

At the same time, however, linear chronology has proven a difficult shadow for literary scholarship to escape. This difficulty is especially visible in two of the most important critical conversations in which *Authorship's Wake* intervenes: let's refer to them as the *after theory* conversation and the *after postmodernism* conversation. In the first, we find books like Terry Eagleton's *After Theory*, Jane Elliott and Derek Attridge's edited collection *Theory after "Theory"* (as well as Ryan's *The Novel after Theory*), each of which engages (with varying levels of skepticism) with the claim that critical theory—at least in the guise in which it initially stormed the Anglo-American academy—has peaked and is now in terminal decline. What, they ask, comes next? The second conversation has to do with the history of literature and culture rather than the history of criticism and theory. It proceeds from the premise that postmodernism, as described by Fredric Jameson and many more, is no longer an adequate descriptor for the field of contemporary culture. Some critics—like Jeffrey Nealon in *Post-Postmodernism* (2012)—see the current moment as an intensification of Jameson's theorization of late capitalist postmodernity.[43] Others—like Stephen Burn in *Jonathan Franzen at the End of Postmodernism* (2008)—see in contemporary literature a number of misgivings with postmodernism's key tenets.[44] With some exceptions—such as Mary K. Holland, who sees in the work of writers like David Foster Wallace and Jonathan Safran Foer "the success of postmodernism rather than its failure"[45]—the *after postmodernism* critics agree that postmodernism is over. What, they too ask, comes next?

What I want to emphasize here is that these two conversations do not just share a similar chronological frame (what comes next?): they are, in an important sense, two versions of the same question. Put another way, it is not just the *after* that *after theory* and *after postmodernism* have in common: *theory* and *postmodernism* too can be understood as two different ways of naming the same larger phenomenon—a particular strategy of resistance against capitalism, white supremacy, and heteropatriarchy. This is a point that is clearly visible in several of the best contributions to these twin fields, in the work of critics like Jeffrey Nealon, Jane Elliott, and Mitchum Huehls. The argument that recurs across the work of all three of these scholars runs something like this: first, that twentieth-century theory *and* literature employed versions of the same strategy in order to critique the powers that be (whichever aspect of those powers we choose to focus on: capitalist, imperialist, patriarchal, white supremacist, heteronormative). Elliott calls this strategy "anti-instrumentalism": a stance that takes instrumental reason—and more specifically "an instrumental, totalizing, or univocal notion of meaning"—as its "bad guy," as the particular form of thinking, making, and being through which capitalism and its henchmen operate.[46] Hence the potential political utility of any number of theoretical projects, from the Frankfurt School critique of instrumental reason and totalitarianism, to Lacan's preference for the radical destabilizing force of the *jouissance* of the Real over the restrictive symbolic order, to deconstruction's insistence that meaning is always undermining itself and never univocal—indeed, most of what we could categorize under the heading of the linguistic turn.[47] So hence too "The Death of the Author" and Barthes's rejection of authorial intention in favor of polysemic textual play. And hence—on the literature side—both modernism and postmodernism, with their aesthetic forms of anti-instrumentalism, whether in the form of modernist fragmentation (Eliot, Woolf) or postmodern metafiction (Nabokov, Borges).[48] All of these concepts and devices function in the service of the same goal: an insistence on openness over closure, on uncertainty over truth claims, on variability over regularity, and on the singular over the universal, as a way to combat the totalizing, standardizing, instrumentalizing force of heteropatriarchal racial capitalism.

What Nealon, Elliott, and Huehls all emphasize, however, is the sense that this strategy of resistance no longer has the critical purchase it once offered—and that both theory and literature are all too aware of this. Elliott, for example, reads Margaret Atwood's *Oryx and Crake* (2003) as a novel about "a tradition of anti-instrumentalism that has become outdated and inadequate."[49] Nealon finds in all sorts of current cultural production—from "anti-postmodern neorealism" to "object-oriented philosophy and speculative realism"[50]—evidence of a turn away from the anti-instrumentalist critique of capitalism. And Huehls sees in contemporary US fiction a realization that emphasizing that which supposedly cannot be instrumentalized—epistemological indeterminacy, affective excess, polyvalent signification—no longer works as a strategy of resistance, because neoliberal capitalism has successfully instrumentalized every aspect of our inner lives.[51] This creeping co-optation of what had previously been means of resistance is what Nealon refers to as "affective capitalism."[52]

To summarize, then, Nealon, Elliott, and Huehls all see critical theory (especially in the French poststructuralist mold) and literature (both modern and postmodern) during the twentieth century as engaged in the same project: the critique of instrumentalism and the defense of uncertainty, singularity, and openness. "The Death of the Author" and the stories of Borges are, under this reading, symptoms of the same larger intellectual orientation. Crucially, though, this set of strategies has lost its effectiveness, and so the question for both theory and literature becomes *what next?* "What comes after theory?" and "what comes after postmodernism?" are therefore two versions—one oriented toward intellectual production, the other toward aesthetic production—of the same larger question, which we could phrase as "what comes after anti-instrumentalism?"

The version of this question that I ask here is "what comes after the death of the author?" By zooming in on one specific aspect of a much broader field, I aim to provide more detailed answers, in the context of a more coherent canon of texts—and because, as I explained above, this canon spans divisions of genre and nation, the fact that they all share a specific central question is all the more important as a unifying factor. At the same time, though—as the overview of nonnormative chronologies at the beginning of this section implies—I want to retain a degree of circumspection with regard to the formulation "what comes after …?" What all of the scholarship I have cited emphasizes is that there is something dubious about the succession-oriented mindset implicit in *after*. The chase for the next new thing, whether it is metaphorized via the linear succession image of *after* (after theory, after postmodernism, after nature, after critique) or via the spiraling, dialectical *turn* (the linguistic turn, the post-critical turn, the ontological turn, the affective turn), cannot rid itself of an urge toward progress that humanities scholarship has spent a great deal of time problematizing. Psychoanalysis has done so in the form of a critique of desire's never-ending succession of objects. Marxism has done so via its critique of capitalism, lurching from crisis to crisis. Is it the case that scholars, titling their books *After Critique* or *Post-Postmodernism*, have overlooked the fact that their own enterprise is similarly entwined in these kinds of destructive, repetitive drives toward the new that is also the same? And if they have, might we therefore want to abandon the preposition *after* and the prefix *post-* altogether? Or would that just be another turn of the screw—an aftering of *after*?

Doing so might not be such a bad idea. It is the tactic that Jason Potts and Daniel Stout take in their edited collection *Theory Aside* (2014), a project rooted in a valuable skepticism of "the theory-as-wholesale-transformation model" and an explicit rejection of "chronological sequence, currency, nextness, or newness" in favor of "aside-ness or adjacency."[53] Nevertheless, though, the preposition in this book's subtitle remains "after," and the image in the first part of the title—the *wake*—is likewise an image of afterness. The decision to stick with the preposition is not just due to the fact that we can be equally suspicious of any other word, as just another "after" in disguise. It is also because *after* is fertile ground. There is a lot already here in the *after*, a lot worth lingering in, rather than turning away from in search of the next new thing. I share *Theory Aside*'s desire "to think specifically about what might already be out there"[54] and try to do so by focusing not on coming up with a new theory of authorship but rather on making visible the fact that there are a number of tremendously worthwhile theories that have been around for a decade or two now, in recently published Barthes lectures and seminars (too easily overshadowed by the canonized polemic of "The Death of the Author"), in generically hard-to-pin-down texts like *The Argonauts*, and in the work of novelists like Zadie Smith. But part of "what might already be out there" is also a fecund body of thinking on afterness that complicates normative notions of linear progression.

Much of the fecundity of *after* is on display in Janet Halley and Andrew Parker's coedited volume, *After Sex? On Writing since Queer Theory* (2011)—a title this study consciously echoes. *After Sex?* includes essays by all of the key figures from what we could call queer theory's anti-chrononormative turn—Freeman, Edelman, Muñoz, Love—and the contributors consistently put an enormous amount of semiotic pressure on the word "after." "Crisp distinctions between before and after," Halley and Parker note, "appealed to no one."[55] Instead, we get multiple senses of afterness: "the 'after' of prosecution and persecution" (as in hunting after something) alongside "the 'after' of belatedness and desire" (as in pining after something), and innumerable other gradations.[56] Sex, for these critics, is (like colonialism) not really something one can ever reach the other side of. As Lauren Berlant writes, "the story of being 'after' or beyonding sex, which is a phrase's fantasy of having passed through a phase, remains unclear."[57]

The phrase "Writing after the Death of the Author" should now, I hope, be a little clearer—or perhaps a little more generatively opaque. The word "writing" indicates that my canon consists of the written word, but not a particular form or genre (literature, theory, fiction, nonfiction) within that category. The lack of quotation marks around "the Death of the Author" in my subtitle indicates that I am not dealing exclusively with the legacy of Barthes's essay, but rather with the larger critique of the author of which "The Death of the Author" is the most canonical example. And "after" signifies a number of possible relations: a relation of chronological sequence—perhaps a "fantasy of having passed through a phase"[58]—but also a relation with a variable affective charge that encompasses desire and hostility. In every chapter, the texts I deal with are profoundly ambivalent in their relationship to the figure of the author and to the idea of that figure's death. The idea of being the sole author of the dictionary that defines you is both amazingly attractive and deeply dangerous.

It is this symbolic range that the word "wake" in *Authorship's Wake* aims toward. As with "after," the term has attracted the attention of a number of humanities scholars, drawn to its productive ambivalence, signifying at once the disturbance spreading out behind an object (especially a ship) moving through water, a ceremonial gathering in honor of the dead prior to the funeral, and (as a verb) to move from sleep to consciousness.[59] All of these senses of the word entail a certain understanding of afterness, as well as a corresponding affective valence: are we striving to escape from the trail left by our predecessors, are we mourning them, or are we dismissing them like a bad dream or false consciousness? In *The Wake of Deconstruction* (1994), Barbara Johnson's early entry in the *after theory* conversation, "wake" marks this ambiguity: the question "of whether there is progress, of whether there is an identifiable lineage or genealogy flowing from deconstruction, whether deconstruction is awake or asleep and whether it's dead or alive and whether it ever was alive."[60] The word's ambiguity functions as the jumping-off point for Johnson's assessment of the legacy of deconstruction in the Anglo-American academy. The fullest exploration of these meanings, though, comes in Christina Sharpe's *In the Wake: On Blackness and Being* (2016). The wake in which Sharpe positions her work is that of the violence of transatlantic slavery; to be Black in the diaspora is to be in the wake.[61] For Sharpe, then, the object whose motion leaves behind the wake is very specifically the slave ship, and the deaths being mourned at/in the wake are starkly real and explicitly racialized. Yet "wake" becomes in her text a marker not just of a violent legacy, but also of an aesthetic, ethical, and political practice that stakes out "ways to imagine otherwise," ways to *wake up*—a practice she names "wake work."[62]

Johnson and Sharpe both take the word "wake" as the starting point for incredibly generative work, some of which I hope to build on in *Authorship's Wake*. Like *The Wake of Deconstruction*, *Authorship's Wake* questions whether the absent presence at its center is "dead or alive and whether it ever was alive."[63] The ambivalence that Johnson's use of the term marks is reflected in the relationships I analyze between post–death of the author texts and their predecessor (literally, one who died before), the figure of the sole, sovereign author. At times these texts mourn, at times they seek a resurrection, and at times they say *good riddance* or make the case that such an understanding of authorship was never anything more than a fantasy. Sharpe's work, by contrast, occupies an important place in relation to this project not only for its careful expansion of the word "wake" but also for what it has to say about the relationship between the literary and the theoretical, the personal and the critical, and the aesthetic and the political. *In the Wake*, like Saidiya Hartman's *Lose Your Mother* (2007) before it, combines scholarship and personal narrative in a manner that challenges easy distinctions between genres. Not only does Sharpe make the claim that aesthetic cultural expression (poems, novels, creative nonfiction) can do the same kind of intellectual, ethical, and political work as criticism and scholarship; her writing itself is also deeply informed by this argument. In this sense, her work also fits alongside *The Argonauts* and *I Love Dick* under the headings of "wild theory" or (in Paul B. Preciado's term, cited by Nelson) "autotheory."[64] *In the Wake* therefore stands as an important example of one of the key arguments of *Authorship's Wake*: that literature and theory are more entangled than they appear. In the chapters that follow I seek, like Sharpe, to make visible the ways in which texts across a variety of modes and forms can take part in the same transgeneric and transnational conversation.

3. Communication, Intention, Agency, Labor

"The Death of the Author" accomplished at least two things. Most obviously, it declared the beginning of a new era of polyvalent textuality unconstrained by the controlling figure of the sovereign author; it insisted on the necessity of "overthrow[ing] the myth" of the omnipotent "Author-God."[65] But at the same time, Barthes's essay also ended up setting into canonical stone a compelling description of this monumental, mythic figure. In killing off the Author, Barthes also memorably clarified for readers the precise version of authorship he sought to erase: nourishing, paternal, autonomous, regal, omniscient. The Author-God—from whom Zadie Smith's "sole author" descends—flashes into being at maximal vitality in "The Death of the Author" and, in the same seven-page stretch, is sentenced to death. He (and the masculine pronouns are no coincidence) is at the same time vividly alive and irreversibly dead. Barthes's essay has many precursors, of course, from Mallarmé's poetry and the *nouveau roman* in nineteenth- and twentieth-century France, to Anglo-American New Criticism and its rejection of authorial intention, stretching all the way back to Plato's denigration of the poets in the *Ion* and the *Republic*.[66] But more than any other text, "The Death of the Author" has set the terms for the conversation that followed—not only by killing the author but also by defining him. If there is a single traumatic event at this project's point of origin, then, it is Barthes's simultaneously affirmative and destructive act. The repercussions of that trauma are the subject of *Authorship's Wake*.

What precisely are those repercussions? What goes on in or at the wake of the Author? In the following chapters, I isolate four key issues at stake and analyze four corresponding sites of activity in the wake of authorship. These issues are, in order: communication, intention, agency, and labor. "The Death of the Author" fundamentally unsettled normative assumptions about all four. Barthes prompted his readers to question whether a literary text could really be thought of as a vehicle of communication, from author to reader. He denied altogether that authorial intention was a meaningful category. He sought to diminish the author's status as a figure of supreme agency, to sever the link between author and authority. And in redefining the nature of a text as "a multi-dimensional space in which a variety of writings, none of them original, blend and clash,"[67] he challenged the notion that an author's labor consists in creating new and original work and suggested instead that writers merely select and combine preexisting material. In each of the chapters of *Authorship's Wake*, I focus on one of these freshly unsettled assumptions in order to assess how writers (novelists, theorists, and producers of less easily categorizable texts) have dealt with "the expanding wedge of ruffled water"[68] that Barthes's disruptive essay left behind.

Broadly speaking, the chapters are arranged according to scale, from smallest to largest. The first focuses on the communicative and ethical stakes of authorship at the interpersonal level, within the family. This chapter begins from Zadie Smith's observation that "tear[ing] down the icon of the author … jettisons the very idea of communication, of any possible genuine link between the person who writes and the person who reads."[69] Is it possible, I ask, to still conceive of writing as having a communicative function if one accepts the argument of "The Death of the Author"? And if so, what kind of aesthetic strategies might one adopt in order to give writing's communicative capacity the best chance of success? The text that I analyze in order to answer these questions is Maggie Nelson's autotheoretical nonfiction prose work *The Argonauts*. A densely allusive book, *The Argonauts* turns to a wide range of theorists, poets, philosophers, and psychoanalysts as Nelson performs for her readers her "particular manner of thinking."[70] Drawing on the thought of several of these interlocutors—Wittgenstein, Barthes, Irigaray—I argue that Nelson's quasi-epistolary project gives us a theory of writing as communication that forges a delicate but nevertheless "genuine link between the person who writes" (Nelson) "and the person who reads" (her son) precisely by acknowledging, after Barthes, that writing is not the site of a transparent and frictionless author-reader communion. Adam Phillips suggests in his critical biography of Donald Winnicott that "our words are not misunderstood, they are just more or less usefully heard."[71] I argue that writing as communication post–death of the author looks less like understanding and more like useful hearing.

Chapter 2 focuses on the interpretive stakes of authorship, and the drama it depicts takes place on a slightly larger stage: the university campus. My focus is divided between two texts: Zadie Smith's 2005 campus novel *On Beauty* and Judith Butler's *Precarious Life* (2004). Both deal, in strikingly similar ways, with the question of freedom of speech and hate speech on campus and in particular with the question of intention. To what extent do a speaker's intentions matter when the words they utter do harm? Both Smith and Butler grapple with this question as it plays out in the early-twenty-first-century North American university. The answers they each provide are inconsistent—but this inconsistency, I argue, is in fact a virtue. In a longstanding debate between the defenders of authorial intention and its detractors, the battle lines have long been drawn up, to the detriment of any nuanced treatment of the politics of speech. Critical theory, I argue, has a lot to learn from a writer like Zadie Smith, for whom "ideological inconsistency is … practically an article of faith."[72] What is most valuable about *On Beauty* and *Precarious Life* is the fact that—even though Butler, unlike Smith, attempts to mask the internal contradictions in her work—each text plays fast and loose with the anti-intentionalism it inherits. Though predominantly loyal to the psychoanalytic and poststructuralist critique of intention and of the sovereign subject more broadly, Smith and Butler nevertheless at times defend the idea of authorial intent. They both acknowledge the fact that intentions are neither entirely accessible nor entirely inaccessible, that they may not be sovereign but they are not wholly powerless either.

At this point, there is a shift in emphasis: whereas the first two chapters frame themselves primarily in terms of aesthetic questions (writing's communicative capacity, authorial intention), the third and fourth are more explicitly political in their orientation. The third concerns the author as a figure of political agency and in particular as a figure of patriarchal power. The texts I work with—Rebecca Solnit's essay "Men Explain Things to Me," Chris Kraus's *I Love Dick*, Sheila Heti's *How Should a Person Be?*, Ben Lerner's *10:04*, and Roland Barthes's Collège de France teaching—all provide resources for understanding the trope I refer to as the *Man Who Holds Forth*: a figure for a kind of excessively agentic and explicitly gendered form of authorship. The Man Who Holds Forth is an author (literal or metaphorical) in the tradition of Barthes's Author-God: confident and secure in his privileged position, wielding his authority (whether earned or not) like a weapon and shutting out and shouting down others—especially women. The first half of the chapter focuses on Kraus, Heti, and Lerner, three of the key figures in English-language autofiction. For all three, I argue, engaging with the trope of the Man Who Holds Forth is a way to negotiate the gendered dynamics of authorship. In the second half, my attention turns to Barthes, who provides a remarkably prescient analysis of the same phenomenon in his 1977 seminar "What Is It to Hold Forth?" Notably absent from this seminar, however, is any consideration of gender: he entirely evades the question of *who it is* who holds forth. I assess the reasons for Barthes's evasiveness in the context of his often antagonistic relationship with feminist, queer, and left politics and ultimately argue that, despite the shortcomings that result from his opacity, Barthes's Collège de France lectures and seminars nevertheless offer a compelling theory of what it might mean to be an author without turning into an authoritarian Man Who Holds Forth.

Finally, the fourth chapter, at the largest scale, analyzes the author as a worker, assessing the representation of authorial labor in the wider context of changes in the forms of property and labor in postwar America. This chapter centers on a reading of David Foster Wallace's unfinished and posthumously published novel about the Internal Revenue Service, *The Pale King* (2011), and it draws on three weeks of research at the Harry Ransom Center, which houses Wallace's papers. I argue that Wallace's novel gives us a theory of writerly labor as a form of *information work*, wherein the worker's activity is primarily selective rather than creative. What a writer does, Wallace suggests, consists not in creating new things from scratch, but rather in assessing a large body of preexisting data and making a choice as to which elements of it are worthy of attention. My focus is therefore on *The Pale King*'s many representations of labor, as performed not only by writers but also by accountants and by cowboys. Ultimately, I argue that Wallace's depiction of the working life of tax accountants employed by the IRS in the 1970s and 1980s is a way of providing the reader with new ways of imagining and theorizing the postwar shift in North America toward an economy based on information as a form of property and as an object of labor—a shift also known under the name of neoliberalism.

Independently, each of these chapters demonstrates how contemporary writers—writers who, like Zadie Smith, were trained in theory's critique of the author during their undergraduate humanities education or who, like Roland Barthes and Judith Butler, took an active role in that critique—have expanded our understanding of what it means to be an author and why it matters, from the smallest scale to the largest. Taken as a whole, they make the case that the question of whether the author is alive or dead is no longer the most important one to be answered. Instead, what I argue in this study is this: that regardless of the author's vital status, we have a lot to learn from the writing that exists in authorship's wake.

Chapter 1

COMMUNICATION: MAGGIE NELSON AND THE LITERARY TEXT AS LETTER

> How can you write, believing in Barthes?
> —Zadie Smith, "Rereading Barthes and Nabokov"

1. Introduction

The question that Zadie Smith asks in the epigraph above is one version of the question this chapter attempts to answer. Smith, in an essay that compares Barthes's "The Death of the Author" with Vladimir Nabokov's "bold assertion of authorial privilege," traces a shift that has taken place in her reasons for reading and her ways of doing so:

> I'm glad I'm not the reader I was in college anymore, and I'll tell you why: it made me feel lonely. Back then I wanted to tear down the icon of the author and abolish, too, the idea of a privileged reader—the text was to be a free, wild thing, open to everyone, belonging to no one, refusing an ultimate meaning. Which was a powerful feeling, but also rather isolating, because it jettisons the very idea of communication, of any possible genuine link between the person who writes and the person who reads. Nowadays I know the true reason I read is to feel less alone, to make a connection with a consciousness other than my own.[1]

"Communication," "a connection with a consciousness other than my own": these are notions we are accustomed to find suspicious. From Wittgenstein through Barthes to Butler (all thinkers with whom this chapter will engage), there are a great many reasons to be skeptical of writing's communicative capacity. Considered from the point of view of the author, however, if writing is to be thought of as an attempt to say something *to* a reader—and for the writer this chapter will focus on, Maggie Nelson, it is—there seems to be little choice other than to place "a cautious faith in the difficult partnership between reader and writer, that discrete struggle to reveal an individual's experience of the world through the unstable medium of language."[2] The partnership is a "difficult" one, the faith the author places in it is "cautious," and the medium through which they "struggle" to convey their experience is "unstable": there is no returning to a naïvely idealistic view of the author as a single speaking subject who expresses their thoughts to another human being through a transparent medium. This chapter is concerned with the question of how literature responds to this bind. How might it be possible to think of writing as a form of communication after the death of the author?

I focus in particular on the prose work of Maggie Nelson, especially her 2015 book *The Argonauts*. *The Argonauts* is a nonfictional account of Nelson's marriage to fluidly gendered artist Harry Dodge and their family together. At the same time, it is also a theoretical conversation with numerous philosophers, writers, artists, and critical theorists on topics including motherhood, queerness, identity politics, and language. The first section of this chapter lays out the stakes of the question of writing as communication and the problems involved. I focus in particular on the idea (a frequent one in Nelson's writing) of the literary text as a letter—that is, the literary text as a form of authored communication. Then, in the second section, I theorize (via Ludwig Wittgenstein, Roland Barthes, Luce Irigaray, and Nelson) how one might think of writing as a form of communication that functions not in spite of the problems discussed in the first section, but by acknowledging them. If we want still to be able to think of literature as a way of "mak[ing] a connection with a consciousness other than my own," I argue that we need to shift our definition of communication toward something like what Adam Phillips refers to as *useful hearing*: "Our words," he suggests, "are not misunderstood, they are just more or less usefully heard."[3] In order to be usefully heard, I argue (following Wittgenstein) that it is necessary for the author to acknowledge the untenability of a notion of aesthetic communication as transparent and that it is precisely this acknowledgment that can create the space necessary for the reader to be able to *usefully hear* or read literature. In the third and final section, I return to *The Argonauts* in order to consider how the theoretical and ethical model of authorship and communication I describe functions in practice—how it manifests in the text's formal characteristics and in its content. The text's fragmentary form, its use of allusions, and the way it figures writing as a form of queer family-making help the text to achieve its communicative goals.

Throughout the chapter, my most important interlocutors (other than Nelson) are writers and thinkers with whom Nelson herself engages in *The Argonauts*: Wittgenstein, Barthes, and Irigaray, as well as Judith Butler, Adam Phillips, Eve Sedgwick, and Donald Winnicott. This is a deliberate decision. It serves partly as a way of better understanding Nelson's relationship with these thinkers but also stems from the desire to consider literature and theory (a categorical distinction that *The Argonauts* blurs) alongside each other, rather than one above the other. In their different modes, genres, and disciplinary contexts, these writers all share certain concerns, and I am interested in staging a conversation between them on relatively level terms, rather than bringing theory from a putative *outside* in order to *apply* to Nelson's text.

2. Letters

2.1. The Literary Text as Letter

In *Bluets* (2009), Maggie Nelson describes her love for the final line—"Sincerely, L. Cohen"—of Leonard Cohen's "Famous Blue Raincoat." "It makes me feel less alone," she writes, "in composing almost everything I write as a letter. I would even go so far as to say that I do not know how to compose otherwise."[4] Whereas "The Death of the Author" made Zadie Smith feel lonely, "Famous Blue Raincoat" has the opposite effect on Nelson. The line "Sincerely, L. Cohen"—a kind of signature, a sign of the song's authoredness—has some kind of communicative or community-forming effect. If "The Death of the Author" forecloses the possibility of communication, an assertion, like Cohen's, of what Smith called "authorial privilege," seems to reopen it. But the point I am interested in here is not primarily the fact that it is an authored discourse that makes Nelson "feel less alone": what she feels less alone *in* is "composing almost everything I write as a letter," and it is this statement of affiliation with the epistolary mode on which I want to focus.

What would it mean to take Nelson's declaration here seriously and to think of her writing as a letter? I want to suggest that doing so is a good way of getting at this chapter's question—how to think of literature as communication after the death of the author—because the letter is the paradigmatic example of a literary form that is both communicative and explicitly authored. Nelson's *The Argonauts* is, I will argue, an attempt to think through how letters function as a communicative and authored form. Furthermore, it does so within a post-death of the author theoretical framework, by drawing on Barthes, Ludwig Wittgenstein, and Judith Butler—that is, the very same thinkers whose work (both before and after Barthes's 1967 essay) has helped render suspect the notion of writing as a form of communication. A reading of Nelson, then, can help get at the question of how literature more generally might function as a communicative form after the death of the author.

To think of literature as a letter is to engage in a conversation about what Janet Gurkin Altman has called epistolarity: "the use of the letter's formal properties to create meaning."[5] Since Altman's *Epistolarity: Approaches to a Form* (1982), the critical debate around the concept has taken place in the context of work in a variety of genres and forms, from actual correspondence, to eighteenth-century epistolary novels, to less obviously letter-like texts, both novelistic and theoretical.[6] A number of characteristics are relatively stable in these discussions: letters and other epistolary texts are thought of as authored, sent to a "specific *you*" as a part of a reciprocal exchange, and necessitated by a spatial separation between sender and receiver.[7] Where critics tend to differ most is in the specific modality of this separation. For Derrida, for example, both the separation and the (connected) possibility of the letter's failure to reach its intended recipient structure the epistolary mode.[8] On the other hand, critics such as Margaretta Jolly—in *In Love and Struggle* (2008)—and Liz Stanley—in 2011's "The Epistolary Gift"—are more interested in the capacity of the letter to *overcome* the separation between writer and reader. Stanley and especially Jolly locate their theorization of the letter as "relational"[9] in a specifically feminist politics: "Feminists—myself included—have idealized letters as ethical forms in which we hope that some equally idealized relational self can finally be expressed."[10] Jolly points to a tension between the masculine-coded genre of autobiography, frequently tied to a notion of the subject as autonomous, and the letter as a relational and feminized form, but suggests that the impact of the ethical turn in critical theory has been to universalize (and thereby to defeminize) relationality.[11]

My concern in this chapter is not so much to insist on the fundamental importance of relationality over separation (or vice versa). Rather, I am interested in the question of how, while acknowledging the separation fundamental to the epistolary mode and the difficulties of bridging it, Nelson nevertheless works toward relationality—that is, toward a communicative effect. An example from *Bluets* is instructive here. Addressing a former lover, she writes:

> I felt no romance when you told me that you carried my last letter with you, everywhere you went, for months on end, unopened. This may have served some purpose for you, but whatever it was, surely it bore little resemblance to mine. I never aimed to give you a talisman, an empty vessel to flood with whatever longing, dread, or sorrow happened to be the day's mood. I wrote it because I had something to say to you.[12]

In a very literal way, this unopened letter is a failed act of communication. Nelson's addressee, she imagines, "reads" the letter (by not reading it) against, or rather entirely independently of, her authorial intentions; he has his own inscrutable agenda for the text. Like the undergraduate Zadie Smith reading "The Death of the Author," for whom the text is "a free, wild thing, open to everyone, belonging to no one, refusing an ultimate meaning," he does with the letter whatever he wishes.[13] Nelson wrote to him because she "had something to say to [him]," but his disregard of her desire forecloses the possibility of communication even before he has the opportunity to (mis)read its actual words. Communication in Nelson's work is never taken for granted, always rendered precarious: nevertheless, the desire—"I had something to say to you"—remains.

2.2. Epistolarity and The Argonauts

Much writing on epistolarity focuses on actual correspondence and therefore frames its project as a shift in critical attention toward the letter's literary qualities.[14] By considering literature as in some sense letter-like, I am engaged in the opposite endeavor.[15] It remains to consider, though, how we might have to rethink epistolarity in the context of *The Argonauts*. Like *Bluets*, the book describes acts of letter-writing, but if we are to take seriously Nelson's claim of affiliation with the epistolary mode, it is important to acknowledge the ways in which her work—and literature in general—departs from the formal properties of the letter, in terms of its relation to the categories of both authorship and readership.

I want to suggest first of all that *The Argonauts* necessitates an especially nuanced approach to the question of epistolary authorship, in part because of the complexities of its relationship to genre. Although I would follow Linda Kauffman in arguing that epistolarity should be considered a mode rather than a genre[16]—that is, a text's epistolarity does not determine its external formal features—I would nevertheless maintain that genre does have a bearing on the particular way in which a text performs epistolarity. *The Argonauts* flouts easy generic categorization, but Nelson has said that she does not mind the book being called "autotheory," a term she takes from Paul B. Preciado's *Testo Junkie* (2008).[17] This term might be understood as linking *The Argonauts* to the tradition of feminist "personal criticism" that Nancy K. Miller analyzes in *Getting Personal*,[18] or to what Nelson has called "Wild Theory."[19] By this, she means "theoretical writing that falls out of boundaries or disciplines, or even sense-making," a category that would also include *Testo Junkie*.[20] *The Argonauts* exists at the intersection of cultural criticism, personal narrative or memoir, queer and feminist theory, anecdote, and other genres.[21] Accordingly, it resists the generic codes that influence a reader's understanding of authorship and, like Miller's personal criticism, questions "the conditions of critical authority."[22] It is difficult, in other words, to gauge the distance between the narrative "I" of the text and the author, and this difficulty necessitates a more nuanced approach to the question of the text's authoredness than considerations of epistolarity often give.

A nuanced approach is especially important given the long history of (mostly male) critics misreading women's writing as simplistically autobiographical, ignoring the way in which "feminist theory has always *built out from* the personal" rather than limiting itself to the private sphere.[23] On the topic of authorial presence, Nelson writes: "If I insist that there is a persona or a performativity at work, I don't mean to say that I'm not myself in my writing, or that my writing somehow isn't me. I'm with Eileen Myles—'My dirty secret has always been that it's of course about me.'"[24] Myles's line stands in contrast to the anti-personalizing maneuvers of "The Death of the Author": whereas for Barthes the text's putative authoredness hides the secret that writing is in fact "the negative where all identity is lost, starting with the very identity of the body writing," Myles imagines the text as veiling the secret presence of the author.[25] But even though Nelson figures her writing as "of course about me," she nevertheless maintains a distinction between that "me" and the "me" that the reader constructs from the text. "I never worry about anyone feeling like they know me [from reading *Bluets*]," she tells *Salon*, "because I know that they don't. I don't mean that to sound glib; it's just literally true."[26] In other words, we might qualify the quotation from Myles—"My dirty secret has always been that it's of course about me"—with a further quotation, this from Judith Butler: "Yes, it is me, but I am not the one you think I am."[27] Or, in the words of Luce Irigaray: "Who I am for you and who I am for me is not the same, and such a gap cannot be overcome."[28]

Compared to an actual letter, then, *The Argonauts* demands that more attention be paid to the question of authorial presence. It also necessitates a rethinking of the nature of the epistolary reader. Literary texts that figure themselves as letters *to the reader* do not address a single "specific *you*" in the same way that real correspondence does; the author cannot know all of their readers in advance of publication.[29] Much epistolary literature, on the other hand, figures itself as a letter to a "specific *you*" who is someone other than the actual reader, putting them in the position of textual eavesdropper. Ta-Nehisi Coates's *Between the World and Me* (2015), for example, is written as a letter to his son, and though Samori Coates is one reader of *Between the World and Me*, he is one among many, and all of them but him read it (not without a sense of voyeurism) as a letter addressed to somebody other than them.[30] In this sense, it might make more sense to understand the literary-text-as-letter in relation to the open letter, which evokes a "wider epistolary community" than just the named addressee.[31]

On the other hand, though, epistolary acts—even open letters—are generally understood as taking place at least potentially in the context of a reciprocal back-and-forth. The addressee can write back. In the case of a published book, however, the reader's ability to respond is considerably compromised—or rather, the reader's response does not for the most part take the form of a text that makes its way back to the author.[32] Nelson's readers may be forgiven for "feeling like they know" her, and they can—and do—email her to tell her as much, but the text itself, in Gillian Beer's words, "reveals, exactly because it attempts to disguise, the *fictive* nature of the dialogue between writer and reader. We appear to be in conversation. Collaboration is implicit. We listen. But we are not heard. The book does not listen to us."[33] The literary-text-as-letter, then, might best be considered something like a last letter, a letter to which the reader cannot respond in kind—it might, that is to say, be considered something like the "last letter" Nelson describes sending to her former lover in *Bluets*, the one he never opens.[34] In its divorce from the chain of responses that characterizes epistolary exchange, therefore, the literary-text-as-letter opens itself even more fundamentally to the possibility of communicative failure: as Plato argues in the *Phaedrus*, the written text (unlike spoken rhetoric) has an existence independent of its author and can therefore be all too easily "ill-treated or unfairly abused."[35] Without recourse to the dialogic possibilities present in both the speech situation and the epistolary exchange, the literary text is at constant risk of misreading.

2.3. *The Risks of Letter-Writing*

If we are to consider a literary text as letter-like, then, it is clear that the possibilities of communication it provides are even more tenuous than those of actual letters, which are themselves already considerably compromised. Whereas *Bluets* starts to gesture toward the pitfalls of letter-writing, though, *The Argonauts* not only furthers this exploration; it also raises the stakes. For Nelson in this text, it is not merely that letters might fail in their communicative intent: they might actually cause harm.

There are several different senses in which *The Argonauts* might be thought of as epistolary. If the book itself is to be understood as a letter, the most obvious candidate for the role of recipient would be Harry, Nelson's partner. The book opens with a dedication—"*for Harry*"—and frequently addresses him in the second person, from the very first paragraph onward.[36] At the very end, however, Harry is referred to not in the second person, but in the third ("Harry now also keeps abreast of the Top 40") and in the first-person plural ("we're still here").[37] Harry is no longer exactly the addressee: the grammar here figures him more as a character (third-person singular) and a co-narrator (first-person plural). Indeed, a few pages prior, Harry does become something like a co-narrator, with the text including lengthy sections written by him.[38] With Harry no longer positioned as the recipient of the book-as-letter, it is Nelson and Harry's infant child Iggy who takes on this role.

Around halfway through the book, Nelson discusses the final section of André Breton's *Mad Love* (1937), which begins "Dear Hazel of Squirrelnut" and addresses his daughter Aube, who was eight months old at the time of *Mad Love*'s composition.[39] At the very end of *The Argonauts*, Nelson returns to Breton, rewriting his letter so as to address Iggy.[40] It is this act of letter-writing that is central to Nelson's interrogation of the stakes and pitfalls of the epistolary mode. These pitfalls concern not only the question of whether communication is possible but also the ethical status of the communicative act: as I'll demonstrate, Nelson suggests that the desire to communicate can easily slide into the desire to subjugate or control.

In her consideration of Breton, Nelson confesses that she has "always been a little spooked by texts addressed to or dedicated to babies." She continues:

> Such gestures are undoubtedly born from love, I know. But the illiteracy of the addressee—not to mention the temporal gap between the moment of the address and that at which the child will have grown into enough of an adult to receive it (presuming one ever becomes an adult, in relation to one's parents)—underscores the discomfiting fact that relation can never be achieved in a simple fashion through writing, if it can be achieved at all. It frightens me to involve a tiny human being in this difficulty, this misfiring, from the start.[41]

Despite these dangers, and despite his "hetero romanticism" (which is "hard to take"), Nelson is "moved" by Breton's letter to Aube.[42] The pitfalls she describes, though, are significant. The goal, as in *Bluets* ("I had something to say to you") is relation, but this relation is far from sure. In fact, the only certainty is the impossibility of achieving this relation "in a simple fashion through writing." This much applies to any act of letter-writing. The particular situation of writing to an infant does not so much exacerbate this difficulty (failure is already certain; it cannot be made more likely): rather, it "underscores" it. When writing to an infant, the recipient of the letter is quite literally unable to read it, and when they are able to do so, it might be a decade and a half later (*Mad Love* imagines Aube at sixteen reading the letter).[43] There is always, in any act of letter-writing, a temporal gap between the letter's composition and its reception, but that gap is here expanded to the point of absurdity, rendering the attempt at communication more precarious than ever. On the other hand, the spatial separation that is conventionally understood as making a letter necessary in the first place does not, in this situation, exist. Breton is right there, looking at his daughter as he writes. Nelson, considering the possibility of writing to Iggy, makes precisely this point: "The baby wasn't separate from me, so what use would it be to write to him as if he were off at sea?"[44] The infant child may not be capable of understanding complex language, but there is something perverse, Nelson suggests, about writing to her baby when she is capable instead of attending to his needs in the present. "*I cannot,*" she writes, "*hold my baby at the same time as I write*": writing here is understood as mutually exclusive with the act of care.[45] The concept of the letter to the infant, then—on top of the difficulties that any letter necessarily involves itself in—is both (from the temporal perspective) extremely fraught and (from the spatial perspective) redundant, even a distraction from more urgent matters.

Furthermore for Nelson, the precariousness of the epistolary relation has an ethical import. To expose a vulnerable "tiny human being" to the "misfiring" of language (her metaphor suggesting a violence whose direction is never under control) is a frightening prospect. "Writing to him felt akin to giving him a name: an act of love, surely, but also one of irrevocable classification, interpellation."[46] The potential violence of the act of writing to Iggy here takes two forms—"classification" and "interpellation"—that allude respectively to Roland Barthes and to Louis Althusser. The former is a major presence throughout *The Argonauts* and the source of its title.[47] Barthes's claim that "all speech is a *classification* and that all classifications are oppressive" is a persistent fear: to write to Iggy would already be to set up terms through which he would be understood.[48] Following Barthes's logic, a letter would not only fail as an act of communication; it would also have an oppressive effect on its addressee: "to utter a discourse is not, as is too often repeated, to *communicate*; it is to *subjugate*."[49]

If Barthes's characterization of language as "fascist" seems hyperbolic, it may help to consider the classificatory power of language alongside Nelson's allusion to its interpellative power.[50] A letter to an infant—especially a published letter—is an act not unlike the famous hailing of Althusser's policeman: before even being able to communicate, before becoming a speaking subject with a fully formed ego, Iggy would be (like Aube—but also, like us all) brought into being from without, without consent.[51] "We develop," Nelson writes, "even in utero, in response to a flow of projections and reflections ricocheting off us. Eventually, we call that snowball a self."[52] To write a letter is to add to that "flow of projections" (and classifications); to publish a letter is to add even more.

But Nelson's tone here—calmer and less dogmatic than Barthes's arguments regarding the fascism of language—indicates that there may be another side to the acts of "classification" and "interpellation." As much as they are operations of power, unwilled by the not-yet-subject on which they act, they also bring about that proto-subject's entry into the world: in Judith Butler's words, subjection is also "the condition of possibility for the emergence of the subject."[53] In *The Neutral*, Barthes acknowledges that, even though "the categories of language are coercive laws, which force one to speak," they are at the same time the laws that "permit communication."[54] That is to say, classification and interpellation are precisely what allow for communication to (potentially) succeed. But the obverse is also true: if the desire to communicate ("I had something to say to you") is, even partially, to be satisfied, then not only must one risk failure (the possibility that the letter is unread or misread); one must also risk a kind of violence.

2.4. Silence

So far, we have established a desire (to communicate, to write a letter), and we have established a set of ways in which that desire either might be frustrated (misreading or not reading, spatial and temporal distance) or might turn out not to be so desirable after all (in that it represents a potential form of violence: classification or interpellation). The question emerges, then: why bother attempting to satisfy this desire, given the risks? Might it be better *not* to try? If speech is classification, and classification is oppressive (and that's when it works), why not try silence? Nelson writes:

> Cordelia could not heave her heart into her mouth. Who can? No matter: her refusal to try famously becomes her badge of honor. But her silence has never moved me, quite: instead it's always struck me as a bit paranoid, sanctimonious—stingy, even.[55]

It is worth emphasizing just how unconventional a reading of Cordelia's silence in the first scene of *King Lear* this is. When I have talked to people about this passage, they have tended understandably to defend Cordelia. There are very good reasons for her silence: Cordelia is not so much refusing to express her love for her father. Rather, she is refusing to participate in a specific game of competitive flattery, a game in which her sisters take part all too eagerly and insincerely. One could justifiably read Cordelia as a kind of linguistic Bartleby figure, heroically trying to evade through her silence the power relations in which her father insists on implicating her.[56] Christina Luckyj describes Cordelia's "willful silence" as a "confrontation with authority's insistence on speech," which might align Cordelia both with Sara Ahmed's archive of willful subjects in her book of the same name and with Barthes's project of resisting the way in which the authority of language "compels speech."[57] To condemn her, as Nelson does, as "a bit paranoid, sanctimonious—stingy, even" is a gesture perilously close to siding with Lear, Goneril, and Regan. Lisa Jardine argues that to do so would be a mistake: the audience, she suggests, should understand that Lear's interpretation of Cordelia's silence as a stingy "denial of filial affection" is a "moral mistake on [his] part."[58] Surely his narcissistic request is more unreasonable, and indeed more paranoid, than Cordelia's silence?

This passage, though, is not primarily an interpretation of *King Lear*. Rather, Cordelia becomes a figure in *The Argonauts* for a certain type of inadequate response to the dilemma with which the text as a whole is concerned. In this particular context, the dilemma is framed, using Shakespeare's terms, as the desire to heave one's heart into one's mouth. In the previous section, I framed it as the desire to write a letter. And in the context of the argument of this chapter, I have framed it in terms of the question of communication. If communication is to take place—despite the fact that nobody can heave their heart into their mouth, despite the fact that letters can go astray—some linguistic act is going to have to take place. Cordelia's silence, in the way Nelson reads it, is a deliberate foreclosure of the possibility of communication before it has even begun. Even if communication fails, and even if it is a potential form of violence, to refuse even to try, for Nelson, is an inadequate response.

And more than inadequate, it is "paranoid." This particular word choice is best understood in relation to Nelson's frequent interlocutor—and one of the "many gendered-mothers of [her] heart," along with James Schuyler, Allen Ginsberg, and Lucille Clifton—Eve Sedgwick.[59] In "Paranoid Reading and Reparative Reading," Sedgwick describes the paranoid mode as being characterized in part by an "aversion to surprise": it assumes the worst, even requires the worst, so that the possibility of a nasty surprise can be eliminated.[60] In her "refusal to try," Nelson's Cordelia excludes surprise—bad or good. She is determined that she cannot heave her heart into her mouth, and her silence only confirms this; afraid of failure, she forecloses the possibility even of partial success. Sedgwick of course contrasts paranoid reading with reparative reading, which acknowledges the necessity of surprise, and the hope of a good surprise.[61] To risk the attempt to communicate, as Nelson does (her book, after all, is published, her letter posted), is to open oneself up to the possibility of surprise and "to surrender the knowing, anxious, paranoid determination that no horror, however apparently unthinkable, shall ever come to the reader *as new*"—or rather, shall ever come to the author as new.[62] Nelson, unlike the paranoid Cordelia, is therefore in some sense engaged in a reparative project. I will return to this idea later, in a discussion of Nelson's rewriting of Breton.

Whether Cordelia's silence is paranoid and sanctimonious or honorable and moving, it is also not exactly a silence. More specifically, it is a silence that says something. From a certain perspective, this need not be a bad thing. For Luckyj, the fact that "Cordelia frames her refusal to speak as itself a speech act" is indicative of the eloquence of her silence, of the fact that it is such an effective response to the dramatic situation.[63] If, on the other hand, we want to follow Nelson in understanding Cordelia's silence not just as an attempt to exempt herself from a morally sullying game but also as a repudiation of the paradigm of communication, then it fails.[64] From this perspective, then, there is no escape from the fascism of language, and Cordelia's silence is a bad form of response not only because of its paranoid "refusal to try" but also because, even on its own terms, her willful non-compliance with the demand to speak does not work—not to mention the fact that it arguably sets off the play's series of tragic events.

3. *Communication, Nonsense, and Space*

For Nelson, then, Cordelia is a figure for a certain type of inadequate response to the difficulties of communication. The Cordelia example helps Nelson to justify her authorial project. It serves as a counterexample, demonstrating why the option of *not* communicating is no option: that is, because it either forecloses the possibility of connection altogether or merely fails on its own terms as an attempt to escape from the communicative paradigm. Ruling out this option, though, does nothing to solve her communicative dilemma: it merely wedges her more tightly between a rock and a hard place. How might one respond to this double bind?

Up to this point, my emphasis has been on difficulties and obstacles, on all the ways in which language and communication fail. But this is only one side of the coin. Nelson tells *Guernica* magazine: "Some people who've read the book say, 'Wow, you're really down on language,' and I think, 'If I were really down on language, I wouldn't be trying to do this in language! I'd be doing something else!' I love language. It doesn't bother me that its effects are partial."[65] Exactly: to say that language's effects are partial is very different from saying that language has no effect at all. It suggests that, even if it is not a complete success, language is nevertheless not a complete failure either. It is partial: it achieves a partial success. So far, I have concentrated solely on the shortcomings and on the ways in which it misfires. At this point, I want to start to change the emphasis. How might communication take place after all, despite the partial nature of the effects of language?

On the very first page of *The Argonauts*, in a passage worth quoting in full, Nelson gives the beginning of an answer:

> Before we met, I had spent a lifetime devoted to Wittgenstein's idea that the inexpressible is contained—inexpressibly!—in the expressed. This idea gets less air time than his more reverential *Whereof one cannot speak thereof one must be silent*, but it is, I think, the deeper idea. Its paradox is, quite literally, *why I write*, or how I feel able to keep writing.
>
> For it doesn't feed or exalt any angst one may feel about the incapacity to express, in words, that which eludes them. It doesn't punish what can be said for what, by definition, it cannot be. Nor does it ham it up by miming a constricted throat: *Lo, what I would say, were words good enough*. Words are good enough.
>
> *It is idle to fault a net for having holes*, my encyclopedia notes.[66]

If Cordelia's silence is "sanctimonious," drawing attention to her supposed moral superiority, Wittgenstein's idea is refreshingly unostentatious. Yes, words fail: "that which eludes them" remains inexpressible. This much is true. But whereas Cordelia, declining even to *try* to heave her heart into her mouth, comes across to Nelson as "stingy," Wittgenstein, shifting the attention away from the limits of the expressible and toward the possibility of expressing (or at least containing) the inexpressible, is comparatively generous. He is not concerned with punishment or self-beratement; he does not demand perfection, instead suggesting that words, though limited, are nevertheless (and here, for the first of many times, Nelson evokes Donald Winnicott) "good enough."

This section considers Wittgenstein's ideas about language's capacity to contain ("inexpressibly!") the inexpressible in more detail. What I want to suggest is this: Wittgenstein, in the *Tractatus Logico-Philosophicus* and in other writings of the same period, is engaged in a similar communicative dilemma to the one I have been discussing up to this point in the context of Nelson. A reading of the early Wittgenstein, then, not only helps lay out some of the specific problems that writing, if it is to be understood as a form of communication, has to overcome; it also offers a response to these problems.

3.1. "Whereof One Cannot Speak"

In the passage quoted above, Nelson is referring to two different sources. The first idea—"that the inexpressible is contained—inexpressibly!—in the expressed"—comes from a letter Wittgenstein wrote to his friend Paul Engelmann in April 1917.[67] The second—"Whereof one cannot speak thereof one must be silent"—is the final line of the *Tractatus Logico-Philosophicus*, which was published in 1921 but which Wittgenstein was working on at the time of the letter to Engelmann.[68] These two ideas, then, are roughly contemporaneous in the development of Wittgenstein's thought, and they represent two sides of his argument in the *Tractatus*. The central question of this text is this: what can be said? Wittgenstein's answer (the short version of it, anyway) is that we can say statements of fact along the lines of natural science (empirically verifiable propositions that show how things stand in the world) and nothing else. Propositions that are not empirically verifiable—that make claims, for example, about subjective experience, values, or belief—are, for Wittgenstein, nonsensical. The limit of language is the limit of natural science, and "what lies on the other side of the limit will be simply nonsense."[69] This allows Wittgenstein to reach his famous conclusion—"Whereof one cannot speak, thereof one must be silent"—and allows for a reading of the *Tractatus* that would prescribe that, outside of statements of empirically verifiable fact, no other form of language should even be attempted.

The famous paradox of the *Tractatus*, though, is that the book itself is, according to Wittgenstein's own definition, nonsensical.[70] The activity of philosophy (and for Wittgenstein, "philosophy is not a theory but an activity") is not the same as natural science: "The result of philosophy is not a number of 'philosophical propositions,' but to make propositions clear."[71] That is, philosophy does not produce propositions that have truth conditions (that make a contingent—verifiable or falsifiable—claim about how things stand in the world). Instead, it aims "to make propositions clear," an activity which involves producing sentences that are *not contingent*, which have *no truth conditions*—and are therefore nonsense. Implicitly, then, there is a second question being asked in the *Tractatus*. Not merely what can be said, but (more interestingly, at least for our purposes) how might we attempt to say what *cannot* be said? Or phrased slightly differently, how might we attempt to speak of that "whereof one cannot speak"? This would suggest that the conclusion that "whereof one cannot speak, thereof one must be silent" might not be the end of the story.

This is where the other Wittgensteinian idea that Nelson cites comes in. In its original context, it reads as follows:

Dear Mr Engelmann,   9.4.17
   Many thanks for your kind letter and the books. The poem by Uhland is really magnificent. And this is how it is: if only you do not try to utter what is unutterable then *nothing* gets lost. But the unutterable will be—unutterably—contained in what has been uttered!...
   Yours
   Wittgenstein[72]

The first thing to note is that this is a letter; the second thing to note is that it is a letter about a poem. Neither of these facts, I want to suggest, are coincidental. Wittgenstein is talking about nineteenth-century German poet Ludwig

Uhland's "Graf Eberhards Weissdorn" ("Count Eberhard's Hawthorn"), which tells of a former soldier who, in old age, sits beneath a hawthorn tree grown from a cutting he had taken many years earlier and which he had attached to his helmet for the duration of his time at war. The poem never directly describes the experiences Count Eberhard went through as a soldier. Instead, the tree metonymically stands for and evokes these experiences: "The branching arch so high, / Whose whisper is so bland, / Reminds him of the past / And Palestina's strand."[73]

What is uttered in this poem is confined more or less to contingent propositions along the lines of those of natural science. Uhland describes actions—"Then in his iron helm / The little sprig he plac'd"[74]—through statements that formally accord with Wittgenstein's picture theory of language: "The picture represents a possible state of affairs in logical space."[75] This is what Uhland's sentences do: they describe a logical relation between a set of elements (in the example above, the *Count*, his *helmet*, and the *sprig of hawthorn*, connected by the action of *placing in*). Even though the story they tell is fictional, they are nevertheless, according to Wittgenstein's definition, grammatical and meaningful propositions: "The picture represents what it represents, independently of its truth or falsehood."[76] The poem therefore does not "try to utter what is unutterable." But what it finally utters is—partly for that reason—not confined to the literal content of these propositions: through the metonymic tree, the (unutterable, because subjective, non-contingent) experiences of the Count are, in Wittgenstein's words, "unutterably ... *contained* in what has been uttered."

Poetry, then, is a discourse that can, for Wittgenstein, contain the unutterable, and it can do so via rhetorical devices such as metonymy—that is, via devices that call upon the reader to do the imaginative work of conceiving the unutterable. And Wittgenstein says this—and his statement, it is important to remember, is, like the statements of the *Tractatus*, technically nonsense—in a letter. The letter, as we have already seen, is an especially precarious form of communication. Or perhaps better: the letter is a form of communication that makes especially visible (that "underscores," to use Nelson's word) the precariousness of all communication. Like the poem's metonymy, the letter calls upon its readers to create meaning, and it cannot necessarily rely upon them to create meaning in a predictable or transparent way. It is peculiarly appropriate, therefore, that this unutterable idea about how we might communicate what cannot easily, if at all, be communicated should be contained in a medium that is itself engaged in the effort to communicate despite the perhaps insurmountable difficulties this effort involves.

When Nelson, on the first page of her book, aligns herself with "Wittgenstein's idea that the inexpressible is contained—inexpressibly!—in the expressed" as opposed to his more well-known "whereof one cannot speak thereof one must be silent," she is aligning herself with the second as opposed to the first of the two questions of the *Tractatus*: not *what can be said?*, but *how might we attempt to say what cannot be said?* Furthermore, this question that the early Wittgenstein and Nelson both grapple with provides, I want to suggest, a way of answering the question that I asked, via Zadie Smith, at the beginning of this chapter: how might it be possible to think of writing as a form of communication after the death of the author?

Wittgenstein attempts in the *Tractatus* to communicate to a reader something which cannot be said: "Its object," he writes in the Preface, "would be attained if there were one person who read it with understanding and to whom it afforded pleasure," but he fears that it "will perhaps only be understood by those who have themselves already thought the thoughts which are expressed in it—or similar thoughts."[77] Communication, for Wittgenstein, is a source of such difficulty because the thoughts he attempts to communicate are not the propositions of natural science. The propositions of natural science can easily be understood because they are formally identical to the reality they describe: "The world is the totality of facts."[78] All that is required to understand such propositions is "to know what is the case, if [they are] true," a process that requires no substantive effort on the part of the reader beyond mere literal comprehension.[79] To engage in philosophy, on the other hand, is to attempt to communicate not facts, but something about facts, which necessarily means speaking nonsense. And if the reader is to get anything from nonsense, they are going to have to do something qualitatively different—something qualitatively *more*—than literal comprehension.

Adam Phillips, writing about Donald Winnicott in a book that Nelson has frequently cited, suggests that, in the analytic situation, "our words are not misunderstood, they are just more or less usefully heard."[80] This, I think, gets at the distinction I am trying to draw between the way that the language of natural science works and the way that the language of philosophy or art (or, indeed, psychoanalysis) works. In natural science, words are either understood or (if the reader does not know or assumes incorrectly the referent of a particular term) misunderstood; the statements of philosophy and art, on the other hand, cannot be transparently understood and cannot be misunderstood in quite such a clearly identifiable (and correctible) way either. Because they rely on the reader or listener (or analysand) to do imaginative work, they can only be "more or less usefully heard." Philosophical and aesthetic language is nonsense, and nonsense cannot be understood; to suggest that it could would be a category error. Nonsense can, however, be "usefully heard."

But what exactly does *useful* mean in this context? Are we to understand it in a narrowly utilitarian or instrumentalizing sense? Is it being employed as a synonym for "appropriable"? *Useful* is one of Phillips's favorite ways to describe the words that are said in the psychoanalytic situation. He uses it in particular to describe narratives, such as the ones told by Freud—"useful fictions but improbable facts"—and by psychoanalysts more generally, who all have "their favorite stories" that they find "useful."[81] In other words, Phillips is suggesting that psychoanalysis has more in common with the nonsense of aesthetic discourse than it does with the sense of natural science. Natural science is useful in the sense of having an easily graspable meaning that can tell us concrete facts about the world around us—concrete facts that indeed *are* the world around us, in the sense that "the world is the totality of facts."[82] But, for Wittgenstein, that is all that natural science is useful for. That is, natural science can record a fact, but it cannot translate a fact into a law; it can tell us what is occurring at a given moment, but not what will occur in the future. "A necessity for one thing to happen because another has happened," Wittgenstein writes, "does not exist."[83]

What Phillips implies is that a useful hearing of a psychoanalytic interpretation might involve departing from the tightly prescribed ways in which one can usefully hear a scientific proposition. The meaning of a psychoanalytic interpretation or any other story is *not* so easily graspable as that of a scientific statement; because it is not empirically verifiable, it is not a code that can be solved, and we cannot access the "intention behind" it.[84] As a result, the usefulness of Freud's "fictions" about the human psyche is, according to Phillips, a little broader than the usefulness of natural science. He suggests that we read Winnicott's stories of mothers and infants somewhat less than literally: "It is not that Winnicott isn't really talking about mothers and babies, but that he is also using mothers and babies to talk about other things as well."[85] That is, the mothers and babies are metonymic: the usefulness of Winnicott's stories relies on the reader to extend their sense beyond its literal meaning. *Useful*, then, when we are talking about aesthetic, philosophical, or psychoanalytic discourse, depends more on the receiver than the sender.

In some sense, this begins to sound like "The Death of the Author" all over again: if the literary text cannot be misunderstood, if the usefulness of its reception is determined entirely on the reader's terms, then it is again "a free, wild thing, open to everyone, belonging to no one, refusing an ultimate meaning" and communication has once more been foreclosed.[86] But I want to suggest that this shift in terms, from *understanding* to *useful hearing*, contains an opening toward a kind of communication between author and reader that not only takes account of the ways in which language can fail—that does not fault the net for having holes, as it were—but also counters the potential ethical violence (classification, interpellation) of communication. The next section, with reference to Wittgenstein, Barthes, and Irigaray, attempts to explain this and to address the question of how a piece of aesthetic or philosophical writing might lend itself to being usefully heard. If an author wants to communicate, wants their readers to be able to usefully hear them, what particular aesthetic strategies can they employ in order to help bring this about?

3.2. Acknowledged Nonsense

At the very end of the *Tractatus*, Wittgenstein draws a comparison between two philosophical methods. "The right method," he suggests, would be "to say nothing except what can be said, i.e. the propositions of natural science, i.e.

something that has nothing to do with philosophy: and then always, when someone else wished to say something metaphysical, to demonstrate to him that he had given no meaning to certain signs in his propositions."[87] This purely negative philosophy has no substantive content whatsoever: the only positive statements it puts forward are entirely nonphilosophical. Wittgenstein imagines that this method, though correct, would be "unsatisfying" to the student being told that his metaphysical propositions were nonsense, but it might nevertheless have a pedagogical effectiveness.[88] Though the philosopher could never actually describe the formal limits of "what can be said" (propositions about the limits of language are beyond the limits of language and thus nonsensical), the student might eventually, by working out the logic behind when the philosopher intervened and when he did not, learn where those limits are. The philosopher would therefore have communicated the limits without attempting to directly utter them; "the unutterable [would have been]—unutterably—*contained* in what [had] been uttered!"[89] As in Uhland's poem, something inexpressible would have been communicated without actually being uttered, via the imaginative work of the interlocutor.

The second method that Wittgenstein describes is the one that he himself employs in the *Tractatus*: "My propositions are elucidatory in this way: he who understands me finally recognizes them as senseless, when he has climbed out through them, on them, over them. (He must so to speak throw away the ladder after has climbed up on it.)"[90] Insofar as Wittgenstein's propositions are nonsense, his approach departs from the "strictly correct method."[91] He has not limited himself to the contingent propositions of natural science: his discourse is philosophical, as well as arguably both ethical *and* aesthetic.[92] Nevertheless, the communicative effect is, if Wittgenstein is successful, the same: the reader, by recognizing Wittgenstein's propositions as nonsense, will have ascertained the limits of what can be said. Again, the reader is required to do some work to get to this point (more than he would have to do in order to understand the propositions of natural science). "He has climbed out through [Wittgenstein's propositions], on them, over them": no ordinary reading.

What is important, and what Wittgenstein emphasizes throughout his work, is that the point of this endeavor to help his readers recognize the limits of language is *not* to teach them to stay within those limits. Rather, as he writes in *Philosophical Investigations*, "what I want to teach is: the transition from unacknowledged nonsense to an acknowledged one."[93] This perhaps explains why Wittgenstein departs from what he views as the "strictly correct method" of philosophy: he can endure writing nonsense, not only because *he* acknowledges it as nonsense but also because Wittgenstein's acknowledged nonsense can—perhaps more effectively than the strategy of limiting oneself to what *can* be said—help his readers acknowledge both his and their own nonsense. In this particular situation, nonsense seems to make *more* sense than sense or at least to be more effective at prompting the reader to make (to construct) sense.

So then in response to the question I asked earlier—what makes a piece of philosophical or aesthetic writing able to be usefully heard?—I want to suggest that a possible answer is *acknowledgment*. Philosophical and aesthetic writing is nonsense, but if it is *acknowledged* nonsense, it might be nonsense that can be usefully heard. To put this another way, stubbornly insisting that relation *can* "be achieved in a simple fashion through writing"[94] (or that what is being said is *not* nonsense) can be counterproductive. On the other hand, an *acknowledgment* of the "discomfiting fact" that relation *cannot* be achieved so simply—that aesthetic discourse is nonsense—can open up a certain degree of space for the reader to be able to usefully hear what the author is trying to communicate.

The passage quoted above, wherein Nelson discusses Wittgenstein, ends as follows: "*It is idle to fault a net for having holes*, my encyclopedia notes."[95] We might rephrase this: it is idle to fault aesthetic writing for being nonsense. And just as faulting a net for its holes is missing the point of what a net *is*, so is faulting aesthetic writing (or philosophy or critical theory) for not being transparently comprehensible in the manner of natural science. A net has holes for a reason: if it did not, it might still catch a fish, but it would bring with it a load of water and be a lot heavier. Maybe the gaps in the language of art (and theory) have a positive function too. Acknowledging that aesthetic writing is nonsense is not so much a ceding of power; it just opens up space for it to be what it is and consequently for it to be read more usefully.

3.3. Space

"Space" is a term I have used twice in the last two paragraphs. It is a term I am using in the sense that Nelson uses it in the following passage from *The Art of Cruelty*:

> In all the work of [Paul] McCarthy and [Mike] Kelley I've seen, no matter how disturbing, I've never felt from them the bossy conviction I feel from so many other artists, to admit that my problems are actually their problems—to admit that they are actually Our Problems. Instead, they inhabit their obsessions so thoroughly, with so blessedly little concern for my wellbeing, as they catapult their feelings, problems, and obsessions into the public sphere, that some space is created.
>
> This space exists when an artist may hope to give other people his or her problems, but also knows that the transmission cannot be surely made, and that the fallout is likely to be unpredictable, disorderly.[96]

The artist-viewer relationship being described here is a long way from Zadie Smith's description of reading in order "to feel less alone, to make a connection with a consciousness other than my own."[97] Nelson describes McCarthy and Kelley as turning their attention inward and away from their audience, having "blessedly little concern for my wellbeing." This is a paradoxical notion: why would lack of concern be a blessing? And if we are trying to move toward a notion of communication that counters the potential for ethical violence we observed earlier, why are we now valorizing a mode of aesthetic relationality that seems above all self-centered? Would concern for the well-being of the audience not be a positive step toward countering the possibility of violence?

Nelson argues the opposite: that "concern for my wellbeing" can itself *be* a form of violence. Roland Barthes and Luce Irigaray are helpful here. In *The Neutral*, Barthes claims that "we have to choose between egotistic discourse and terroristic discourse."[98] This choice corresponds to the comparison Nelson is setting up here between McCarthy and Kelley on the one hand and artists who impose upon the audience with a "bossy conviction to admit that my problems are actually their problems" on the other. It is a choice between two different ways of communicating with one's interlocutor. Terroristic discourse demands that the interlocutor relate to the speaker entirely on the speaker's terms or not at all. The speaker has already decided what the grounds of identification are—what "Our Problems" are—and asks the interlocutor, *are you with us or against us?* This is what Barthes refers to as "the terrorism of the question."[99] Concern for the audience's well-being can all too easily turn into an attempt to lay out in advance the exact way in which they will experience the artwork or text. "I'd much rather the artist be thinking about his or her own experience," Nelson writes, "than trying to micromanage mine."[100]

Egotistic discourse, on the other hand—where the artist is "thinking about his or her own experience" and thoroughly "inhabit[ing] their obsessions"—disavows the "terroristic" mode of relation that compels the reader to either accept or reject the author's terms and in doing so gives the reader space to relate on *their* terms. This is the mode that Barthes himself adopts, by reading "a text written in the 'I' mode, a little diary fragment."[101] The move from the first-person plural ("Our Problems") of terroristic discourse to the singular ("the 'I' mode") does not foreclose the possibility of communication; the self-centeredness of an approach like McCarthy's or Kelley's is not alienating for the viewer, or at least not for Nelson. The turn toward the self is not necessarily a turn away from the other: in this case, it is a way of relating to the other on more ethical terms.

The reason for this, Nelson suggests, is that McCarthy and Kelley have not abandoned the desire to "give other people [their] problems." Their turn inward comes from their understanding that "the transmission cannot be surely made, and that the fallout is likely to be unpredictable, disorderly." That is, they acknowledge what Nelson acknowledges in *The Argonauts*: "the discomfiting fact that relation can never be achieved in a simple fashion through writing"—or visual art—"if it can be achieved at all."[102] Or, in Wittgenstein's terms, they acknowledge the nonsensical status of their discourse.

This pattern—the desire for relationality, the realization and acknowledgment of the difficulties it involves, and the retreat backward that does not abandon the hope of achieving communication but does counter communication's potential ethical violence—is the same pattern that Irigaray draws out in *To Be Two* (1994). Her description of relationality takes place in a different context—specifically, in the context of the relationship of love between two human subjects, especially between two human subjects of different sexes—but the ethical paradigm she sets out is nevertheless useful for explaining how there can be such thing as having "blessedly little concern" for the well-being of one's interlocutor, specifically in the context of the mediated encounter between author and reader.

Irigaray's ethics in *To Be Two* is an ethics of two-ness, of "being with" the other "while remaining myself."[103] The mode of relationality she argues for values a certain "insuperable gap" between—rather than a seamless union of—subjects.[104] Distinguishing her project from Hegel, Heidegger, Sartre, and others, whom she sees as embodying a male tradition of privileging the subject-object relationship over the subject-subject relationship, Irigaray argues that respecting "the other as other"—the other as another subject, rather than as an object—requires "leav[ing] *space* ... around and within the other."[105] "If I become the other," she writes, "I abolish the two poles I–you, she–he. Thus the relationship between two disappears and, with it, a possible dialogue and a possible intersubjective dialectic ... Such becoming annuls communication-between."[106] In a similar manner to Nelson, she draws a correlation between the fraughtness of the intersubjective relation and the productivity of the space between subjects. For Irigaray, annulling that space "annuls communication-between," just as the "bossy conviction" that Nelson describes forecloses communication by failing to take account of the difficulty of giving other people one's problems—a difficulty that, when acknowledged, creates space.

Irigaray's theorization of the ethical encounter in *To Be Two* is—compared to, for example, Emmanuel Levinas's or Judith Butler's—particularly helpful for understanding the kind of necessarily indirect encounter that takes place through the medium of the work of art, especially the literary text. Levinas, via his theorization of the face, focuses on the embodied and visual aspect of the encounter and the proximity it involves; Butler, although she suggests in *Frames of War* that an ethical encounter can still occur without physical proximity (through a photograph, for example), nevertheless follows Levinas, arguing that "the norms that would allocate who is and is not human arrive in visual form."[107] Like Butler, Irigaray focuses on the remoteness of one subject from another and the tenuousness of the link between them, but for her, *seeing* the other is not necessary or even necessarily desirable: "In blindness," she writes, "we remain distinct, one towards the other ... we listen always and anew to each other so that the irreducible can remain": words are more important than the image.[108] And distance is not what keeps subjects apart, what prevents the encounter, but what "allows us to approach each other."[109] In the epistolary encounter of the literary-text-as-letter, an ethics of the face along Levinasian lines is difficult to conceive: the other as face may not always coincide with the literal face, but it is nevertheless primarily encountered visually, as a body (whether that body is present physically or only in a photograph).[110] An ethics of remoteness and space along the lines of Irigaray, on the other hand, shares much more with the kind of relationality that can take place between the author (as letter-writer) and reader.

From this perspective, we can read the idea of an artist having "blessedly little concern" for the well-being of their audience not as a narcissistic ethical failure, but as the kind of return to the self that acknowledges that there can be something sustaining about the "insuperable gap" between subjects. Not seeking to overcome this gap aids rather than hinders the possibility of "communication-between."[111]

Furthermore, I want to suggest that the kind of "egotistic" return to the self involved in this mode of relationality that I am attempting to theorize might also be understood as a kind of *authoredness*. What Nelson calls thoroughly inhabiting one's obsessions, what Barthes calls egotistic discourse, and what Irigaray calls "your repose with yourself, in yourself," is not so far in the end from what Zadie Smith calls the "bold assertion of authorial privilege."[112] Although, as discussed above, Nelson's characterization of the artist-viewer relationship in the context of Paul McCarthy's and Mike Kelley's work initially sounds very different from Smith's description of reading in order "to feel less alone," I hope to have shown that they are not so different after all.[113] Asserting "authorial privilege" by writing in the first-person singular rather than the first-person plural or by thinking about one's own experience rather than "trying to micromanage" the audience's allows for rather than forecloses the possibility of a "genuine link between the person who writes and the person who reads."[114]

3.4. The Work of the Reader

The final part of this chapter returns to *The Argonauts* in order to consider how the model of authorial communication that this second section has laid out ends up working in practice. Before that, however, and by way of transition to it, I want to consider a potential pitfall of this communicative model. In my discussion of Wittgenstein and metonymy, I suggested that the unutterable might be contained via devices that call upon the reader to do the imaginative work of conceiving it. In order to *usefully hear* the nonsense of aesthetic discourse, the reader is asked to put in effort. And in the ethical relationship that allows the reader space to relate to the text on their own terms from the far side of an "insuperable gap," there is once more a shift in the distribution of the aesthetic labor involved in the author-reader encounter: the reader takes over from the author much of the work of creating a connection. Might this not become—well, exhausting? Could there not be a point where the reader decides that it is no longer worth it? Does this ethical model imply an aesthetics that places too much value on difficulty, to potentially exclusionary effect?

The aesthetic strategy Nelson admires in McCarthy and Kelley is in some sense similar to John Ashbery's, as described by Adam Phillips in *Missing Out* (2012):

> When Ashbery was asked in an interview why his poetry was so difficult, he replied that when you talk to other people they eventually lose interest, but that when you talk to yourself, people want to listen in … what Ashbery is suggesting in his whimsically shrewd way is that *the wish to communicate estranges people from each other*.[115]

The point Phillips makes here (via Ashbery) is astute and corroborates the story I have been telling about counterproductive attempts to relate to the other and the positive function of seemingly egotistic discourse. But Ashbery's poetry, as this passage acknowledges, is notoriously difficult; it approaches nonsense, and not just in Wittgenstein's sense of the word. Yes, difficulty might make people "want to listen in," but how long is this strategy effective as a way of maintaining a connection?[116] And might it work better in poetry than in—for example—the 140 prose pages of *The Argonauts*? In some sense, this last question is redundant: *The Argonauts* is extremely lucidly written, like all of Nelson's prose, though as I will discuss below, it is a text that is difficult in other ways. But listening to someone talking to themselves, even if what they are saying is not exhaustingly hard to comprehend, may just become rather boring. If the literary-text-as-letter is going to be successful in its attempt to communicate, it has to hold its reader's attention, and that requires more than just an ethics of space or an acknowledgment of its nonsensical status. To put it another way: just because it's OK that nets have holes doesn't mean that there's no such thing as "a crappy net."[117] This section has focused on the importance of acknowledging the holes in the net. In the final third of this chapter, I want to ask what, beyond having holes, a net has to do in order to be effective. Addressing this question requires returning once more to *The Argonauts*.

4. The Argonauts *and the Ethics of Space*

In the passage from *The Art of Cruelty* discussed at length above, Nelson describes her experience of viewing Paul McCarthy's *Caribbean Pirates* as "memorably spacey": despite "the work's relentless assault," Nelson does not feel assaulted; it succeeds in creating the space that I have argued is necessary for communication to take place. I want now to consider the experience of reading *The Argonauts*—a very different work to the "gore-fest" of *Caribbean Pirates*.[118] To what extent does Nelson's text create space? And what other strategies does it adopt in its attempt to communicate?

In order to begin answering these questions, I want to start with a short close reading of a passage from the text, which spans two and a half pages and takes place about a third of the way through *The Argonauts*.[119] It consists of three sections, divided into four, two, and two paragraphs respectively. The following paraphrase (in which I have numbered the three sections and their constituent paragraphs) highlights the structure of the passage and summarizes (quoting where appropriate) the ideas it puts forward and the events it describes:

1.1 As Michael Snediker points out in *Queer Optimism* (2008), Donald Winnicott takes his patients' problems seriously but does not wax lyrical about them.
1.2 "Lyrical waxing," Snediker suggests, "often signals (or occasions) an infatuation with overarching concepts or figures that can run roughshod over the specificities of the situation at hand." Nelson supports this point with an example from Winnicott, who accuses Freud of falling prey to such an infatuation in his writings on the death drive.
1.3 The propensity toward lyrical waxing has a particular tendency to arise when writers try "to pay homage, in their writing, to a beloved": love letters, ostensibly written to a specific person, can all too easily turn into generic hymns of praise. Here Nelson recounts a story Wayne Koestenbaum had told her; Koestenbaum also cites Derrida's *The Post Card*.
1.4 Nelson fears this possibility in her own writing. Referring both backward (to the passage from Wittgenstein on the first page of the text) and forward (to the brief discussion of Cordelia that takes place a couple of pages later), she writes: "The inexpressible may be contained (inexpressibly!) in the expressed, but the older I get, the more fearful I become of this nothingness, this waxing lyrical about those I love the most (Cordelia)."

2.1 Nelson finishes a first draft of *The Argonauts* and gives it to Harry. They try to address Harry's feelings of exposure and misrepresentation (of being waxed lyrical about) and Nelson's protectiveness of her writing.
2.2 Nelson and Harry attempt to negotiate what Nelson calls in *The Art of Cruelty* "the essentially unsolvable ethical mess that is autobiographical writing": the fact that "one person's interpretation of events that involved others"—that is, what autobiographical writing *is*—"nearly always make[s] someone feel betrayed."[120]

3.1 They had previously had an idea to write a book together, inspired by Gilles Deleuze and Claire Parnet's *Dialogues II* (1977), in which the voices of the two coauthors merge.
3.2 Nelson subsequently realized that she "wasn't ready to lose sight of *my own me*."

This passage is, I think, a fairly representative example of the issues *The Argonauts* deals with and the ways in which it deals with them. "I am,"

Nelson writes, "interested in offering up my experience and performing my particular manner of thinking, for whatever they are worth."[121] Here, she does both, recounting an aspect of her experience (her relationship with Harry) and performing her "particular manner of thinking," which is (in this book) fragmentary and densely allusive. Over the course of these eight paragraphs, Nelson makes reference to Winnicott, Snediker, Freud, Koestenbaum, Derrida, Shakespeare, William James, and Deleuze and Parnet. In addition to these connections between *The Argonauts* and other texts, the reader also makes connections within the text: back to the previous passages on Wittgenstein and forward to the discussion of Cordelia—though this single-word allusion to a discussion that has not yet occurred only really functions as such on a second reading. The passage moves from idea to idea rapidly—Nelson's description of herself as "a serial minimalist" is apt[122]—but explains each one lucidly. The way each paragraph relates to the next is fairly easy to discern, but the principle of combination is not plot-based; instead, the text moves forward based on associations between ideas, between experiences, and between ideas and experiences. Both aspects of the word Nelson uses to describe the book's genre—autotheory: self and theory—are not only fully on display but also deeply enmeshed within one other.

In what follows, I want to focus on two of the formal characteristics—fragments and allusions—and one of the thematic concerns—family-making—that are on display here.

4.1. Fragments

There are several models for Nelson's use of fragmentary form in *The Argonauts*. Perhaps the most prominent are two of the thinkers this chapter has already considered in detail: Barthes and Wittgenstein. The *Tractatus Logico-Philosophicus* and *Philosophical Investigations* are both written in numbered sections which at times approach the aphoristic, but which also have a very definite and specific order and structure. Discussing the *Tractatus*, Alfred Nordmann writes:

> Each of the remarks is introduced by its own number, set off from the ones that precede and follow it, thus literally surrounded by a bit of *space*. This physical *space* on the page corresponds to a *space* of thought of which the recorded remark is only an index or vestige, perhaps an invitation to move into this larger *space* by reenacting the conditions that may have produced the remark.[123]

Nordmann suggests that Wittgenstein's use of fragments creates not only a "physical space on the page" but also a "space of thought" for the reader. This argument has an obvious resonance with the one I have been making about the way that acknowledging the difficulties of communication can provide a reader with the necessary space to usefully hear a literary text. It suggests that the use of fragments can be a formal way of maintaining this productive gap: separated from a clear linear trajectory, each numbered remark in the *Tractatus* is an "invitation" for the reader to recreate the thought process evoked by the fragment. Nordmann's choice of word here is important: "invitation" figures the work the reader is prompted to do not so much as an obligation but as an opportunity. That is, it counteracts the possibility discussed above that an ethics of space could lead to an aesthetics that demands that the reader take on all the work of sense-making.

Discussing *Bluets*—which evokes Wittgenstein by referring to its 240 numbered fragments as "propositions"—Nelson broaches this question of the distribution of labor between author and reader:

> I'm sure one could write a book of very disconnected fragments that didn't so overtly weave into a whole—I've read many of them—but it's also true that the mind will always work overtime to put disparate things together; the Surrealists mined that tendency for all it was worth. I think that's a cool approach, to let the reader make the connections, but it's important to me as a writer to make sure that the connections, when made, actually point toward what I want to be pointing at, rather than just reflecting the human brain's capacity to make a bridge.[124]

There is a negotiation here: Nelson does not just scatter the pieces and leave the reader to pick them up and assemble them. They are written, chosen, and scattered in such a way as to allow the assemblage to "point toward what I want to be pointing at," which is something other than merely the act of assembling per se. Like *Bluets*, *The Argonauts* also arranges its pieces in a deliberate way. As discussed above, there are clearly discernable threads that link one paragraph to the next. But at the same time, the text displays a degree of ambivalence about the possibility of attempting to guide the reader too much: "I labor grimly on these sentences," she writes, "wondering all the while if prose is but the gravestone marking the forsaking of wildness (fidelity to sense-making, to assertion, to *argument*, however loose)."[125] Here, Nelson expresses an anxiety that her lucid prose is a misguided attempt to take on too much of the labor of "sense-making" herself, depriving readers of this opportunity by presenting them with an "assertion" or an "argument"—labels Nelson elsewhere explicitly distances her project from.[126] "Assertion" is a term she associates in particular with Barthes, who strives in *Roland Barthes by Roland Barthes* (1975) to outplay language's declamatory nature. In a passage that Nelson quotes, he considers the "absurd remedy" of "add[ing] to each sentence some little phrase of uncertainty," but his most notable method of responding to this bind is precisely his use of fragments.[127] The "breach" in continuity that Barthes's fragments bring about, he suggests, has the effect of preventing "a meaning from 'taking'":[128] that is, the fragments preserve a degree of fluidity, of resistance to fixed meaning, or of what Nelson might call "wildness." Fragments outplay the assertiveness—and with it, the potential violence—of linear, argumentative prose.

4.2. Allusions and Family-Making

From its title onward, *The Argonauts* is densely allusive. In an interview with Michael Silverblatt for *KCRW's Bookworm* podcast, Nelson locates her book within "a long tradition of books that like to provide your reading genealogy to other people in hopes of sharing references … as a form of … intellectual family-making."[129] Nelson is both reader and author, and she figures her connections both to the writers she reads and to the readers who read her as familial (in many cases these two categories cross over, as in the case of Fred Moten, Wayne Koestenbaum, or Eula Biss, who, as well as being quoted in *The Argonauts*, provide blurbs for it). This project of family-making has particular resonances with what Nelson refers to as "the long history of queers constructing their own families—be they composed of peers or mentors or lovers or ex-lovers or children or non-human animals."[130] The allusions in *The Argonauts* may, Nelson acknowledges, have an intimidating effect ("depending on … where you're at in your life when you encounter things that you don't know"), but the goal, for her, is to provide clear explanations of her reading list so that "if you're interested in it you can go find it."[131] At one point she even directly addresses the reader to this end: "I won't reproduce the image here," she writes, "but I encourage you to find [Dodie Bellamy's] *The Buddhist* and consult it."[132]

The parallel between reading/writing on the one hand and family-making (in particular motherhood) on the other is developed throughout *The Argonauts*.[133] Nelson is concerned not only to counter the ways in which maternity has been figured as antithetical to highbrow art and theory and to radical queer politics but also to underline the real and material connections between authorship and motherhood: "I estimate that about nine-tenths of the words in this book were written 'free,' the other one-tenth, hooked up to a hospital-grade breast pump: words piled into one machine, milk siphoned out by another."[134] Although (as discussed in Section 1.3) there is a sense in which maternal care and writing are mutually exclusive—"I cannot hold my baby at the same time as I write"[135]—motherhood also provides models for the kind of relationality to which writing can aspire. Nelson describes pumping milk as follows:

> While pumping milk may be about nourishment, it isn't really about communion. A human mother expresses milk because sometimes she can't be there to nurse her baby, either by choice or by necessity. Pumping is thus an admission of distance, of maternal finitude. But it is a separation, a finitude, suffused with best intentions. Milk or no milk, this is often the best we've got to give.[136]

The parallels with the model of authorship I have laid out in this chapter are striking: there is a necessary separation, an acknowledgment of the "distance" between two humans, twinned with a desire to connect, to give to the other. Writing "isn't really about communion," but it is nevertheless "suffused with best intentions." Milk and words are "the best we've got to give"—and even if they are finite, they can still be "good enough."[137]

These parallel thematic strands come together one final time at the very end of *The Argonauts*, when Nelson returns to Breton's *Mad Love* and feels finally able to rewrite it to address her son. It is worth comparing her version to the original:[138]

Mad Love	*The Argonauts*
You were thought of as possible, as certain, in the very moment	I want you to know, <u>you were thought of as possible</u>—never <u>as certain</u>, but always as possible—not <u>in</u> any single <u>moment</u>, but over many months, even years, of trying, of waiting, of calling—<u>when, in a love</u>
when, in a love deeply sure of itself,	sometimes <u>sure of itself</u>, sometimes shaken by bewilderment and change, but always committed to the charge of ever-deepening
a man and a woman	understanding—two human animals, one of whom is blessedly neither male nor female, the other of whom is female (more or less),
wanted you to be.	deeply, doggedly, wildly <u>wanted you to be</u>.

Nelson's emendations here serve several different functions. They are a queering of Breton's text, an undercutting of Breton's "hetero romanticism," and a reflection of the specificities of the particular relationship Nelson is describing and performing.[139] She emphasizes the communicative intent ("I want you to know"), the complexities of the context of Iggy's conception and of the gender identities of his parents, and the strength and nature of her and Harry's desire for Iggy to exist. The letter to Iggy is an act of communication as family-making in several senses: it concerns a literal genealogy between mother and son, a literary genealogy between one writer and another, and an "intellectual family-making" between author and reader: not just Iggy, but all of the book's readers. It is a communicative act that acknowledges the difficulties of communication—the fact that "relation can never be achieved in a simple fashion through writing"[140]—and in so doing creates the space that allows its readers (us and Iggy) to receive, usefully, Nelson's letter.

Chapter 2

INTENTION: THE INCONSISTENT ANTI-INTENTIONALISM OF ZADIE SMITH AND JUDITH BUTLER

> I'm forced to recognize that ideological inconsistency is, for me, practically an article of faith.
> —Zadie Smith, *Changing My Mind*

1. Introduction

1.1. Consulting the Oracle

In 2014, I gave a conference paper on the novelist, essayist, and photographer Teju Cole. I was interested in one of his many experiments with social media and digital texts; Cole's first book *Every Day Is for the Thief* (published in Nigeria in 2007, and revised and republished in the United States and the UK in 2014) began life as a blogging project, and his experiments with Twitter have found wide acclaim.[1] The particular project I wanted to discuss, though, was a series of annotations he had made on the website genius.com (known at the time as Rap Genius). Rap Genius's key feature is the ability to add marginal notes to text, from song lyrics to poetry and fiction, and in June 2013, Teju Cole uploaded the first three paragraphs of his 2011 novel *Open City* and added seven annotations, pointing out a series of allusions to *Beowulf*, Kazuo Ishiguro, Ernest Hemingway, Talib Kweli, Julian Barnes, J. M. Coetzee, and the Russian composer Rodion Shchedrin. I was interested in the ways in which a digital platform like this might affect our understanding of authorship and how readers relate to authors and their work.

The day before I was due to give the paper, I returned to the Genius page with Cole's annotations and noticed that an eighth annotation had been added— this one not by Cole, but by an ordinary user of the site, who pointed out that *Open City*'s comparison between bird migrations and human wanderings in its second paragraph bears a resemblance to the opening of *The Great Gatsby*.[2] The connection is fairly tenuous. I can find two lines in *Gatsby*'s first chapter that could be read as making this comparison, neither of them especially connected to *Open City*: a few pages in, Nick imagines the "perpetual wonder" of gulls flying over the elliptical landmasses of East and West Egg; later on (more promisingly), Daisy decides that a bird on her lawn "must be a nightingale come over on the Cunard or White Star Line."³ A bird imagined crossing the Atlantic on a human vessel in the 1925 novel, and a human "watching bird migrations" before beginning his own "aimless wandering" in the 2011 book—the connection is there.⁴

But I was unsure as to the status of this connection. Could it have been an intentional allusion? To what extent was it different from the connections that Cole himself pointed out in his annotations? What difference does a statement from the author make? When Teju Cole tweeted a link to the annotations, he described them as covering "all the allusions" on the first page of *Open City*.⁵ There are two important pieces of information being conveyed there: first, that the seven annotations explain *all* of the allusions, implying that, according to Cole, any further connections to be drawn between this excerpt and other texts (like *The Great Gatsby*) are not allusions. And second, that the seven connections that Cole annotates *are allusions*. And we generally understand allusiveness as, by definition, a matter determined by authorial intention, meaning that it makes a certain amount of sense to give some credence to Cole's statements of his intent. All of this would suggest that there *is* a key qualitative difference between the connections that Cole points out and the connection to Fitzgerald that somebody else pointed out.

As soon as authorial intention comes into the picture, though, things get complicated—not least because of the potential for committing the intentional fallacy. And indeed, the situation I am describing, in which I was faced with a text and was unsure as to whether a line from it ought to be considered an allusion, is precisely the situation described by William K. Wimsatt Jr. and Monroe C. Beardsley in their canonical 1946 essay, "The Intentional Fallacy." What ought a critic to do, they ask, if, reading T. S. Eliot's "The Love Song of J. Alfred Prufrock," they come across a line that bears a resemblance to a John Donne poem? In their hypothetical situation, the critic commits the mistake of "writ[ing] to Eliot and ask[ing] what he meant, or if he had Donne in mind."⁶ Wimsatt and Beardsley contend that, were Eliot to respond, "such an answer to such an inquiry would have nothing to do with the poem 'Prufrock'; it would not be a critical inquiry ... Critical inquiries are not settled by consulting the oracle."⁷ Wimsatt and Beardsley draw a clear line between what is internal to the text and therefore relevant and what is external and therefore irrelevant.

It had been a while since I had read "The Intentional Fallacy," however, and I had forgotten about this moment from their essay. So I made the very same mistake that Wimsatt and Beardsley's hypothetical critic does: I tried to settle a critical inquiry by "consulting the oracle." I tweeted at Cole, asking him if he had seen the new annotation and asking him if he had had *The Great Gatsby* in mind. Two hours later he responded: "I didn't have Gatsby in mind, no."⁸

At this point, I did reread "The Intentional Fallacy" and was startled to see the way in which Wimsatt and Beardsley's hypothetical situation had just come to life, as well as embarrassed at having committed such a cardinal error. According to critical orthodoxy, I ought to dismiss Cole's response as outside the proper sphere of investigation—but I was nevertheless reluctant to simply ignore this new piece of information, that Cole had confirmed that he *was not* deliberately alluding to *The Great Gatsby*. As an undergraduate, I had been well trained in avoiding the intentional fallacy. I had been happy to skirt around the issue of intentionality by discussing texts instead in terms of their effect and by thinking about connections between texts in terms of intertextuality rather than allusiveness or influence. "The Intentional Fallacy" has had a lasting effect on the way we think about literary interpretation and especially the way we teach literary interpretation: an approach that disavows extrinsic material in favor of an in-depth engagement with the text itself has an understandable pedagogical appeal.[9] But this coming-to-life of Wimsatt and Beardsley's essay had the effect of making visible and newly precarious my previously unquestioned assumption that the intentional fallacy was indeed a fallacy. Is it really preferable to avoid talking about authorial intention? Is it even really possible?

In this chapter, I want to think about situations in which our increasingly sophisticated ways of not talking about authorial intention fail. Situations in which intention becomes an important category, one that we feel the need to engage with. Situations in which we realize that, while avoiding discussions of intention solves certain problems, it creates others.

1.2. Intention and the Authorship Debates

In the decades since its publication, Wimsatt and Beardsley's essay has been canonized as a precursor to the critical theoretical debate about literary authorship that raged throughout the second half of the twentieth century. As Seán Burke notes in his anthology *Authorship: From Plato to the Postmodern*, questions of intention and the degree of both its accessibility and its relevance to interpretation have remained central to these conversations.[10] Wimsatt and Beardsley famously argue that authorial intention is neither accessible nor relevant. Their essay can be understood as part of a wider modernist and New Critical adherence to a theory of authorial impersonality, most canonically expressed by T. S. Eliot in "Tradition and the Individual Talent" (1919), in which meaning is understood as being located not in the author (and their intent) or the reader (and the effect it has upon them) but in the text itself. Since then, the intentionalism debates have tended to revolve around this same set of terms: text, author, and reader; meaning, intention, and effect. In "The Death of the Author" (1967), Roland Barthes of course goes even further than the New Critics, shifting the emphasis radically away from the author and their intention, and toward both the text and ultimately the reader—albeit a reader understood not as an individual human but as an impersonal site of the text's destination.[11] The same year, in an attempt to defend the author against modernist "assault," E. D. Hirsch makes the case in *Validity in Interpretation* that the meaning of a text is identical with "what the author meant"; the experience the reader has of the work, for Hirsch, is mere "significance" and remains secondary to intentional meaning.[12] A decade and a half later, Steven Knapp and Walter Benn Michaels out-Hirsch Hirsch: for them, Hirsch fails to follow through on his attempt to reattach meaning to what the author meant. Knapp and Michaels hold that, if Hirsch had truly understood the inseparability of intention and meaning—that "what a text means and what its author intends it to mean are identical"—then he would realize that the so-called problem of intention never existed in the first place.[13] And yet, despite Knapp and Michaels making the case that the entire enterprise of theorizing interpretation and intention should come to an end, intention remains a problem to which critics return again and again.[14] And, as we will see, the continued fascination with authorial intention is not just limited to academia: it also includes more public thinkers, like the novelist and essayist Zadie Smith.

This literary-studies debate about the supposed death of the author should also of course be understood in the context of a larger conversation in critical theory. This is the conversation that Seán Burke calls "the death of man" and that Fredric Jameson calls the "death of the subject."[15] Here, too, intention is a key issue—not specifically the intention of literary authors, but rather the intentions of speaking subjects more generally. Judith Butler, drawing a helpful connection between these two conversations, refers to the critique of the "author-subject": that is, the critique of the subject understood as the author of itself, as autonomous, as sovereign, and as fully intentional.[16] This critique goes back to the three thinkers Paul Ricoeur describes as the masters of a hermeneutics of suspicion: Marx, Nietzsche, and Freud.[17] The last couple of decades, however, have seen a backlash against the critique of the author-subject and against critique—with its characteristic strategies of demystification, negation, and suspicion—in general. This backlash is especially visible in the turn to surface reading and other forms of post-critical reading exemplified by Rita Felski's *The Limits of Critique* (2015)[18] and in the turn to beauty and aesthetics that we see in Elaine Scarry's *On Beauty and Being Just* (1999).[19]

In both of these conversations, then, the battle lines have been drawn up. Either we remain committed to the project of the critique of the author-subject or we push back against it. We are resolutely anti-intentionalist, or—even if we do not hold steadfastly to the untenable belief that intentions are transparently accessible and fully realizable—we resist anti-intentionalism. On the first side, we have most of progressive critical theory, including its psychoanalytic, Marxist, feminist, and queer versions. And on the other side, we have critics like Knapp and Michaels, Felski, and Scarry and those invested in the claim that "intention is an essential concept for literary study" like Joshua Gang and Kaye Mitchell.[20]

Generally speaking, Judith Butler has been understood as a member of the first camp and Zadie Smith as a member of the second. My claim in this chapter is that neither thinker fits quite so easily into these categories and that their inconsistency is precisely what's most interesting and useful about them.

We have very good reasons for understanding Butler as a thinker who remains fully committed to the critique of the author-subject. In fact, as Mari Ruti argues in *Between Levinas and Lacan* and "The Bad Habits of Critical Theory," Butler's later work remains committed to this project to a fault.[21] She also remains committed to critique more generally: see her contribution to *Is Critique Secular?* in 2009, and her 2016 *PMLA* article on Marx's "ruthless critique."[22] But what interests me most about Butler are the occasions when her "allegiance to the ritual of slaying the humanist subject" falters.[23] Especially in *Precarious Life: The Powers of Mourning and Violence* (2004), we can see moments when Butler displays some hesitation about the continued imperative to decenter, disrupt, and demystify the author-subject.

On the other hand, Zadie Smith's work has most often been understood as pushing back against the critique of intention. Supporting this conclusion is her essay "Rereading Barthes and Nabokov," in which she explicitly rebuffs the anti-intentionalism of Barthes's "The Death of the Author." My discussion of Smith focuses mostly on her 2005 novel, *On Beauty*, which has also been read along these lines. Anette Pankratz, for example, understands it as an instance of the author "writ[ing] back" to the declaration of the death of the author, and Dorothy Hale points out that Smith "overturn[s] both modernist pieties about the value of authorial impersonality and postmodernist pieties about the impersonal sources of all subjective agency."[24] The fact that *On Beauty*, as its title suggests, draws heavily on Elaine Scarry's book also fits neatly with this reading. As Smith tells us in the novel's acknowledgments, she found in Scarry not only a title but also "a chapter heading and a good deal of inspiration."[25] Scarry's argument in *On Beauty and Being Just* is that beauty has both a pedagogical and an ethical value. It is "a starting place for education" because it creates within us a sense of conviction about the truth of the beautiful object—as Roland Barthes puts it, a beautiful work of art makes us say "That's it, that's absolutely it!"—and thereby makes us eager to search for truth in other avenues.[26] And beauty has an ethical force because it teaches us to be attentive to and protective of beautiful objects and then to extend that "standard of care ... to more ordinary objects" in the wider world.[27] Zadie Smith, though, is particularly interested in the reasons why Scarry feels she has to make this argument in the first place: that she understands the academic humanities, in no small part because of the influence of critique, as having lost—or, worse, willingly sacrificed—the ability to appreciate the beauty of the works of art they study. Scarry, that is, takes anti-intentionalism to task for stripping literature of beauty and therefore stripping literary studies of their pedagogical and ethical value. My claim, though, is that *On Beauty*'s position with regard to the critique of intention is, to its credit, considerably more complex and that it is in fact predominantly—albeit inconsistently—anti-intentionalist.

The inconsistencies that characterize both Butler's and Smith's anti-intentionalism become especially visible in one particular context: discussions of hate speech and freedom of speech on university campuses. For both writers, this particular issue puts us in the same double bind that my initial anecdote made visible: how do we avoid falling prey to the intentional fallacy while still maintaining our ability to engage in a nuanced way with issues that are hard to discuss without recourse to a vocabulary of intentionality? As long as we remain dogmatically committed to an inflexible version of anti-intentionalism, we remain unable to have a productive discussion about hate speech and academic freedom. And as the debates around freedom of expression, content warnings, student activism, and safe spaces on campus continue to demonstrate, the need for a nuanced way of approaching these issues is more urgent than ever.[28]

My contention is that, as long as we remain dogmatically committed to one side of the battle lines or the other, that is not going to happen. Understanding Smith and Butler as inconsistent and as valuable precisely *for their inconsistency*, therefore, is one way of thinking through how to start righting that wrong.

2. On Beauty *and Anti-Intentionalism*

2.1. Zadie Smith and the Return to Authorial Intention

One may as well begin with Zadie Smith's essay, "Rereading Barthes and Nabokov." Published in 2009's *Changing My Mind*, the essay is Smith's most explicit published engagement with the question of authorial intention. It also shares a part of its genesis with *On Beauty*, in 2002–3, the year that Smith spent as a Fellow at the Radcliffe Institute for Advanced Study at Harvard University. The essay, Smith writes, "began life as a lecture, given at Harvard University, although it has been revised so extensively almost nothing of the original remains."[29] *On Beauty*, too, began life that year: Smith wrote part of the novel there, and, as many critics have noted, its setting is conspicuously similar to Harvard—where, notably, Elaine Scarry also teaches.[30]

Novel and essay also both draw heavily on Smith's undergraduate training at Cambridge, where she read Barthes for the first time. There she was taught "the New Criticism, very formally, and then later on … a kind of structuralist and postmodern criticism," two schools of criticism she understands as having in common "the idea of a text separated and not being absolutely dependent on the personality of the author." Within this way of thinking, "you can't know who this writer is really, it's useless knowledge … biography wasn't just a stain, it was banished."[31] In "Rereading Barthes and Nabokov," on the other hand, Smith—while acknowledging how taken she initially was with this critical dogma (exemplified in the essay by "The Death of the Author")—stakes out a position that opposes the anti-intentionalism in which she was trained.

Smith figures her changing relationship with Barthes—and with French theory more broadly—as a process of maturation, even a Künstlerroman: that is, her discovery, initial fascination, and eventual disillusionment with Barthes runs parallel to her process of becoming a writer. In school, she describes being taught "passive and authoritarian reading styles," in which texts were to be understood along rigid and literal lines, with little room for interpretative freedom.[32] Little wonder, then, that reading "The Death of the Author" in university was a moment of liberation, and indeed the moment in which Smith the reader started to become Smith the writer (she began her first novel, *White Teeth*, during her time at Cambridge): Barthes gave Smith the license to read a novel "upside down, back to front or in entirely anachronistic terms." "That kind of freedom," she tells us, "makes writers of readers."[33] This becoming-writer of the reader is of course entirely consistent with Barthes's project in the late 1960s and early 1970s, in *The Pleasure of the Text* and *S/Z*, or in "From Work to Text." In the latter, Barthes draws a distinction between the (bad) work (which he would elsewhere describe as "readerly") and the (good) Text (which corresponds to his definition of the "writerly" in *S/Z*): the Text, for him, "requires that one try to abolish (or at the very least to diminish) the distance between writing and reading."[34] The Text undoes the training of "the (secondary) School," which, for Barthes as for Smith, teaches students only "to *read* (well) and no longer to write."[35]

But if reading Barthes and learning to read literature as Text rather than work blurs the lines between reader and writer, that is not to say that this early-Barthesean approach makes for an effective way of thinking about actually *being a writer*. When Smith actually "became a writer," she tells us:

Writing became my discipline, my practice, and I felt the need to believe in it as an intentional, directional act, an expression of an individual consciousness ... Barthes, though, had no interest in what the author felt or wished you to feel, which is where my trouble starts.[36]

This is Smith's story of development, from reader, to reader-writer, to writer. As a reader in secondary school, she is taught to read passively and literally, accepting without question that the seeming intentions of the text determine its meaning: that "*Hard Times* = British education system in Victorian England."[37] As an undergraduate reader-writer, the "freedom of movement" she gains from Barthes allows her to read the text "against the grain," to become as much a "producer" as a "consumer" of text.[38] And finally, as a published author, she leaves Barthes and her anti-intentionalist training behind, returning to the assertion of authorial intention.

If we take this narrative of development seriously, it would seem to make sense to understand Smith alongside the group of artists that Walter Benn Michaels focuses on in his 2015 book *The Beauty of a Social Problem: Photography,*

Autonomy, Economy. In that book, Michaels is interested in a group of writers and photographers (among them Maggie Nelson), whom he sees as defined by their "simultaneous assertion of form and meaning":

> All of them were born after 1965 (and most in the 1970s), which is to say they were born and raised and began to study and produce art in a world where artistic ambition—especially insofar as form might be thought to establish the work's autonomy, or *meaning might be understood as a function of the artist's intentions*—was often identified with the critique of both.[39]

In other words, Michaels is telling a story about the history of artistic production in which a group of young artists does precisely what Zadie Smith (born in 1975) describes herself as doing in "Rereading Barthes and Nabokov": they rebel against their anti-intentionalist education, asserting their work as meaningful (and meaningful because of their artistic intentions) despite having been trained to believe, à la Barthes, that good, ambitious art (Text, rather than work) involves precisely the *critique* of artistic intention.

Michaels's study, then, begins from a similar starting point to both this chapter and this book as a whole: writers born mostly in the 1960s and 1970s (Zadie Smith in 1975, as well as Maggie Nelson in 1973, and David Foster Wallace in 1962—Chris Kraus, slightly older, was born in 1955; Teju Cole, with whom this chapter began, was born in 1975, a few months before Smith), who "began to study and produce art in a world where artistic ambition was often identified with the critique of" authorial autonomy and intention—and indeed, the critique of authorship per se. Michaels sees the critique of authorship as ultimately complicit with neoliberalism: demolishing the hierarchies between author and reader might make us better able to resist hierarchies based on race, gender, or sexuality, but it cannot do anything about the larger structural problems of rising economic inequality; furthermore, in its insistence on "the primacy of the beholder," the "neoliberal aesthetics" of the death of the author tends to reduce the work of art to a mere commodity for the beholder/consumer to do with as they please.[40] Hence, Michaels sees the *reassertion* of authorial ambition in writers like Nelson as progressive rather than reactionary. But as far as Zadie Smith—and in particular, *On Beauty*—is concerned, I want for the moment to leave open the question of her reassertion of authorship. While *On Beauty* undoubtedly provides some important resistance against the critique of the author-subject, and the critique of intentionality in particular, that is not to say that it makes the case for returning to an understanding of human beings as entirely self-knowing, autonomous, and capable of knowing and fulfilling their intentions. In what follows, I assess the novel's treatment of intention, paying close attention to both the ways in which it is asserted and the ways in which it proves inaccessible, indistinct, or insufficient.

2.2. On Beauty *against the Critique of Intention*

As I mentioned in the introduction to this chapter, *On Beauty* has for the most part been read as a reassertion of authorial ambition and intentionality, along the lines of Smith's statement of her poetics in "Rereading Barthes and Nabokov." Part of the basis of this argument lies in the fact that the novel heavily draws on E. M. Forster's *Howards End* (1910): for that reason, it is easy to read it, as many critics initially did, as a throwback to a bygone era, taking its inspiration not merely from modernism, but specifically from Forster, by reputation the most old-fashioned and formally traditional of the modernists.[41] As Frank Kermode notes in his review of *On Beauty* in the *London Review of Books*, Forster was, moreover, a novelist who (more than his contemporaries) valued "authority" and was "modestly certain of possessing" it, interrupting his narration to make preacherly announcements. In her choice of Forster as her model, then, it is easy to read Smith as expressing nostalgia for a time before "The Death of the Author" and "The Intentional Fallacy," a time when writing was understood (as Smith wants to understand it in "Rereading Barthes and Nabokov") as an "intentional, directional act, an expression of an individual consciousness."[42]

Such a reading finds further support in Smith's treatment of her protagonist, Howard Belsey. Howard is a British professor of Art History teaching at East Coast elite university Wellington College. His theoretical allegiances are unambiguously on the side of the critique of the author-subject:

> "What we're trying to ... *interrogate* here," he says, "is the mytheme of artist as autonomous individual with privileged insight into the human. What is it about these texts—these images as narration—that is implicitly applying for the quasi-mystical notion of genius?"[43]

The word "mytheme" here indicates Howard's background in the structuralism of Lévi-Strauss (*Structural Anthropology*) and Barthes (*Mythologies*), and his investment in the demystification of "the quasi-mystical notion of genius" indicates his commitment both to the critique of the author and to ideological critique more generally. His forthcoming book, fittingly, is titled *Against Rembrandt: Interrogating a Master*.[44] Howard is the epitome of those "postmodernist pieties about the impersonal sources of all subjective agency." And Smith is very clear about the ways in which such pieties not only fail but actually make Howard a pretty terrible person.

Howard's dogmatic allegiance to the critique of the author-subject makes him, as the body of criticism on the novel has consistently noted, a failure in both pedagogical and ethical terms.[45] As a teacher, Howard's approach, as much as it has in common with the Barthes of "The Death of the Author," does not have the same liberatory effect that that essay had on Smith at Cambridge. The version of (American) secondary education that Smith presents in *On Beauty* is far more positive than the version of (British) secondary education she described in "Rereading Barthes and Nabokov," to the point where the transition from high school to undergraduate work becomes a step backward: a college education, in *On Beauty*, serves to stamp out any pleasure students might have taken in art. Howard's loyal Kentuckian Teaching Assistant, Smith J. Miller, would have us believe that this is exactly what a college education ought to do, but his view is one that the novel finds sorely wanting: "Ah'm dealing with these kids who are still saying *Ah really like the part when* and *Ah love the way*—you know, that's their high-school-analysis level."⁴⁶ Sure, "*Ah really like the part when*" is not an especially sophisticated reaction to a literary text, but academic sophistication tends in *On Beauty* to go along with a whole host of undesirable characteristics. Specifically, for characters like Howard and his undergraduate daughter Zora, sophistication comes at the cost of the ability to take pleasure in art.

What is important for Smith about "*Ah really like the part when* and *Ah love the way*" is the fact that there is an aesthetic pleasure being taken. This is the same aesthetic pleasure that is expressed by Katie Armstrong, a sixteen-year-old freshman from South Bend, Indiana, who, despite the brevity of her appearance in the novel (disappearing after a mere six pages), is the source of some of *On Beauty*'s most thoughtful and generous thinking about art.⁴⁷ Katie used to dream, we are told, "about one day attending a college class about Rembrandt with other intelligent people who loved Rembrandt and weren't ashamed to express this love."⁴⁸ Howard's is not such a class. She finds the conversation dominated by two professors' daughters and a young Heideggerian named Mike, who, intelligent as he seems to Katie, certainly does not seem like he loves Rembrandt. Howard, for his part, alienates her with poststructuralist jargon—"she felt the professor to be speaking a different language"—misnames her—"Kathy—everything good?"—and effectively pushes her out of both his class and the novel, never to be heard from again.⁴⁹ The pedagogical environment she dreamt of, in which aesthetic pleasure is something to be celebrated rather than a source of shame, never materializes.

Instead, we get a classroom where the pleasures taken are of a different nature. Unlike Katie and the other freshmen who "*like*" and "*love*" literature so unashamedly, Zora is described by Smith J. Miller as "lahk a text-eating machine," "rip[ping] apart" Joyce and Eliot, "strip[ping] the area of sentiment."⁵⁰ It is not that Zora gains no pleasure from reading. Rather, it is that her pleasure stems not from an act of appreciation (like Katie's), but from an act of critique. In this sense, she is her father's daughter. Howard, as his wife Kiki tells him, is prone to similar acts of demolition and uncovering: "all you ever do is rip into everybody else."⁵¹ It is in this kind of act, rather than in contemplating a Rembrandt painting, that Howard gets his kicks:

> To enact with one sudden tug (like a boy removing his friend's shorts in front of the opposing team) a complete exposure, a cataclysmic embarrassment—this is one of the purest academic pleasures. One doesn't have to deserve it; one has only to leave oneself open to it.⁵²

Enacting "complete exposure": this is the familiar language of Ricoeur's hermeneutics of suspicion, the dominant logic of critique that Rita Felski describes as the imperative "to *expose* hidden truths and draw out unflattering and counterintuitive meanings that others fail to see."[53] I will return to this idea in more detail later (Section 2.4), in an extended engagement with Felski and the expansive critical conversation around the limitations of critique. For now, the key point is this: in *On Beauty*, the persistent need to critique, to subject the text and its author (or the painting and its artist) to forceful interrogation (ripping, stripping, eating), is associated not only with ethical failure but also with a kind of immaturity. Howard is, in the novel's judgment, worse and less mature than the freshmen with their "*Ah really like the part when*": he is no better than "a boy removing his friend's shorts in front of the opposing team." And behind it all, providing theoretical support for his ethically indefensible actions—cheating on his wife not once but twice, alienating his family and his students—is the death of the author and the critique of authorial intention.

So *On Beauty* critiques the critique of intention. So far, so much like Walter Benn Michaels's argument in *The Beauty of a Social Problem*. But is the critique of the critique of intention the same as the reassertion of intention? In order to start answering this question, it is necessary to look at the novel more broadly, rather than just reading its characters as representative of certain views and the novel's sympathetic or unsympathetic treatment of those characters as evidence of its position with respect to their views. In particular, it helps to look at the way Smith treats psychoanalysis, the example par excellence of a theory that undermines the idea of the sovereign intention.

2.3. On Beauty *and Psychoanalysis*

In "Rereading Barthes and Nabokov," the flipside of Barthes's power-to-the-reader thesis is the "bold assertion of authorial privilege" that Smith admires in Nabokov.[54] And in Smith's argument, such an assertion of the right to actualize authorial intentions goes hand in hand with an aversion to psychoanalysis: "Nabokov's profound hostility to Freud was no random whim—it was the theory of the unconscious itself that horrified him. He couldn't stand to admit the existence of a secondary power directing and diverting his own. Few writers can."[55] Nabokov cannot stand Freud because Freud critiques the idea of the author-subject as fully intentional, as fully in control. Smith, on the other hand, although she admits to "a vocational need to believe in Nabokov's vision of total control," has a far more ambivalent attitude toward Freud.[56] *White Teeth*, for example, engages with *Beyond the Pleasure Principle* and its theorization of trauma, the death drive, and the repetition compulsion to great effect, and ultimately sides with Freud in his critique of the voluntaristic, pleasure-driven subject.[57] And in *On Beauty*, Smith is dismissive of a certain vulgar Freudianism, but much more sympathetic to the basic psychoanalytic insight that our conscious intentions are constantly and fundamentally undermined by the unconscious.

The first of the two extramarital affairs that Howard has is with his colleague and long-time friend, the poet Claire Malcolm. Claire goes twice a week to see a psychiatrist in Boston named Dr Byford, who interprets her symptoms as part of "a pattern ... rooted in her earliest babyhood": Claire is, according to Dr Byford, "a woman still controlled by the traumas of her girlhood."[58] This version of psychoanalysis is not one that is presented in an especially positive light. And it is certainly one that Lacan, with his disdain for American ego-psychology, would scoff at, not least because Dr Byford sees the unconscious residues of trauma as immunizing Claire against all responsibility—"It made more sense to put her three-year-old self in the dock"—whereas Lacan sees the psychoanalytic discovery as making the subject precisely *more* responsible for their actions.[59] This crude version of psychoanalysis is essentially a story told to explain away irrational behavior, for the purposes of comfort and stability. In this sense, it is very similar to the liberal "creation myths" about conservatives that Howard's right-wing rival Monty Kipps derides: "you liberals," he tells Kiki, "choose to believe that conservatives are motivated by a deep self-hatred, by some form of ... *psychological flaw*. But, my dear, that's the most comforting fairytale of them all!"[60] Such a belief is comforting to liberals, Monty suggests, because it allows them to understand conservativism as an irrational behavior that can be explained away as a "psychological flaw"; if it weren't for this flaw, conservatives would turn out to be liberals like everyone else. Under this view, everyone has the right intentions—Claire wants to be a good, happy subject, and conservatives want to be good, happy liberals—but they are just held back by their inconvenient traumas and psychological flaws, and if those could just be corrected, everything would be fine.

But there is a better, less trite reading of psychoanalysis that informs *On Beauty*, and it is one in which we are not reducible to comprehensible, pleasure-driven intentions and the obstacles that stand in their way. Smith is especially interested in the role of the body in relation to our conscious intentions, and in that sense, the closest theoretical parallel to what she does with psychoanalysis, I would suggest, is Shoshana Felman's *The Scandal of the Speaking Body: Don Juan with J. L. Austin, or Seduction in Two Languages*. Originally published in French in as *Le Scandale du corps parlant* in 1980, then translated into English under the title *The Literary Speech Act* in 1983, before being republished with its new, more faithful title in 2003, Felman's project in this book is to bring together Lacanian psychoanalysis and J. L. Austin's work on the performative in order to theorize the speech act as a specifically *bodily* act. For Felman, "the relation between language and the body" is one "of incongruity and inseparability."[61] Judith Butler summarizes her argument as follows: Felman "suggests that the speech act, as the act of a speaking body, is always to some extent unknowing about what it performs, that *it always says something that it does not intend*, and that it is not the emblem of mastery or control that it sometimes purports to be."[62] Felman's reading of Freud (alongside Austin and Lacan) is one that undermines the sovereign intentional subject much more profoundly than

Dr Byford's clichéd ego-psychology. For Felman, "Freud discovers not simply that the act subverts knowledge"—this would be Byford's reading—"but also that it is precisely from the *breach in knowledge*"—that is, the unconscious—"that the act takes its performative *power*: it is the very *knowledge that cannot know itself*"—again, the unconscious, here in Lacan's definition—"that, in man, *acts*."[63] To put that more simply, the unconscious is not a mere obstacle to the speech act: it is a fundamental part of what speaks. And it is through the body that this unconscious-driven, perpetually misfiring speech act takes place.

A similar interpretation of the Freudian insight is visible in *On Beauty*, in which Smith's speaking bodies always say and do things that they do not intend. The most important example here is Kiki, who is all too aware of the ways in which her body, combined with the cultural history in which it is entwined, exceeds her intentions:

> Kiki suspected already that this would be one of those familiar exchanges in which her enormous spellbinding bosom would play a subtle (or not so subtle, depending on the person) silent third role in the conversation … The size was sexual and at the same time more than sexual: sex was only one small element of its symbolic range. If she were white, maybe it would refer only to sex, but she was not. And so her chest gave off a mass of signals beyond her direct control: sassy, sisterly, predatory, motherly, threatening, comforting … Her body had directed her to a new personality; people expected new things of her, some of them good, some not.[64]

Here, as in *The Scandal of the Speaking Body*, the body is "that which acts in excess of what is said."[65] But Smith also departs from Felman, in that she is much more interested in the social. In this specific example, Smith is interested in the part that race plays in the Black female body's excessive signification. And more broadly, she is interested in the ways in which our intentions are undermined by *other people*—by the conscious intentions and by the unconscious drives and desires of those with whom we share the world.

In *On Beauty*, then, Smith draws on Freud's analysis of the ways in which the unconscious undermines our conscious intentions, but she is also interested in the many other forces that undermine our intentions. To put it another way, she draws on the psychoanalytic insight about the ways in which our intentions fail because of our selves but adds to this a consideration of the ways in which our intentions fail because of others. Thus, on the one hand, Smith consistently demonstrates the ways in which our unconscious drives us toward things from which our pleasure-driven intentions would run the opposite way. This tendency is visible in a passage in which Howard goes wandering and ends up, without realizing, on the doorstep of the father he has conscientiously avoided for four years: "He had no plans—or at least, his conscious mind told him he had none. His subconscious had other ideas."[66] It is also visible in the way that Claire offers herself to Howard, even though "she had not really known why," even though she is in a stable relationship with someone else, and even though she had "no sexual desire whatsoever" for him.[67] But on the other hand, Smith also brings out the complex negotiation that takes place between our desires (conscious and unconscious) and the desires of others—family, friends, or lovers. Sometimes our intentions fail because another character has the opposite intention: "I know that wasn't your original intention, Howard, but given the circumstances …"[68] Sometimes they go awry because another character has the *same* intention, as when Howard and Kiki fight: "Howard was intent on slamming the door behind him, and Kiki was equally determined to kick it shut. The force of it knocked the plaster picture to the floor."[69] And sometimes, as in the example discussed above, they fail because of the complex interaction between our intentions, our bodies, the racial imaginaries through which others see them, and our corresponding perceptions of those others' perceptions.

2.4. On Beauty *and Critique*

We are now in a better position to answer the question I posed at the beginning of my discussion of *On Beauty*: to what extent does the novel push back against the critique of intention? The answer, evidently, is complex. On the one hand, it does exactly that, in that it finds the academic critique of the author-subject sorely wanting in both pedagogical and ethical terms. On the other hand, it draws on and even extends this critique, demonstrating the myriad ways in which intention is undermined by the self, by others, and by the histories and cultural codes in which we are enmeshed.

My claim is this: Zadie Smith does not fit with Walter Benn Michaels's group of young artists rebelling against their anti-intentional training quite as easily as she initially appears to, in that her quarrel is not with anti-intentionalism per se, but rather with *bad readings* of anti-intentionalism, like Dr Byford's Freud-lite and Howard's empty poststructuralist posturing. Or to put it another way, it's not so much the critique of *intention* that Smith is pushing back against in *On Beauty*. Rather, it's the *critique* of intention: critique, and the pleasure taken in it, the pleasure taken in "complete exposure," in ripping texts apart and stripping them down.[70] Thus, I would contend that when critics focus on the novel's relationship with E. M. Forster and liberal humanism and suggest that the novel sits astride "postmodernism's emphasis on the random or contingent" and "liberal humanism's confident assertion of the autonomous individual, supremely responsible for his or her own acts," they misread the novel.[71] I am in agreement that the random and the contingent, in the guise of the unconscious, the body, and society, inform Smith's novelistic universe. But I do not think that it is the autonomous, intentional subject of liberal humanism that is the other side of this coin in *On Beauty*. To put it another way, whereas some critics read *On Beauty* as occupying a middle ground between postmodernism and what came before it (the era of E. M. Forster's liberal humanism), I argue that the novel can be better understood as embodying the tension between postmodernism and what comes *after* it. When Smith parodies "postmodernism's emphasis on the random or contingent," she is not trying to make a case for the reassertion of the fully intentional subject; she is not trying to turn the clock back.[72] Rather, she is making a case against some of the unwanted side effects of the *critique* of that subject and a case against critique in general. In this sense, the novel is less a throwback to the lost era of Forster than it is a participant in a very current debate in the humanities about the limits of critique.

Conversations about the limits of critique go back much further than Rita Felski's 2015 book of that name. Susan Sontag's "Against Interpretation" (1966) is one frequently cited predecessor to the current conversation. The late work of Roland Barthes can be read as another. But the two most recent instantiations of the debate—the turn to aesthetics and discussions of beauty and the turn to surface reading and other forms of post-critical reading—have led to a renewed and expanded degree of attention being paid to how we read texts and why. Up to this point, *On Beauty* has been read as participating in only the first of these critical conversations: because of its extended engagement with Elaine Scarry's *On Beauty and Being Just*, Smith's novel has frequently been understood as participating in the critical renewal of interest in aesthetics of which Scarry's book is a key part.[73] My claim is that Smith's novel might be more usefully understood in relation to both the turn to beauty *and* the turn to surface reading, in that both these critical turns share with *On Beauty* a turn *against* critique.

These two turns understand critique as an approach characterized by the same kinds of interpretive practices that Ricoeur analyzed in his influential work on the hermeneutics of suspicion and its chief practitioners, Freud, Marx, and Nietzsche. The Enlightenment subject—the author-subject, the intentional subject—was the victim par excellence of the aggressive, suspicious modes of reading practiced by these thinkers and their descendants, from Barthes to Butler. The turn to beauty and the turn to surface reading both spring from the conviction that such a reading practice is limited and even harmful. Elaine Scarry suggests in *On Beauty and Being Just* that, after several decades spent exposing the complicity of canonical works of art with oppressive power structures, we have forgotten, and indeed "banish[ed]" from discussion, a significant part of what made those works of art worthy of attention in the first place: their beauty.[74] Rita Felski, in *The Limits of Critique*, argues along similar lines that critique has, through overuse, lost any of the political bite it once had, becoming little more than a series of rote exercises in literary detective work.[75] Bruno Latour even points to the appropriation of critique by such reactionary causes as climate change denial: further evidence that critique has, in his phrase, "run out of steam."[76]

What ought to replace critique and the hermeneutics of suspicion, of course, is another question entirely and one to which a great many answers have been proposed. "Surface reading" proper is associated primarily with Stephen Best and Sharon Marcus's fall 2009 special issue of *Representations* on *The Way We Read Now* (which opens with Best and Marcus's "Surface Reading: An Introduction"), but I am using the term here, as has become common practice, to refer metonymically to a wider range of reading practices that Felski has characterized as "postcritical": "just reading," "reading with the grain," and "denotative reading," as well as the anthropology- and sociology-influenced methodologies that Heather Love has discussed under the title of "the descriptive turn."[77] These reading practices share, at least to a certain degree, an interest in the literal over the figurative, in surfaces over depths, and in description over interpretation. In these allegiances, the turn to surface reading shares at least some of its tenets with the turn to beauty. The thinkers writing under that banner, including Scarry, Denis Donoghue, and Alexander Nehamas, have tended to advocate, both explicitly and by example, for approaches that pay attention to the aesthetic and affective power of the work of art, not in order to demystify it, but in order to emphasize what can be learnt from it.

Such approaches have not been met with universal acceptance, and even within the list of thinkers cited above there is a significant degree of disagreement. Felski and Schmitt, for example, both maintain that the Best-and-Marcus version of surface reading is logically suspect in its reliance on the surface/depth binary.[78] More broadly, surface reading and its cousins have been frequently perceived as harboring an anti-intellectual strain. Sianne Ngai, for example, has expressed reservations about the way that surface reading, in rejecting interpretation, seems paradoxically to want to see more about the objects it studies by knowing *less*. Ngai holds, on the other hand, that the more you know about a work of art, the more you see. And for her, knowing more about a work of art—knowing, for example, that *Mansfield Park* is about imperialism—does not damage our aesthetic relationship to the work, as Scarry's argument implies, but enhances it.[79] And to extend Ngai's point, if, as Scarry and Felski advocate, literary criticism were to move away from the kind of cultural criticism exemplified by Edward Said's iconic argument about *Mansfield Park*, it would also lose a significant degree of its claim to political value.

Where, then, does *On Beauty* stand in the context of this conversation? And if, as I have argued, *On Beauty* can be understood as making a case against critique, what is it making a case *for*? For the most part, the body of criticism on the novel has read it as making the same argument as Scarry—that like Scarry, Smith is making a case for the importance of beauty as the grounds of an ethics and for the importance of the university's role as an arbiter and conservator (rather than a demystifier or critic) of the beautiful.[80] The case for the importance of beauty and the university's role in its preservation is perhaps most clearly visible in the novel's ending. Here, finally, Howard begins to regain both the humanity and the appreciation for beauty that he has gone without (to no good end) for the preceding 440 pages.

The final pages of the novel describe a lecture on Rembrandt that Howard is scheduled to give at a gallery in Boston. Just as he begins his lecture, however, Howard realizes that he has left his notes in the car. Instead, he ends up clicking through the slideshow of Rembrandt paintings, in complete silence, until he reaches the final slide: a painting of Rembrandt's love, Hendrickje. Howard announces its title and date, and "said no more."[81] In a silence disturbed only by the perplexed muttering of his audience, Howard zooms in on Hendrickje, until her "fleshiness filled the wall."[82] In the novel's final paragraph, Smith describes the painting, and a fleeting moment of connection that takes place between Howard, on stage, and his now-estranged wife Kiki, in the audience. The narration then returns to describing the painting, and Rembrandt's depiction of Hendrickje's skin, with its "ever present human hint of yellow, intimation of what is to come."[83] And there the novel ends.

How are we to understand this? Howard's silence here is presented as, paradoxically, his most eloquent moment as an art historian: despite the confusion of most of his "faintly frowning" audience, it is the connection with Kiki that counts.[84] A key part of the reason for this, as Fiona Tolan, Kathleen Wall, and John Su have all pointed out, is that in this moment "Howard seems to appreciate a kind of beauty in the painting that he had previously attempted to deconstruct."[85] And appreciation of beauty, as in Scarry's argument, has a positive ethical outcome: "The recognition of the beauty of the other finally enables Howard to relinquish his selfishness."[86] But an important question remains: what, having abandoned critique for appreciation and recognition, does criticism look like? Does it exist at all? Does it consist merely in selecting beautiful objects and standing silently in front of them? What, if anything, does Howard's silence say?

This silence is the nearest the novel comes to offering us a model of post-critical reading; if there is an answer to the question of what the novel presents as a viable alternative to critique, it is in Howard's silence that we are most likely to find it. In one sense, then, the ending feels like a cop-out, as if, when faced with the question of what comes after critique, the novel declines to answer and promptly shuts up shop. In another sense, we could understand it as a parody of surface reading: if we abandon critique, then we have nothing left to say; surface reading can be no more than what Heather Love calls (albeit less pejoratively) "thin description," if that.[87] Or is this another moment of the author pushing back against the declaration of their death? If, as Susan Sontag claims, "interpretation is the revenge of the intellect upon art," then is Howard's failure to carry through his planned critique of Rembrandt an instance of the revenge of art—and the revenge of the artist—upon the intellect?[88] In a different essay, Sontag provides us with a whole host of other potential ways of reading Howard's silence: silence as "a metaphor for a cleansed, non-interfering vision"—that is, a kind of noninterpretive (noncritical) way of seeing, like surface reading.[89] Silence as "certifying the absence or renunciation of thought" or, conversely, as "certifying the completion of thought."⁹⁰ Silence as a gesture toward "the ineffable" evoked by the beauty of the painting.⁹¹ Silence, in its lack of determinacy, seems richer and more full of potential than a voiced, effable piece of criticism could ever be.

And perhaps this is the point: silence is more compelling than critique in this moment because it is roomier, because it contains multitudes, whereas critique, at least as Howard practices it, is narrow, singular, and predictable.⁹² We already know exactly how Howard's interrogation of Rembrandt and "the quasi-mystical notion of genius" would go, but his silence, on the other hand, is represented as an opening toward new possibilities.⁹³ If arguments against critique like Felski's and Scarry's are persuasive, then I would contend that they are most so when they are arguments against *the dominance of* critique, rather than arguments against critique per se—when they are arguments against critique as dogma, as *doxa*, as automatism, as bad habit.⁹⁴ Howard's brand of critique does not fail because it is *wrong*: Smith agrees with him that humans *are not* fully intentional, autonomous, sovereign subjects. It fails because it is dogmatic and inflexible, because it has become rote: Howard has been delivering exactly the same undergraduate course on "Constructing the Human: 1600–1700" for six years.⁹⁵ Conversations about the limits of critique can be exciting in the way they prompt us to think about new possible ways of doing criticism outside of critique—not in prescribing one particular way of doing criticism as a new norm. They are exciting in their orientation toward the future. This openness, this sense of new possibilities, is what I would argue is most valuable about Howard's silence. It is a sort of death—Howard literally "croak[s]" the title of the painting and "said no more," as if uttering his last words⁹⁶—but it is also a rebirth. The last line of the novel again: "the even present human hint of yellow, *intimation of what is to come.*"⁹⁷

3. The Humanities Quandary

3.1. Judith Butler and the Humanities Quandary

I want to turn now to Judith Butler and to a story she tells at the beginning of the final chapter of *Precarious Life: The Powers of Mourning and Violence*— published one year before *On Beauty*. It is a story that is strikingly similar to an episode from Smith's novel. In these two moments, both of which take place in universities, at meetings of faculty and administration, the focus is on a professor whose theoretical allegiance is with the critique of the author-subject, who is faced with a double bind. Both Howard Belsey and Judith Butler, committed as they are to the critique of intention, find themselves unable to respond to pressing problems without recourse to the vocabulary of intentionality. Accordingly, these are moments that get to the heart of the issues I am dealing with in this chapter. Specifically, through Butler I want to firmly ground the critique of intention in the genealogy of the critique of the subject, and through Smith, I want to start to think about the connection between the critique of intention and the topic of hate speech and academic freedom. Let us start with Butler.

Judith Butler's story is of a meeting she attended, in which she hears a university press director describe a separate meeting, in which a president of a university discussed the crisis in the humanities. "I'm not sure whether he [the press director] was saying that the university president was saying that the humanities had lost their moral authority, but it sounded like this was, in fact, someone's view, and that it was a view to take seriously."[98] There are several layers of reported speech here, which makes it difficult to ascertain the origin of the address: Butler hears "someone's view," which may or may not have been the president's view, which is reported by the press director and, then, through Butler, to the reader. Whoever's the view is though, it concerns the humanities' loss of moral "authority": that word is worth noting, because, as we will see, the story Butler is telling here is a story about authorship.

The press director's report prompts a discussion in the meeting Butler is attending, a discussion

> in which it was not always possible to tell which view was owned by whom, or whether anyone really was willing to own a view. It was a discussion that turned on the question, Have the humanities undermined themselves, with all their relativism and questioning and "critique," or have the humanities been undermined by all those who *oppose* all that relativism and questioning and "critique"?[99]

So if the humanities have lost their authority, then two opposing answers are being proposed here as to how this came about. One: that it is the fault of the humanities themselves, because of their devotion to the project of "relativism and questioning and 'critique'"—and we should understand the discourse of anti-intentionalism and the author's death (the project of cutting the tether, as Butler will put it in the next paragraph, between discourse and authors) as a central part of that project. According to this argument, the death of the author has, ironically, become disempowering precisely for the author's killers—for professors like Howard, with his interrogation of "the mytheme of artist as autonomous individual"[100]—who failed to anticipate that their own authority would vanish along with (or, more pessimistically, instead of) the authority of, say, Rembrandt, or the white-male-dominated literary canon. The opposite argument is that the humanities have had their authority "undermined by all those who *oppose*" the critique of the author-subject. In this case, the irony has a slightly different cast: in attempting to uphold authorship in the face of attacks from the marauding postmodern relativists, those who wish to see the authority of the humanities preserved—like Howard's conservative rival Monty, author of a very different book on Rembrandt—have unwittingly contributed to its depletion.

But there is another loss of authority going on here, at the level of the discussion itself: the views being shared in the meeting cannot easily be tied to an owner, so it becomes difficult not only to know who, if anyone, has undermined the humanities but even to know who is claiming what in response to this question. Did the university press director think that the humanities had lost their authority? Did the president? Who, among the other participants in the discussion, thought what? "It was not always possible to tell."[101] The humanities seem to have lost their authority, and so do the participants in the meeting.

Butler continues:

> I started to wonder whether I was not in the middle of the humanities quandary itself, the one in which no one knows who is speaking and in what voice, and with what intent. Does anyone stand by the words they utter? Can we still trace those words to a speaker or, indeed, a writer? And which message, exactly, was being sent?[102]

At this point, it becomes clear that what Butler is really talking about is authorship. The "humanities quandary" she describes is a quandary of authorship. The categories at stake—identity, voice, intention, responsibility, origin, meaning: these are the categories of the authorship debates. To be in the humanities quandary, or even to be in the humanities per se, is for Butler to subject these categories to "questioning" and "critique."

All of which makes it hard to say anything very definite about the crisis in the humanities. Which is a problem:

> Although I did not know in whose voice this person was speaking, whether the voice was his own or not, I did feel that I was being addressed, and that something called the humanities was being derided from some direction or another. To respond to this address seems an important obligation during these times.[103]

Butler is in a double bind. Near the beginning of this chapter, I said that I was interested in the moments of hesitation about the continued imperative to decenter, disrupt, and demystify the author-subject on display in *Precarious Life*. This is one such moment. Faced with an address of no clearly discernible origin, Butler has no recourse to the kind of model of authorship (the author as a single speaking subject who expresses their intentions through a transparent medium) that would help her to engage on level terms with this address. She writes:

> Of course, it would be paradoxical if I were now to argue that what we really need is to tether discourse to authors, and in that way we will reestablish both authors and authority. *I did my own bit of work, along with many of you, in trying to cut that tether.*[104]

Butler's early work, most famously *Gender Trouble* (1990), is deeply invested in the critique of the Enlightenment subject, understood as autonomous, rational, sovereign, implicitly white, straight, and male, and capable of expressing his intentions. Part of that critique is the critique of the author, the cutting of the "tether" between discourse and authors. In the context of *Gender Trouble*'s argument about gender and performance, for example, we can think of the subversive repetitions of gender performativity that Butler observes in drag shows as cutting the tether between the performer (the author) on the one hand and gender performance and expression (discourse) on the other.[105] Alternatively, in 1997's *Excitable Speech*, witness the focus on "*untethering* the speech act from the sovereign subject" so as to theorize a version of subjectivity that understands humans as "operating with a linguistic field of enabling constraints," thereby helping Butler to reconceptualize agency as non-sovereign and nonautonomous.[106] Butler, then, did her "own bit of work" in cutting that tether—as, she ventures, did "many of you," her imagined readers. That is to say, much of the impetus of critical theory in the last few decades of the twentieth century has been to further the critique of the Enlightenment subject that begins with Marx, Freud, and Nietzsche, and their hermeneutics of suspicion.

But in this moment, Butler expresses a degree of hesitance regarding this project: as the conditional mood of the quotation ("Of course, it would be ...") implies, the next sentence begins with the conjunction "but."[107] That moment of hesitation—*yes, it's important to critique the Enlightenment subject, but ...*—is the moment I am interested in here. Butler's hesitation comes from the fact that, as she suggests, the effect of several decades spent disestablishing authors and authority has been to make it more difficult to think through "the structure of address" and to "respond" to the specific address that she has just described. Having comprehensively deconstructed notions of authority—the authority of the canon, of oppressive norms of gender and sexuality, of colonial and imperial power, and of the author—it then becomes difficult for humanities scholars to claim the "moral authority" that (according to an unnamed university president, but also according to many participants in a broader conversation under the banner of the Crisis in the Humanities) the humanities have lost. In that sense, Butler seems to side implicitly—and unexpectedly— with the argument that "the humanities undermined themselves, with all their relativism and questioning and 'critique.'"

But Butler remains committed to critique and the cutting of the tether between discourse and authors. Her aim—and here, I hope, the parallels between Butler's project and Smith's should start to become visible—is not to undo the important work of decades of critical theory and continental philosophy by attempting "the rehabilitation of the author-subject *per se*."[108] Rather, it is to preserve the insights provided by the critique of the author-subject while still maintaining the space to be able to talk about, and even sometimes to claim, authority and agency. This is a project that is all the more important in the context of the crisis in the humanities, and it is the project of much of Butler's more recent and more politically oriented work.[109] Speaking more broadly, it is also the project of much work from the last three decades in feminist theory, critical race theory, queer theory, and affect theory.[110] Drawing on that work, it is also a key part of the project of *Authorship's Wake*. And, I am arguing, it is a project that we can understand Zadie Smith's work as participating in.

As much as Butler is aware of the limitations of the critique of the author-subject, then, she still remains invested in it as a project. In her moment of hesitation, she does express a desire for the "return" of "a consideration of the structure of address," but this return is not a step backward. It is the opposite of a reactionary move. If the political motivation of the critique of the author-subject was in part to enable oppressed subjects of all stripes to resist oppressive power structures, then Butler's return to the "structure of address" is motivated by precisely the same desire: "It is about *a mode of response*," she writes, "that follows upon having been addressed, a comportment toward the Other"—and in "Other" we can also read "Author" and "Authority"—"only after the Other has made a demand upon me, accused me of a failing, or asked me to assume a responsibility."[111] Butler's project is not just to critique the author-subject. Rather, she focuses on the power structures that put some in a position of authority and exclude others, aiming both to critique authority *and* to enable those excluded from authority to respond—or, in bell hooks's phrase, to "talk back."[112] Just as Sara Ahmed in *Willful Subjects* returns to the idea of will or volition in order to "deepen" rather than refute "the critique of the volitional subject," so Butler in *Precarious Life* returns to the ideas of address, authority, and intention in order to deepen the critique of the author-subject.[113]

3.2. Howard Belsey and the Humanities Quandary

In this passage from *Precarious Life*, it was Butler who found herself in the "humanities quandary." In a parallel episode in *On Beauty*, on the other hand, Howard Belsey finds himself in the same dilemma. Whereas the broader context of Butler's account is the crisis in the humanities, the episode from Smith's novel takes place in the context of a debate around freedom of speech on campus. This debate is of course but one instantiation of a continuing conversation about speech, safety, and freedoms in universities, most recently discussed via the questions of content warnings, no platform policies, safe spaces, and student activism. In *On Beauty*, the issue at stake is a series of lectures to be delivered by Monty Kipps, with the Stanley-Fish-esque title "Taking the Liberal Out of the Liberal Arts." Just as E. M. Forster frames *Howards End* around the tension between two families with different sets of values, so Smith frames *On Beauty* around the rivalry between Howard (white, from a working-class background, left-leaning) and Monty (a wealthy Black conservative), and the tensions— ideological and romantic—between the Belsey and the Kipps families. Howard's and Monty's enmity comes to a head during this meeting, in which Howard asks that the faculty "be given a proposed outline of these lectures; or, failing that, we shall be told this morning *what the intention of the lectures is.*"[114]

Howard's request is fueled partly by his dislike of Kipps, partly by his theoretical allegiances, and partly by concern that—based on Monty's history of "reductive and offensive public statements ... about homosexuality and race and gender"—the content of his lectures may "contravene the internal 'hate laws' of" Wellington College.[115] He presents himself as being against no-platform policies, stating that it is not his habit or taste "to ban speakers of different political colors from my own from this campus."[116] But nevertheless, he asks for "an outline of the lectures he *intends* to give" or to be told "the *intention* of the lectures."[117] In other words, he commits the intentional fallacy—a fact Monty seizes on with glee:

> I am afraid I am quite unable to answer his frankly bizarre request for their "intention". In fact, I admit it surprises and delights me that a self-professed "textual anarchist" like Dr Belsey should be so passionate to know the *intention* of a piece of writing.[118]

Monty seizes here on the inconsistency between Howard's anti-intentionalist theoretical stance and his request that Monty divulge his "intention," leaving Howard in a double bind not unlike the one faced by Butler. Like her, he finds himself in need of the very same ideas that prop up the "mytheme of the artist as autonomous individual," which he has been so committed to interrogating: intentionality, determinacy of signification, the author as the origin of the text and guardian of its meaning.[119] Sticking to his poststructuralist guns would mean ceding to Monty's arguments; maintaining his request for Monty's intention entails facing accusations of hypocrisy. He doubles down on the latter, interrupting Kipps's vague outline of the proposed lectures, not this time to ask what their intention is, but, more intentional-fallaciously still, to claim knowledge of Monty's "clear intention of antagonizing and alienating various minority groups on this campus."[120] At this point, the meeting turns into a carnivalesque face-off: with Howard having adopted the nominally conservative position of claiming that intention is accessible and relevant, Monty mimics the opposite view:

> Now is it not *you*, Dr, who speaks of the instability of textual meaning? Is it not *you*, Dr, who speaks of the indeterminacy of all sign systems? How, then, can I possibly predict *before* I give my lectures how the "multivalency" ... of my own text will be received in the "heterogeneous consciousnesses" of my audience?[121]

Butler's "humanities quandary" reemerges: "no one knows who is speaking and in what voice, and with what intent."[122] Howard, like Butler, is being implicitly accused of having undermined the humanities with his anti-authorial relativism and critique, but this accusation comes at him in the voice of precisely his own anti-authorialism. Who is speaking and in what voice? Monty is speaking, but in a warped version of Howard's own "textual anarchist" voice. He adopts Howard's Barthesean approach in both content and form: his speech is a tissue of unattributed citations ("the 'multivalency' ... of my own text"; "the 'heterogeneous consciousnesses' of my audience"), making it impossible for Howard to work out exactly what he is being accused of or by whom.

In some sense, this scene does the same thing as the passages from the novel I discussed above, in which Smith parodies Howard's theoretical jargon and makes visible his hypocrisy and dogmatism. But there is also a more profound point being made here, one that really does make a case not just against bad versions of anti-intentionalism, but against anti-intentionalism per se. This, in other words, is the point at which Smith's anti-intentionalism truly becomes inconsistent, where she starts to make the case that, while human intentions are consistently undermined from both within and without, and never easily accessible, sometimes we still need to be able to make reference to them; sometimes we need a bit of room to be able to commit the intentional fallacy. Here she makes visible the fact that it is really hard to have a nuanced conversation about hate speech without recourse to the vocabulary of intention. At some level, even if intention is not fully accessible, even if we cannot know for sure that Monty has "the clear intention of antagonizing and alienating various minority groups on campus," we nevertheless find that without the vocabulary of intentionality, it becomes much harder to hold someone responsible for a potentially homophobic, misogynist, or racist text. Like Butler, I am not interested in "the rehabilitation of the author-subject *per se*."[123] But Smith raises an important question here, which is worth considering at more length. Is it possible to talk about hate speech while maintaining one's commitment to anti-intentionalism? To answer this question, I want to go back to Butler, to the chapter that precedes the one discussed above, a chapter that revolves around the question of hate speech, a chapter in which Butler provides a trenchant critique of an attempt to talk about hate speech without committing the intentional fallacy—and in so doing unexpectedly ends up going against her anti-intentionalist background.

3.3. "In Effect If Not in Intent"

Precarious Life's fourth chapter, "The Charge of Anti-Semitism: Jews, Israel, and the Risks of Public Critique," is not Butler's first engagement with the topic of hate speech. Nor is it typical of her approach. In order to bring out what is different and valuable about her work in this chapter, it is worth contextualizing it by comparison to her much more extensive treatment of the topic in 1997's *Excitable Speech: A Politics of the Performative*. As that book's subtitle suggests, Butler's main project is to translate the insights about performativity she developed in *Gender Trouble* into the scene of the politics of speech: speech understood as having a performative function and as having concrete political stakes (fighting words, regulated speech, hate speech). Butler understands hate speech as form of injurious speech but also wants to maintain that its effects are not as determined as somebody like Catharine MacKinnon—who argues in *Only Words* that pornography authoritatively and deterministically "wields a performative power" that cannot but injure women—would maintain.[124] Hate speech, for Butler, is a citation, a repetition of a term that carries with it a long history of sedimented meanings, just like the gender norms that she analyzes in *Gender Trouble*. Hence its degree of authority is unstable: where there is repetition, for Butler, there is the possibility of subversion. Hate speech attempts to silence its addressee, and may well succeed, but it may also provide the addressee with the unexpected opportunity to expropriate its power via a process of subversive resignification that, like the drag performances of *Gender Trouble*, contains the possibility of resistance. This possibility is what Butler (who draws her theory of power in *Excitable Speech* from Foucault) understands by agency. She maintains that her critique of sovereignty and of the author-subject does not mean "the demolition of agency," but rather that "agency begins where sovereignty wanes": agency for Butler is always situated and conditioned, and always preceded by "a linguistic field of enabling constraints."[125]

Here we can see the same orientation toward authority discussed above: Butler aims to critique it *and* to enable those excluded from it to respond to it—even if, in so doing, she limits the ability to respond to a matter of subversive resignification and "unexpected rejoinder[s]."[126] What is important to note regarding the role of intention in hate speech is that it is anything but deterministic. This is very much an anti-intentionalist discussion of hate speech. The person who utters the hate speech cannot ensure that their utterance is (to use the vocabulary of J. L. Austin, on whom Butler continues to draw here) felicitous: "the subject does not exercise sovereign power over what it says."[127] Or as Monty Kipps puts it, they cannot know "how the 'multivalency' ... of [their] text will be received in the 'heterogeneous consciousnesses' of [their] audience."[128] In this sense, Butler's view would be aligned with Howard in his distaste for banning speakers—Butler is consistently wary of institutional control of speech[129]—but would depart from him when he asks for Monty's intention. The intention of the one who utters hate speech, in Butler, matters little. Her focus instead is on the addressee of hate speech and the ways in which they can resist the violent interpellations of the one addressing.[130]

In "The Charge of Anti-Semitism," however, Butler's focus shifts away from the addressee of hate speech and toward the addressee of the *charge* of hate speech. And in this shift, Butler ends up doing two important things. First, she demonstrates the ways in which the framework of intention and effect elides the ability to talk about hate speech with any nuance. And second, against her anti-intentionalist history (on full display in *Excitable Speech*), she carves out a certain degree of space for intentionality.

If *Excitable Speech* is an argument against institutional control over speech (see especially Chapter 2's extended critique of the then-current "Don't ask, don't tell" policy regarding homosexuality in the US military), "The Charge of Anti-Semitism" is a more extended analysis of the consequences of such institutional control, specifically in the context of the university campus. The chapter's starting point is a statement made by then-president of Harvard, Lawrence Summers, on September 17, 2002—around the time, it is worth noting, that Zadie Smith would have arrived at Harvard as a Radcliffe Fellow.[131] Butler begins as follows:

> When the President of Harvard University, Lawrence Summers, remarked that to criticize Israel at this time and to call upon universities to divest from Israel are "actions that are anti-Semitic in their effect, if not their intent," he introduced a distinction between an effective and intentional anti-Semitism that is controversial at best.[132]

Although Butler frames this chapter in her preface to *Precarious Life* as primarily a discussion of the censorship of certain kinds of critical speech, the chapter turns, as its opening sentence makes clear, on a discussion of intention and its relationship to effect.[133] Her argument about Summers's controversial distinction between intent and effect runs as follows. First, she points out that what Summers is talking about is a kind of speech act that has an anti-Semitic *effect* "even if [anti-Semitism] is not part of the conscious *intention* of those who make the utterance itself."[134] That is, we have something like the inverse of the situation that Butler imagines in *Excitable Speech*. There we had an utterance that, because of the potential for subversive repetition, may *fail to have* an injurious effect *despite* having a conscious intention to injure. Here, we have an utterance that supposedly *does have* an injurious effect, despite there having been *no* conscious intent to injure. What remains the same, importantly, is that intention is beside the point. Summers, like the Butler of *Excitable Speech*, approaches hate speech from a specifically anti-intentionalist point of view. Of course, his reasons for adopting this perspective seem to be different from Butler's: whereas anti-intentionalism is part and parcel of the critique of the author-subject to which Butler is committed, Summers seems to be avoiding imputing the intentions of the intellectuals he discusses for more pragmatic reasons. It is a group of "serious and thoughtful people," he tells us, in "progressive intellectual communities," whom Summers is accusing of effective anti-Semitism—some of them, presumably, his own colleagues. Accordingly it makes sense for Summers to avoid giving the impression that he believes them to be harboring hateful views (intentional anti-Semitism), even if the alternative is rather patronizing ("I know you don't really *mean* to be anti-Semitic, but …"). Alternatively, we could read Summers's abstention from making any inference about intentions as a way of countering the potential charge of having committed the intentional fallacy. As the twentieth-century authorship debates establish, from Wimsatt and Beardsley, to Barthes, to E. D. Hirsch, to Knapp and Michaels, making judgments about intention is always fraught with a lack of verifiability and the potential for denial. Regardless of the particular reasons for Summers's anti-intentional method, though, what is interesting and unexpected here is that, in arguing against his approach, Butler ends up departing in an important way from her own position in *Excitable Speech*.

Her argument continues by examining two separate interpretations of what Summers could mean by effective anti-Semitism. The first possibility she considers is that Summers is imagining that, in "the public sphere of the US," there exists a dominant "acoustic frame" that governs the reception of criticisms of Israel, such that these criticisms cannot but be heard as anti-Semitic.[135] In this case, "we are asked to conjure a listener who attributes intention to the speaker," which means that "the only way to understand *effective* anti-Semitism would be to presuppose *intentional* anti-Semitism."[136] Under that possibility, then, the intent/effect distinction that Summers tries to draw collapses, in that the *effect* of the utterance is imagined as retroactively determining its *intention*, even if the intention was entirely different.

The second possibility Butler considers is "that critical statements *will be used* by those who have anti-Semitic intent."[137] Butler acknowledges that a criticism of Israel does indeed run the risk of being exploited in this way but maintains that if Summers is going to claim that this risk means that those criticisms have a determinately anti-Semitic effect, then he is ceding far too much power to the imagined exploiters. "Here again," she writes, "the distinction between effective anti-Semitism and intended anti-Semitism folds, insofar as the only way a statement can become effectively anti-Semitic is if there is, somewhere, an intention to use the statement for anti-Semitic aims, an intention imagined as enormously effective in realizing its aims."[138] It is worth pausing over this. In that last phrase—"an intention imagined as enormously effective in realizing its aims"—Butler is presenting her argument as a critique of sovereign intentionality. It is the same move she uses in *Excitable Speech*, when she critiques Althusser's theory of interpellation for similarly relying on an idea of the policeman's speech act of hailing the subject as sovereign, as "enormously effective in realizing its aims."[139] But in this chapter, the anti-intentional rhetoric belies the larger point she is making: namely, that under both the possible interpretations she considers, she argues that Summers gives too much interpretive power to the reception of an utterance and not enough interpretive power to the one who utters it. In other words, she is putting forward a defense of intention.

This point emerges all the more clearly a few pages later:

> According to Summers, there are some forms of anti-Semitism that are characterized retroactively by those who decide upon their status. This means that nothing should be said or done that will be taken to be anti-Semitic by

> others. But what if the others who are listening are wrong? If we take one form of anti-Semitism to be defined retroactively by those who listen to a certain set of speech acts, or witness a certain set of protests against Israel, then what is left of the possibility of legitimate protests against a given state, either by its own population or by those who live outside those borders? If we say that every time "Israel" is uttered, the speaker really means "Jews," then we have foreclosed in advance the possibility that the speaker really means "Israel."[140]

"But what if the others who are listening are wrong?" What if the speaker meant what they said? What if their intention really was that transparent and accessible? This is Butler at her most un-Butlerian, her most anti-anti-intentional. It is Butler, against all odds, advocating something like surface reading, or at least leaving open the possibility that surface reading might, in some circumstances, have better interpretations than suspicious, paranoid, depth reading. In *Excitable Speech*, she argued that the addressee of an utterance can subversively resignify it, short-circuiting its intentions. Here, she critiques Summers for arguing what appears to be the same thing: that utterances can be "characterized retroactively by those who decide upon their status."

But my point here is not to criticize Butler for her inconsistency. Insofar as I disagree with Butler, it is for the way she tries to mask her inconsistency. My contention, on the other hand, is that the contradiction between her position in *Excitable Speech* and her position in "The Charge of Anti-Semitism" is evidence that sometimes—and hate speech is a case in point—inconsistency is necessary.

In *Excitable Speech*, Butler talks about speech acts that contain the possibility of failure. Speech acts where the effect does not match the intent. Infelicitous speech acts. And in that book, she wants for those speech acts to be infelicitous because she is invested in the project of giving the addressees of hate speech agency, and agency, for Butler, is a matter of subversive repetition—a matter of subverting the intentions of a speech act. In "The Charge of Anti-Semitism," she is also talking about infelicitous speech acts. But here, she wants for them to be *felicitous*: she wants for somebody to be able to voice a criticism of Israel, and for that criticism to be read precisely *as a criticism of Israel*, as intended. There, she was talking about turning actual hate speech into something that resists hate speech. Here, she is talking about statements that are not hate speech and safeguarding their status as not-hate-speech. There, she needed to be able to counter an understanding of speech as fully and sovereignly intentional. Here, she needs to be able to counter an understanding of speech in which intentions are irrelevant. Yes, there is an inconsistency regarding the status of intention there, but it is for good reason. It is important to be able to think both the subversive repetition of hate speech and the academic freedom to voice criticisms of Israel at the same time, and doing so means saying, essentially, that no, intentions are not deterministic or sovereign—*and* no, intentions are not irrelevant either.

4. Conclusion

What my reading of Butler's "The Charge of Anti-Semitism" in relation to *Excitable Speech* has tried to provide, then, is a defense of intention—but also, more importantly, a defense of inconsistency. In Section 3.2, after looking at Smith's treatment of the "humanities quandary," I asked whether it is possible to talk about hate speech while maintaining one's commitment to anti-intentionalism. My answer to that question, as should now be evident, is no. Importantly, though, answering *no* to this question is not the same as saying that we need to return to an understanding of intention as sovereign and transparent. When we talk about hate speech purely in terms of intention, imagining the intentions of the speaker to be fully successful in realizing their aims (as Catharine MacKinnon talks about pornography), then we foreclose the possibility of resistance: this is the lesson of *Excitable Speech*. And when we talk about hate speech purely in terms of effect, imagining the intentions of the speaker to be irrelevant (as Lawrence Summers talks about anti-Semitism), then we foreclose via an act of censorship the possibility of public critique: this is the lesson of "The Charge of Anti-Semitism." Butler may attempt to frame the latter as a critique of intention, but my sense is that, ironically enough, we would be better off reading Butler against her stated intentions in this case. What I have tried to show is that a degree of inconsistency in her argument is a virtue.

In fact, it is precisely the virtue after which Zadie Smith titles her essay collection (the one that includes her defense of authorship, "Rereading Barthes and Nabokov"): *Changing My Mind*. In the foreword, she talks about the ways in which her writing has grown with her:

> *Changing My Mind* seemed an apt, confessional title to describe this process. Reading through these pieces, though, I'm forced to recognize that ideological inconsistency is, for me, practically an article of faith.[141]

"Ideological inconsistency" is not generally understood as a positive attribute in critical theory. As Roland Barthes tells us, "fickleness is never well regarded ... what the Doxa admires is immutability, the persistence of an opinion."[142] What Barthes admires, on the other hand, is something closer to what Smith calls "ideological inconsistency": "Change, vary, but in a nondogmatic way, like the shimmering of mottled silk (that is to say, without fanfare) on the curtain of life."[143] That Smith's defense of the kind of flexibility that might otherwise be condemned as fickleness is so close to Barthes's is of course ironic: in "Rereading Barthes and Nabokov" it is Barthes's supposed *inflexibility* on the question of authorship which she contrasts with her own change of mind, whereas in reality Barthes too changed his mind, varied, in a nondogmatic way. Smith, both in *Changing My Mind* and in her fiction, can be profitably understood as allied in an important way with Barthes. Like Barthes, and like that other marginal figure of twentieth-century theory Walter Benjamin[144] (and indeed like the subject of the previous chapter, Maggie Nelson), Smith is a thinker who prefers flexibility to commitment, eclecticism to correctness, variety to consistency. The kind of shimmering inconsistency that all of these thinkers embody could also be termed, following Barthes, *nuance*. Nuance is a quality Barthes associates not so much with critical theory, semiology, or structuralism, but with literature: literature, he writes in *The Neutral*, is "a teacher of nuance."[145] Part of the impetus behind reading literature and theory together in this study is to let literature teach theory nuance, or to bring out the nuances (the inconsistencies) that theory often wants to mask over.[146]

The first half of this chapter ended with a discussion of the last scene of *On Beauty* in the context of the critical conversations around the limits of critique. There, I argued that, rather than coming out in favor of a specific alternative to critique, *On Beauty* is ultimately an argument against dogmatism and inflexibility. In other words, it is an argument for "ideological inconsistency," for the possibility of changing and varying in a nondogmatic way.[147] This commitment to change rather than to rote critical procedures—what Barthes would call a commitment to *paradoxa* against *doxa*[148]—is also what I identified as most persuasive in arguments like Felski's against the dominance of critique as a method of interpretation. It is also—though Butler might not admit it—what I think is useful about "The Charge of Anti-Semitism" in relation to *Excitable Speech*. Her inconsistency is precisely what allows for an understanding of intentionality that escapes the dogmatism of MacKinnon on the one side and Summers on the other.

If we want to be able to talk about intention without falling into a dogmatism that elides possibilities—of agency and of criticism—then we had better be prepared to sacrifice our allegiance to ideological consistency. And, as we will see in more detail in the next chapter, who better to turn to for ideological inconsistency than Roland Barthes?

Chapter 3

AGENCY: ROLAND BARTHES AND THE MEN WHO HOLD FORTH

> After two quick glasses of Sancerre, the distinguished male author started holding forth.
>
> —Ben Lerner, *10:04*

1. Introduction

1.1. "Mr. Very Important"

Rebecca Solnit's 2008 essay "Men Explain Things to Me" begins with a story about what would later come to be termed "mansplaining." It is a story about gender, power, and privilege. It is also a story about authorship.

Solnit describes attending a party hosted by "an imposing man who'd made a lot of money," a man who insists that she and her friend stay a little longer so that he can talk to her:

> He kept us waiting while the other guests drifted out into the summer night, and then sat us down at his authentically grainy wood table and said to me, "So? I hear you've written a couple of books."
>
> I replied, "Several, actually."[1]

The older man initially acknowledges the fact that Solnit is an author—or at least that she has "written a couple of books"—but behaves in such a way to minimize her authority while maximizing his own. He reduces her "six or seven [books] out by then" to "a couple" and speaks to her "in the way you encourage your friend's seven-year-old daughter to describe flute practice."[2] Having mentioned to the man that she has recently published a book on the photographer Eadweard Muybridge, he insists on telling her about "the *very important* Muybridge book that came out this year"—failing to remember (and then refusing to acknowledge when told) that the book he is explaining to Solnit is the book she herself has written.[3]

Solnit refers to the older man as "Mr. Very Important," reflecting the way that he has appropriated the authority of the "*very important*" book he is explaining.[4] As Mr. Very Important talks, she tells us, he adopts "that smug look I know so well in a man holding forth, eyes fixed on the fuzzy far horizon of his own authority."[5] Solnit provides here a useful definition of this chapter's central term—*holding forth*—as well as the first example of the chapter's central figure: the Man Who Holds Forth.

To hold forth, as this passage employs the term, is to talk at somebody but not to them: the man's eyes are fixed not on his interlocutor, but on "the fuzzy far horizon of his own authority"—and *authority* is a significant word here, implying two of the key connotations of holding forth: power and authorship. Holding forth, in the way I use the term in this chapter, operates at the intersection of authorship and authority, at the intersection of the author and the authoritarian. If the previous chapter focused on the hermeneutic stakes of authorship, this chapter focuses on the political stakes: the author as a figure of power, of authority, of agency—and its counterpart, the author who speaks back to power and authority, who exerts agency against structures of domination. The Man Who Holds Forth is a figure for the first type of author, and holding forth—in Solnit's essay and in the other texts this chapter examines—is the style of discourse he employs. It is a manner of speaking that is ultimately oriented toward little more than shoring up one's own power and privilege, proudly exercising one's ability to speak and be heard while foreclosing anyone else's chance to do the same. Holding forth is the dark side of authorship: authorship characterized by excessive confidence in one's own agency and authorial status; the author who holds forth understands himself, to use Barthes's phrase in "The Death of the Author," as "Author-God."[6] If the twentieth-century authorship debates can be understood in part as a fight to provide authorial recognition to new voices (female voices, nonwhite voices, queer voices), then Men Who Hold Forth like Mr. Very Important are in some sense figures for the opposite side of that fight: those who refuse to recognize the authorial status of other, less privileged but more qualified people. Solnit continues:

> So, Mr. Very Important was going on smugly about this book I should have known when Sallie interrupted him, to say, "That's her book." Or tried to interrupt him anyway.
>
> But he just continued on his way. She had to say, "That's her book" three or four times before he finally took it in. And then, as if in a nineteenth-century novel, he went ashen. That I was indeed the author of the very important book it turned out he hadn't read, just read about in the *New York Times Book Review* a few months earlier, so confused the neat categories into which his world was sorted that he was stunned speechless—for a moment, before he began holding forth again. Being women, we were politely out of earshot before we started laughing, and we've never really stopped.[7]

The turn is immensely satisfying. Mr. Very Important, previously so confident in his own "authority," blunders onward (the forward momentum of "holding *forth*") like the cartoon character who runs over the edge of the cliff but stays suspended for a moment, legs still turning, before gravity kicks in. He takes a while to process that he is no longer the holder of authority, and even then cannot adjust his discursive style to reflect the changed dynamic in the conversation. Solnit turns him from an author-figure into a character in somebody else's book, both figuratively ("as if in a nineteenth-century novel") and literally, for this is her essay that we are reading. She stakes her claim to authority and authorship: "I was indeed the author of the very important book it turned out he hadn't read." Solnit's is the story, then, of the death of one author and the birth of another. Not, as in Barthes's essay, the death of the author and the birth of the reader, but the death of the (male, privileged) author and the birth of the (female, hitherto excluded) author.

1.2. "Men Explain Things to Me" in Context

In her 2014 postscript to "Men Explain Things to Me," Solnit reflects on the essay's reception: "It spread quickly ... and has never stopped going around, being reposted and shared and commented upon. It's circulated like nothing else I've done. It struck a chord."[8] Solnit credits the piece's success in part to the political context in the United States at the time: the 2012 electoral season, when the piece was especially widely circulated, was characterized by a particularly vehement conversation about the "crazy pro-rape, anti-fact statements of male conservatives" like Representative Todd Akin (R-Missouri) who took it upon himself to explain to the world "that we don't need abortion for women who are raped, because 'if it's a legitimate rape, the female body has ways to try to shut the whole thing down.'"[9] Solnit's essay became a key point of reference in the wide-ranging conversation about gender, power, and discourse that followed. I also want, though, to locate "Men Explain Things to Me" in a literary historical context, in terms of both the literary works that testify to the resonance of the chord Solnit's piece struck and the preexisting critical and theoretical conversations that "Men Explain Things to Me" draws on and develops.

First, Solnit's 2008 essay and its continued circulation throughout the Obama era coincide with the rising popularity in North America of autofiction: a genre this chapter will leave relatively loosely defined as narratives, usually first-person, that combine nonfictional and fictional modes and which claim a degree of identity between narrator and author.[10] And autofiction, as the first part of this chapter will argue, has often shared with "Men Explain Things to Me" an interest in the phenomenon of authoritative and authorial men who hold forth and the question of how to deal with them. This connection is especially visible in three of the most prominent examples of recent North American autofiction: Sheila Heti's *How Should a Person Be?* (2012), Ben Lerner's *10:04* (2014), and Chris Kraus's *I Love Dick* (which was originally published in 1997, but enjoyed a major revival in the Obama years, including a television series from Amazon Studios, the pilot of which premiered in 2016). Like Solnit, Heti and Kraus both come at this topic from an explicitly feminist perspective, and their critique of men who explain things to them is directly tied to their assertion of their own authorial status. And even a book like Lerner's, which is by no means an avowedly feminist work, takes up the trope of the "distinguished male author" who is prone to "holding forth."[11] These three texts, and the success they have found in the years following the publication of Solnit's essay, are all evidence of a broader cultural interest in (and critique of) the figure of the overconfident, patronizingly authoritative, and incurably verbose male.

Second, "Men Explain Things to Me," in its resistance to figures of male authority and its insistence on the importance of female authorship, has roots in a feminist conversation about authorship and gender that was at its most active in the 1980s and 1990s and that focused on the legacy of Barthes's "The Death of the Author" (and poststructuralist anti-authorialism more broadly). At the heart of this conversation, which I discuss in detail in the second half of the chapter, was the following question: does declaring the death of the author make room for a broader critique of patriarchal authority, or does it militate against feminist efforts to bring more female authors into the straight-, white-, and male-dominated literary canon by dismissing the importance of authorship just at the historical moment when women—and other people previously excluded from the canon—were making progress toward being accepted as authors? To put it another way, are Barthes and his fellow poststructuralist critics throwing their toys out of the stroller rather than agreeing to share them with their new feminist siblings? This second possibility—that poststructuralist theory's attempt to erase the author and the subject is effectively the straight, white, male canon's last stand—is the one that Zadie Smith summarizes when she notes: "It does seem rather hard to have to give up on subjectivity when you've only recently got free of objectification."[12] Solnit's essay insists in the face of resistance that female authorship is enormously important and argues that women's "status as human beings" is directly tied to their being heard and believed—to their being taken seriously as authors.[13] All too aware of the hard battle women have fought to get free of objectification, Solnit has no intention of giving up on her status as either a human subject or an author. In this sense, her position has strong ties to the anti-Barthesean view that authorship is not a category to be dismissed after all.

I begin this chapter with a reading of "Men Explain Things to Me" for several reasons. First, it introduces the chapter's key concern: the proximity between authorship and authority; the connections between authorship, agency, power, privilege, and gender. Second, it introduces the chapter's key figure: the *Man Who Holds Forth*, understood as a figure for a kind of excessively agentic authorship, for the author who is too secure in his position of privileged authority, and who is more interested in flaunting and strengthening his authority than sharing it. Finally, it introduces two of the chapter's key literary-historical contexts: the prominence of autofiction in North America since

2008 and the feminist pushback against poststructuralism and "The Death of the Author" that began in the 1980s.

My main focus, though, is not Rebecca Solnit but Roland Barthes. The Barthes I focus on, however, is more closely aligned with Solnit than one might expect. Like Solnit, he is interested in the connections between authorship, power, and privilege. And like Solnit, he is interested in the idea of *holding forth*—which, like Solnit, he understands as a figure for excessive authority and verbosity, a manner of discourse associated with an excessively agentic kind of author. His late work in particular—and this chapter will focus on his teaching during the last three and a half years of his life—offers, I argue, important resources for thinking through the proximity between authorship and authority and for analyzing the trope of the male author who holds forth, who explains things to women, who "mansplains."

What is curiously and problematically absent from Barthes's analysis of authorship, agency, and holding forth, however, is any consideration of the particular lines along which authorial agency tends to operate or the exclusions on which the category of authorship has historically been based—whether in terms of gender, race, sexuality, class, or any other factor. In fact, the most prominent example of somebody who "holds forth" that Barthes analyzes is a young woman—in stark contrast to Solnit's rich, older "Mr. Very Important" and to the various male holders-forth in *I Love Dick, How Should a Person Be?*, and *10:04*. Here and elsewhere, Barthes seems to willfully refuse to engage with the politics of authorship, with the question that Kraus describes in *I Love Dick* as "the only question": "who gets to speak and why?"[14] Barthes provides an astute analysis of the phenomenon of holding forth—but he is much less strong on the question of *who gets to hold forth and why*. This conspicuous absence is symptomatic of Barthes's widespread and widely criticized tendency to seemingly elide questions of politics, especially with regard to identity—a tendency that has led him, justifiably, to be critiqued by feminists, taken to task by queer critics, and charged with orientalism. Nevertheless, Barthes has recently begun again to find favor among writers and critics, especially in queer and feminist circles: for one notable example, we can turn back to the text at the center of this study's first chapter, Maggie Nelson's *The Argonauts*. This chapter ultimately makes the case for reading Barthes alongside analyses of authorship (like Solnit's, Kraus's, Heti's, and Lerner's) that engage more directly with the question of who gets to speak and why and the gendered dynamics of holding forth. Despite its shortcomings, Barthes's analysis of *holding forth* is remarkably prescient in the way it anticipates a conversation that Solnit's essay jump-started in North America thirty years later. This is the story, then, of how Roland Barthes almost invented mansplaining, but completely overlooked the *man* part.

The first half of the argument (Sections 2.1–2.4) is a comparative reading of Kraus, Heti, Lerner, and Barthes and the way in which each of them deals with the phenomenon of *holding forth*. *I Love Dick, How Should a Person Be?*, and *10:04* are all—like much autofiction—engaged in questions of authorship. *I Love Dick* and *How Should a Person Be?* are narratives about becoming an author and about negotiating the challenges of female authorship—challenges often embodied by male figures of authority. Kraus focuses specifically on the authorial legitimacy of critical theory (embodied in *I Love Dick* by Walter Benjamin) and her attempts to legitimize herself as a theoretical authority. Heti, on the other hand, focuses on the pedagogical aspects of holding forth, via her analysis of men "who wanted to teach me something."[15] And whereas Kraus and Heti write about their attempts to achieve authorial status, Lerner in *10:04* is concerned with how one deals with authorial status once one has achieved it. *10:04* centers on the question of how to negotiate one's position of privilege, how to be an author without turning into the kind of excessively confident, patronizing authority-figure he describes in this chapter's epigraph: "After two quick glasses of Sancerre, the distinguished male author started holding forth."[16] When read in conjunction with Kraus, Heti, and Lerner, Barthes's analysis of holding forth in his 1977 seminar "What Is It to Hold Forth?" is notable not only for its prescience but also for its failure to address the gendered dynamics of holding forth. The chapter's first half ends, then, by setting up the questions that the second half attempts to answer: why does Barthes evade the question of *who it is* who holds forth and to what extent should this evasiveness be considered a failure on his part?

In the second half, I attempt to answer these questions by considering in detail the history of Barthes's contentious relationship with feminism, as well as his equally contentious relationships with queer politics and with left politics in the wake of May 1968. These three critiques of Barthes's supposedly apolitical stance, I argue, all turn on the same question: do we ultimately place more value on commitment, persistence, and direct political engagement, or do we (like Barthes and a number of his more sympathetic readers) instead prioritize the possibility of a break with the false choices of orthodox politics and the potential for a more nuanced approach that would expand the sphere of the political? My argument ultimately hews closer to the second option: by reading Barthes alongside texts like Kraus, Heti, and Lerner that engage explicitly with questions of gender and identity, I try to counter Barthes's frequently frustrating evasiveness, but I also recognize the value of his nuanced take on the structures of power inherent in every discourse. The chapter closes by considering in detail Barthes's attempts to negotiate the structures of power inherent in *his own discourse*, as a teacher and a writer during his tenure at the Collège de France. Here I analyze Barthes's attempts to deal with his own position of privilege: to teach without holding forth, to be an author without being an authoritarian.

Barthes's notes for the four lecture courses he gave at the Collège, as well as partial records of three seminars he ran, are collected in three volumes, published in French in 2002 and 2003, and translated into English over the course of the following decade. *How to Live Together* (published in French in 2002 and in English in 2013) gathers his lectures and seminars from the 1976–7 academic year; *The Neutral* (2002 in French, 2005 in English) contains his 1977–8 lecture course; finally, *The Preparation of the Novel* includes his lectures and seminars from both 1978–9 and 1979–80 and was published in French in 2003 and in English in 2011. Read together, these volumes—despite the fact that they are very much *not* books in the proper sense, that they are, in Lucy O'Meara's words, "quasi-archival" texts[17]—represent Barthes's most prolonged and sophisticated analysis of the relationship between authorship and agency.

The Collège de France years begin with two explorations of agency in an interpersonal context: of the question of how to balance individual ways of living in a social context without creating oppressive (authoritarian) structures and of the hazards of excessive agency. These are the subjects of the 1977 lecture course, "How to Live Together," and its corresponding seminar, "What Is It to Hold Forth?" (discussed in this chapter's first section). From February until June of 1978, Barthes expanded on the theoretical groundwork of these explorations in his lecture course "The Neutral" and began to link his ideas more explicitly to writing and literature, investigating the possibility that literature might be able to create the kinds of utopian spaces of non-oppressive relationality that he had discussed in "How to Live Together." This connection between power structures and literature—between agency and authorship—came to the forefront in the lecture courses of 1978–9 and 1979–80: the two parts of "The Preparation of the Novel," "From Life to the Work" and "The Work as Will." In these lectures, Barthes—the theorist who had declared the death of the author and told the audience of his inaugural lecture at the Collège that language is fascist[18]—set out to become an author himself and to work out what a writing that wasn't oppressive and dictatorial would look like: to try for himself to be an author without being an authoritarian.[19] And furthermore, throughout these courses and seminars, Barthes not only attempted to *theorize* forms of non-oppressive agency and nonauthoritarian authorship; he also, building on his previous experience leading seminars at the École pratique des hautes études in the 1960s and 1970s, tried to embody these qualities in his pedagogy.

2. Autofiction versus the Man Who Holds Forth

2.1. I Love Dick

I Love Dick is a book about becoming an author and a record of that becoming. It consists largely of letters written from Chris Kraus to "an English cultural critic who's recently relocated from Melbourne to Los Angeles" named Dick.[20] Dick's surname is not included in the text, though Joan Hawkins's afterword to the 2006 critical edition of the novel acknowledges the widely known fact that the title character is Dick Hebdige, who according to rumor "tried to block publication of *I Love Dick* by threatening to sue Kraus for invasion of privacy."[21] It is Kraus's first book: prior to its publication, she had been a filmmaker, and an editor at Semiotext(e) with her partner at the time Sylvère Lotringer, who also appears in the book as the third point of its love triangle. Asked in an interview "when was the pivotal moment when you realized that you had become a writer," Kraus replies: "It was when I started writing those crazy letters to Dick. It was only later I realized I was actually writing a *book*."[22] The resulting book, then, is proof and record of Kraus's achievement of the status of author—a status she achieves through the process of writing letters to Dick, the "important cultural critic"—Kraus's phrasing here recalls Solnit's Mr. Very Important—whom Kraus renders "a blank screen": he does not write back until the last four pages of the text, essentially disappearing as the focus shifts onto Kraus's writing on art, theory, and politics.[23] As Anna Watkins Fisher writes, Kraus's letters become "a means of transforming Dick from subject to *object*, writer to *text*, critic to *critique*."[24] Like "Men Explain Things to Me," *I Love Dick* is the story of the death of a (male, privileged) author and the birth of a (female, hitherto excluded) author.

I Love Dick is also, though, a record of Kraus becoming a very specific type of author: a theorist. The book's recent canonization as the forerunner to the early twenty-first-century wave of North American autofiction has arguably overshadowed the fact that it is just as engaged with the world of critical theory as it is with the world of fiction.[25] *I Love Dick* is, Kraus maintains, fictional—but only in the sense that *everything* is fictional: "As soon as you write something down," Kraus says, "it's fiction. I don't think fiction is necessarily about inventing fake stories."[26] "Everything that happens in it happened first in life," she wrote in *The Guardian* in 2016, "but that doesn't mean that it's a memoir"; memoir, she says elsewhere, "implies the neoliberal illusion of the autonomous individual"—a turn of phrase that clearly signals her grounding in critical theory.[27] *I Love Dick* was originally published as part of Semiotext(e)'s Native Agents series, which Kraus started and still edits:

> I started the Native Agents series for Semiotext(e) in 1990, when Semiotext(e) was well-known for publishing French theory, with the idea of transferring some of French theory's legitimacy to some friends in New York, all of them women, who could best be described as post-New York School writers.[28]

Semiotext(e)'s iconic Foreign Agents series had at that point published books by authors like Jean Baudrillard, Deleuze and Guattari, Paul Virilio, and Antonio Negri. All of them, Kraus notes, were white men.[29] A key part of the project of Native Agents, then, was to extend the authorial legitimacy that white male theory had enjoyed to female and queer writers—in part because, as Kraus recalls, it was predominantly female and queer writers who were taking up "the legacy of French theory … in the United States."[30] The texts in the Native Agents series, she says, "are like psychic corollaries to the theory and activist works: *this* is what these forces yield in people's lives."[31] And Kraus "learned how to write," she recounts, "largely by reading and editing the first Native Agents books."[32]

This context, then, helps to explain why it is that *I Love Dick*'s examples of the figure of the man who holds forth are white male critical theorists: first, the title character, and second, in the passage I will discuss below, Walter Benjamin.

McKenzie Wark argues that Kraus's books are not just about the question that she asks in *I Love Dick*: "who gets to speak and why?"[33] They are also, Wark suggests, about the question of "who decides who gets paid to say or write what about whom?": not only the question of who writes but also the question of who gets to be *recognized as a writer*.[34] They are about "showing the means of production of theory" and the means of production of the *theorist*, the author of theory.[35] *I Love Dick* is for Wark "a record of the breakthrough into a method for being a theoretical girl"; this method entails taking *"high theory"* down a notch from the "position of strength" from which it insists on speaking, bringing theory into the real, embodied life of someone perceived as weak, as a failure—that is, herself; high theory becomes *"low theory."*[36] This is precisely what Kraus does in her analysis of R. B. Kitaj's painting *The Autumn of Central Paris (after Walter Benjamin) 1972/1973*. Kraus writes:

> This painting is a dictionary of everything we know about the brilliant café world of Paris and Vienna in the 20s. All the images and tropes we've read about this time are closely flanked, jammed up against each other, sliding down from the top left of the frame to the bottom right. History as a Jumble Sale... Walter Benjamin sits presiding at a café table with a young man turned away from us and a doe-eyed, pretty, serious young woman... The young woman's looking up at Walter and she's listening. Though his mouth is momentarily shut, he's obviously Holding Forth and he looks terrific in his tinted eyeglasses, waving a cigarette beyond his fleshy sculpted face, so poised.[37]

How does Kraus's depiction of "Holding Forth" compare to Solnit's? Perhaps the first difference to observe is the fact that in this passage "Holding Forth" (which Kraus notably capitalizes) is not only or even primarily a matter of speech; Benjamin's mouth is "momentarily shut." Kraus recognizes it is a pose, a way of occupying space: Benjamin is "presiding" at the table, towering over the young woman who is "looking up at" him. He is charismatic, engaging her attention and looking "terrific." A second key difference is the way that Kraus figures herself in relation to the man holding forth. The trio at the table—a prominent cultural figure, a man, and a woman—echoes the novel's love triangle and its opening scene where Chris and Sylvère dine with Dick; following this reading would place Kraus in a similar position to Solnit, as the female witness to male holding forth. But the passage makes a point of repudiating such a reading: Kraus sees a reflection of herself not in the painting's silent interlocutor, but in a figure who is entirely ignoring the man holding forth. She identifies not with the "serious young woman" seated next to Benjamin, but with the "rakish, yellow coated punk (that's me!) with shocking bright red hair" seated alone and to the right, facing away from the philosopher.[38] By doing so, Kraus is simultaneously acknowledging Benjamin's centrality to the painting (he is the one "presiding") and declaring him irrelevant to her (as far as the yellow-coated punk is concerned, Benjamin might as well not be there). He is just a man explaining things to a woman, while she, the punk with the flaming red hair, ignores him, turning away instead to "see the future at the top of the frame."[39]

But what is especially curious about this passage is the way that, despite her dismissal of Benjamin as a Dick-ish holder forth, she also appropriates, without credit, his ideas. Kraus's reading of Kitaj's painting draws on Benjamin's own iconic reading of Paul Klee's painting *Angelus Novus* in "Theses on the Philosophy of History." The famous passage from Benjamin—the ninth of his eighteen theses—uses Klee's painting in order to explain his understanding of history, progress, and the relationship between the past and the future. The "angel of history" Benjamin sees in the painting is facing toward the viewer and toward the past but is being propelled by a storm from Paradise "into the future to which his back is turned, while the pile of debris before him"—the "wreckage" of history—"grows skyward."[40] To any theoretically savvy reader—and Dick, the nominal addressee, is of course nothing if not theoretically savvy—Kraus's appropriation of Benjamin is impossible to miss. She describes the history of 1920s Europe as a collapsing accumulation of heaped images, "sliding down" the painting: "History as a Jumble Sale." On the next page, she describes the way that, just outside the café, the painting's characters "are all poised in some relation to a nameless future that opens at the top right of the frame," and she figures one of these characters—the "young blonde woman in a big black dress" at the right-hand edge of the painting—as an analog for Benjamin's angel: like the angel of history, the young blonde woman is, Kraus notes, "facing us" and facing toward the debris of the past in the foreground, turning her back conspicuously to the future.[41] And if this is not already enough, Kraus's reading ends as follows: "We're touched by the nostalgia, seeing Walter at the center of our extended European family, but our smarter selves find greater satisfaction knowing history as we understand it is really just an avalanche of garbage toppling down."[42] "Our smarter selves": that is, those who like Kraus have read Benjamin's claim that history is "one single catastrophe which keeps piling wreckage upon wreckage."[43] This passage contains in miniature all of *I Love Dick*'s key motifs: it is a passage in which Kraus critiques and more or less entirely effaces the authority of a theorist who is prone to "Holding Forth" and one in which she appropriates his authority for herself, using the theorist as a way of becoming herself an author and a theorist.

One final question to consider, though: why Benjamin? In some sense Benjamin is an unlikely choice to serve as a figure of male theoretical authority. He is well known for never having achieved the same kind of professional success as his Frankfurt School colleagues, for never finishing what he conceived of as his magnum opus, *The Arcades Project*, and for dying tragically as a refugee from the Nazis in a small village in the Pyrenees. Moreover, McKenzie Wark even places Benjamin in the same "low theory" category as Kraus: Benjamin, she tells *Berfrois*, was not a philosopher, but someone "doing 'low theory'": "The self-conscious attempt to construct conceptual practices outside of formal settings."[44] In his persistent marginality throughout his lifetime, Benjamin is arguably closer to Kraus than her dismissal of him in this passage would indicate. There is, however, a stark contrast between the biographical Benjamin and today's Benjamin, the name on the cover of the imposing, thousand-plus-page *Arcades Project* and a multivolume set of *Selected Writings* from Harvard University Press; the Benjamin whose "The Work of Art in the Age of Mechanical Reproduction" is on a thousand college syllabuses; the Benjamin who has spawned his own "industry."[45] The practitioner of low theory is today firmly entrenched in the canon of high theory. What Kraus does by appropriating Benjamin's ideas, I would suggest, is to re-embed this posthumously authorized theory into something like its original "low" context, by putting it into her own voice, the voice of someone excluded from the academy and denied theoretical legitimacy. Kraus started Native Agents with the idea of "transferring some of French theory's legitimacy" to a group of female American writers. In *I Love Dick* she continues that project: taking the legitimacy of (in this case German) theory for herself. And it is impossible to deny the book's success: having spent a decade in relative obscurity before its republication in 2006, *I Love Dick* now has a TV adaptation, celebrity fans, and a number of writers who cite it as an influence.[46] Like Benjamin, Kraus has spawned an industry.

2.2. How Should a Person Be?

One of the most prominent writers to cite the influence of *I Love Dick* is Sheila Heti, who begins her interview with Kraus in *The Believer* as follows: "I know there was a time before I read Chris Kraus's *I Love Dick* (in fact, that time was only five years ago), but it's hard to imagine; some works of art do this to you."[47] Like Kraus's book, Heti's *How Should a Person Be?* (published in Canada in 2010 and in the United States in a revised edition in 2012) is a story about authorship: it is framed around its protagonist's failed attempt to write a play. Like *I Love Dick*, the narrator and protagonist shares a name and other details with the book's author (the 2012 cover of *How Should a Person Be?* calls it "a novel from life"). And like its predecessor, *How Should a Person Be?* met with a mixed response on its publication—a response inextricably tied to its author's gender. Michelle Dean describes the reception of *How Should a Person Be?* as follows:

> The book comes out, a couple of years later than anticipated, because the business of publishing literary fiction is a thing that cannot be rushed. Young women flock to it. They declare that everyone could benefit from reading it. Perhaps because it is listening for that call, no less than *The New Yorker* decides to review it. (They ignored your last book.) And not just any

review: They assign it to one of the last rock-star literary critics left, a man so acclaimed he can plausibly write a book about how "fiction"—not just one novel, but all of them—works. He concludes that your book does not, in fact, work. And though he just recently raved about a book very similar to yours (that one was written by a man, but one of the same age and same meandering disposition, one who also mixed fiction and fact), the critic's lukewarm review is written with the air of one holding the offending item out at arm's length, sniffing warily.[48]

The rock-star literary critic, of course, is James Wood. And the "very similar" book, which Wood raved about, is Ben Lerner's first novel, *Leaving the Atocha Station* (2011).

Despite Wood's unfavorable judgment—though perhaps helped by a very positive review by Chris Kraus in the *Los Angeles Review of Books*[49]—the next few years saw *How Should a Person Be?*, alongside Lerner's two novels—*Atocha* and *10:04* (2014)—become canonized as the foremost examples of North American autofiction. *I Love Dick* has been frequently mentioned as a forerunner to both writers: Joanna Walsh writes in *The Guardian* that without Kraus's book, "Sheila Heti might never have asked *How Should a Person Be?*, and Ben Lerner might never have written *Leaving the Atocha Station*. A whole generation of writers owes her."[50] And both Heti and Lerner pick up, in different ways, on the figure of the man who holds forth.

What is most noticeable about Heti's take on the trope is her emphasis on pedagogy. Solnit describes men who explain things to her, Kraus describes men who Hold Forth, and Heti describes men who want to teach her something. The pedagogical aspect of this figure is in fact already present in Solnit's essay: Solnit quotes Chaucer's description of the Clerk in *The Canterbury Tales*—"gladly would he learn and gladly teach"—as a way of contrasting Mr. Very Important (who is interested only in teaching and is not even expert in what he professes to be able to explain) with other "lovely men" in her life who have enabled rather than effaced her authorial work.[51] For her, the desire to teach others, when uncoupled from the desire to learn, is a suspect one. Heti's critique of men who want to teach her something, though, goes much further than either Solnit's or Kraus's work in its analysis of the power dynamics of the pedagogical relationship and the usefulness (or not) of the pedagogical metaphor in the first place.

How Should a Person Be? contains many figures who could be described as men who want to teach women things. There is Uri, Sheila's boss at a salon, who declares "I have decided to teach you everything I know."[52] And Sheila describes the experience of sleeping with the dominant and controlling Israel as him "teaching [her] a lesson."[53] The first instance, though, of the phrase that becomes a refrain in the novel—"another man who wants to teach me something"—comes when Sheila's friend Margaux (based on the painter Margaux Williamson) describes the end of a brief friendship with Eli, another artist: "'He's just another man who wants to teach me something,' she said."[54] The second instance is in Sheila's voice. After a long conversation with Solomon, a shopkeeper who talks over her and fails to listen to her, she writes: "I left the copy shop frustrated and upset. He was just another man who wanted to teach me something."[55] Uri, Israel, Eli, Solomon: even if some of these men (like Uri) are relatively benign and the behavior of others (like Israel) crosses over into abuse, they are nevertheless all relatively consistent with Solnit's Mr. Very Important and Kraus's Dick and Walter Benjamin: men who tend to shore up their own power at the expense of women whose authority they minimize.

The third and final occasion when this phrase is used, though, is considerably more complex—in part because this time Sheila uses it to describe *herself*: "I was just another man who wanted to teach me something!"[56] This line comes at the end of a section in which Sheila analyzes her own submissiveness to authority, her confusion as to whether she has been submitting to Israel's demands because she wants to or because she has been feeling "guilt-drenched empathy" for his "perversions."[57] Having been searching for authority figures to learn from throughout the novel, Sheila feels unable to "untangle how you imagined other people wanted you to behave from how *you* wanted to behave."[58] In Lacanian terms, she perceives herself as incapable of differentiating her own desire from the desire of the big Other. Or in the terms of the pedagogical metaphor that runs throughout the novel, she no longer knows how to unravel her own desire as a student from what she perceives as her teacher's desire.

The chapter ends as follows:

> I saw it all so clearly: I had come to New York as a student, like it was my teacher. And hadn't I *always* gone into the world making everyone and everything a lesson in how I should be? Somehow I had turned myself into the worst thing in the world: I was just another man who wanted to teach me something![59]

Up to this point, Sheila has understood the world through the metaphor of pedagogy: Sheila the student and the others (usually men) who teach her. Here, though, that relatively stable frame of understanding collapses in on itself. She describes herself as both student and teacher—or rather, as so dedicated to the role of student (in the art of how a person should be) that she has made "everyone and everything" into a "lesson," thereby becoming in some sense her own teacher. Her desire and her teacher's desire (her desire and the desire of the big Other) are impossible to untangle. The figure of the "man who wants to teach me something," then, is not only toxic in the obvious sense—that it is based on a notion of men as authority figures and women as passive receivers of male wisdom. It is also toxic in its reliance on the pedagogical metaphor: by viewing the world through this metaphor, seeking out lessons in "everyone and everything," Sheila ends up feeling both lost and complicit in her own lostness—making it all the more difficult to find herself again. She is only able to do so, and is only able to finally finish her authorial project—not the play she had been commissioned to write, but the novel we are reading—once she has ceased to see everyone around her as potential teachers. The novel's penultimate chapter gives us one final pedagogical metaphor, in a fable about a gravedigger, described as "a loyal man, solid and unshakable," with no interest in teaching or performing for others.[60] This is the novel's last lesson in how a person should be, and it gives us a less toxic alternative to the figure of the "man who wants to teach me something." The gravedigger "*taught himself* to dig well, and did."[61] *How Should a Person Be?* is a critique of didacticism—of men who want to teach Sheila things and of Sheila's tendency to look to others as teachers and authority figures. What the novel argues for in its stead is autodidacticism and self-authorship.

2.3. 10:04

If *How Should a Person Be?* can therefore be understood as engaged in a similar endeavor to *I Love Dick* and "Men Explain Things to Me"—the project of claiming female authorship—Ben Lerner's *10:04*, on the other hand, can be understood as engaged in a complementary project: it is a novel about the perils of male authorship. Like *How Should a Person Be?* and *Leaving the Atocha Station*, *10:04* is, in Rachel Sagner Buurma and Laura Heffernan's formulation, a "novel of commission": a novel about the process of writing a work commissioned by a literary institution and which considers in detail "the institution's presence in the writing process."[62] But whereas Heti's novel and Lerner's first novel focus on writers who have yet to achieve broad institutional acceptance, and whose creative projects, like Sheila's abandoned play, tend toward failure, *10:04* is more interested in how a writer deals with success. It begins after "an outrageously expensive celebratory meal in Chelsea that included baby octopuses the chef had literally massaged to death"; the meal is to celebrate having sold a proposal for a novel, for which the protagonist—whose name is Ben and whose biography coincides more or less with his author's—receives a "strong six-figure" advance.[63] And although Ben may struggle throughout the course of *10:04* with the process of creating what becomes *10:04*, the fact remains that, from the very beginning, he is framed as a writer whose authorial status is accepted by the institutions that surround him: the university—he has an academic teaching job and joins a panel with two well-known writers at Columbia's School of the Arts—and the publishing industry—his book proposal sparked "a competitive auction among the major New York houses."[64]

As the passage quoted above from Michelle Dean's review of *How Should a Person Be?* demonstrates, this degree of canonical acceptance (by luminaries such as James Wood) is common to both the protagonist and the author of *10:04*. *Leaving the Atocha Station* was, as Kate Zambreno points out in *Heroines* (2012)—a book edited by Chris Kraus—"feted as the tale of our times, written about rapturously" in reviews: "I mean, it's a beautiful book," Zambreno writes, "but I don't get all the adulation. The narrative of the nervous girl would never receive that treatment."⁶⁵ *10:04* is in some sense an attempt on Lerner's part to respond in an ethical way to his position of privilege and his new degree of institutional acceptance.

Beyond his narrator's frequent habit of doubting his own legitimacy, questioning whether he deserves the success he has found, Lerner's most important strategy for dealing with his authorial status is to try to share his status with others and to be a voice for other stories.⁶⁶ In her review of *10:04* for the *Los Angeles Review of Books*, Maggie Nelson—whose own strategies for dealing with the ethical dilemmas of authorship I have already discussed in Chapter 1—draws attention to Ben's "eagerness to listen to other people from varying walks of life," arguing that, even if those other people's stories still come to us via Lerner, *10:04* nevertheless succeeds in providing "an experience of a certain kind of openness and curiosity." And this openness, she points out, is juxtaposed with the behavior of one of the book's minor characters: a male author who had been on the same panel at Columbia, one "so distinguished I'd often thought of [him] as dead."⁶⁷ At dinner, following the panel, this author emerges as Lerner's Man Who Holds Forth:

> After two quick glasses of Sancerre, the distinguished male author started *holding forth*, periodically tugging at his salt-and-pepper beard, moving from one anecdote about a famous friend or triumphant experience to another without pausing for the possibility of response, and it was clear to everyone at the table who had any experience with men and alcohol—especially men who had won international literary prizes—that he was not going to stop talking at any point in the meal.⁶⁸

The "distinguished male author," "so distinguished I'd often thought of [him] as dead": it is clear that we are dealing here with the figure of the excessively agentic author, like the author whose death Barthes declared, or like Solnit's Mr. Very Important.⁶⁹ Like the latter, Lerner's "distinguished male author" remains anonymous, referred to only in terms of his gender and his status (as well as his age: the "salt-and-pepper beard"). And like Heti's men who want to teach her something and Kraus's Walter Benjamin, he insists on talking at and over women:

> The distinguished professor was sitting immediately across from the distinguished male author and seemed more than happy to receive his logorrhea; a younger woman—probably also an English professor, but too young to be distinguished—was sitting beside him, smiling bravely, realizing her evening was doomed.⁷⁰

Most of the key characteristics of this figure that we have seen in Solnit, Kraus, and Heti are here: the attempts to shore up his own importance (here with reference to his "famous friend[s]" and "triumphant experience[s]"), the tendency to dominate the conversation (he does not pause in his discourse "for the possibility of response"), and rude behavior that seems to be especially targeted at those who do not share his level of privilege: "When a young Latino man tried to refill his glass of water from a pitcher, the distinguished male author snapped in Spanish, without looking at the man, that he was having sparkling water."[71] The dynamic Lerner describes is explicitly a gendered one: the other Columbia panelist is a "distinguished female author," who is equally accomplished, but shares with Ben what Nelson identifies as the "eagerness to listen to other people from varying walks of life."

The key thing that sets Lerner's treatment of the Man Who Holds Forth apart from Solnit's, Kraus's, and Heti's is the attitude of *10:04*'s protagonist toward him. In "Men Explain Things to Me," *I Love Dick*, and *How Should a Person Be?*, the narrators (and to some degree the authors) are women who have been forced to prove their authorial status to a patriarchal establishment that tends to discredit female authors. In *10:04*, on the other hand, the narrator (and to some degree the author) is a man who has been accepted as part of that patriarchal establishment and who therefore no longer needs to prove his authorial status. *10:04*'s "distinguished male author," then, is not so much an antagonist as a nightmare version of what the protagonist might become and what he consciously seeks to avoid becoming.[72]

2.4. "What Is It to Hold Forth?"

The four writers I have examined so far—Solnit, Kraus, Heti, and Lerner—all share one important characteristic: they associate "holding forth" primarily with men. By 2012, when, as Rebecca Solnit writes, "the term 'mansplained'— one of *The New York Times*'s words of the year for 2010—was being used in mainstream political journalism," such an association had been firmly entrenched in popular culture.[73] Read today, then, what is most striking about Barthes's analysis of holding forth in his 1977 seminar is not just its prescience—its in-depth consideration of a phenomenon that would not be the subject of widespread cultural interest until several decades later—but also, problematically, its stubborn refusal to address the genderedness of holding forth. Throughout the three sessions of the seminar that Barthes leads, he consistently evades any implication that men, rather than women, are socialized so as to be more inclined to hold forth. And in fact, when he gives a list of examples of holding forth, Barthes chooses to focus his most pointed critique against a young woman.[74]

In the second half of this chapter, I will address in detail the question of Barthes's reticence regarding questions of gender and regarding questions of politics and identity more generally. Here, I focus on the specifics of his study of holding forth, turning in particular to the January 12, 1977, session of his Collège de France seminar "What Is It to Hold Forth? Research on Invested

Speech." I provide an overview of the ways in which Barthes unpacks and investigates the idea, demonstrating on the one hand how it both anticipates and extends the understanding of holding forth that Solnit, Kraus, Heti, and Lerner give us and on the other hand the ways in which it notably falls short of the concrete and directly political analysis that the previously discussed thinkers offer.

The January 12 session was the first of eleven that comprised the seminar, which ran until the end of March. Barthes also led the final two sessions, which are included in *How to Live Together* under the title "Charlus-Discourse": they consist for the most part of an analysis of a scene from Proust in which Charlus addresses the narrator. These sessions are less directly relevant to the phenomenon of holding forth, however: Barthes explicitly denies that Charlus-Discourse is an "example" or a "representative" of "holding forth"; instead, these sessions are a return to the kind of close reading of a single text that Barthes performs in *S/Z*, this time with more attention paid to the power dynamics of the speech situation.[75] The remaining eight sessions of "What Is It to Hold Forth?" were led by other speakers and covered a range of related topics; there are no published records of these other sessions beyond a list of speakers and their subjects (which, tantalizingly for our purposes, included a session on "Woman as object of speech" led by one of Barthes's students, Cosette Martel). As a result, my analysis focuses almost entirely on Barthes's opening session, in which he considers explicitly and in detail the question of what it is to hold forth.

The first issue that ought to be addressed is one of translation: to what extent is Barthes actually talking about the same thing as Solnit, Kraus, Heti, and Lerner, given that he is writing (or rather teaching) in a different language? "Holding forth"—as translator Kate Briggs renders it in the English edition of *How to Live Together*—is a translation of the French idiom "tenir un discours": literally, to hold a discourse. In her preface, Briggs describes the field of meaning of this expression as encompassing both "to make or deliver a speech" and "to have or hold to a position or point of view."[76] It is possible to make a case for the more literal option that Briggs occasionally uses, "to sustain a discourse": by keeping the word "discourse," this translation would maintain the link with the seminars Barthes had given the previous two years at the École pratique des hautes études on "le discours amoureux" (the basis for his published book, *A Lover's Discourse*), and the seminar on holding forth does indeed pick up on many of the same themes as the seminars on the lover's discourse.[77] Overall, though, I would suggest that "to hold forth" is a fitting translation for "tenir un discours" and that when Barthes discusses the concept, he is talking about more or less the same phenomenon as Solnit, Kraus, Heti, and Lerner. For one thing, Barthes emphasizes that it is "to hold/to sustain/*tenir* and not discourse/*discours*" that is the "key word" in the idiom: the fact that Briggs's translation does not contain a direct translation for *discours*, this would imply, is of relatively little significance.[78] Most importantly, though, the way that Barthes discusses the idea of *tenir un discours* in this seminar is—with the notable exception of its gendered associations—closely aligned with the way that Solnit, Kraus, Heti, and Lerner discuss holding forth.

The majority of Barthes's opening session on *tenir un discours* is devoted to a close unpacking of the phrase, both in its individual elements and as a whole. Throughout this unpacking, there are "two basic semes" (or units of meaning) that keep coming back: "Power, force, subjection, ascendancy" and "duration, persistence."[79] Holding forth, for Barthes, is a question of power maintained over time—just as *holding* involves both power (gripping that which is held) and the persistence of that power over time (holding *on*). More specifically, that power is primarily linguistic: the "one point of return" in the seminar, around which Barthes and the other speakers circle, is "language as force"— "the intimidation of language."[80] In this sense, the seminar is an expansion of Barthes's remarks in his inaugural lecture at the Collège de France, where he (infamously) discusses the "fascism" of language.[81] There, Barthes sets out his intention to focus on the power structures inherent in language and to be a critic of the "'authorized' voices which authorize themselves to utter the discourse of all power: the discourse of arrogance."[82] In a phrase like this, we can hear clear echoes of both Barthes's earlier critique of "authorized" voices in "The Death of the Author" and the critiques of arrogant authorial figures in "Men Explain Things to Me," *I Love Dick*, *How Should a Person Be?*, and *10:04*. *Tenir un discours*, for Barthes, refers to this "discourse of arrogance": holding forth is "an ostentatious performance of speech," one in which the speaker shows off, plays a role, and does so with "an intentionality of force, coercion, subjection."[83] Whereas the corresponding lecture course on "How to Live Together" explores the possibilities of a utopian form of sociability, in which power dynamics are neutralized, the seminar on holding forth presents, in editor Claude Coste's words, "the dark side of Living-Together," in which the social sphere is understood as a dystopic arena of linguistic power struggle.[84]

Like for Solnit, Kraus, Heti, and Lerner, then, the person who holds forth is for Barthes a figure for a bad form of excessively agentic authorship. At the same time, he acknowledges (like Kraus and Heti) that there is a certain seductiveness in holding forth: see *I Love Dick*'s Walter Benjamin, looking "terrific in his tinted eyeglasses," or *How Should a Person Be?*'s Israel, "the sexiest guy in the city"; similarly, Barthes admits that he "take[s] pleasure in being subjected to" the power of the one who holds forth.[85] Like for Kraus too, holding forth in Barthes's analysis is gestural as well as verbal: it is "a body ... asserting itself," like Benjamin "presiding at a café table," towering over his companions.[86] And like for Heti, holding forth has pedagogical stakes: as I will discuss later on, Barthes puts a great deal of effort in his Collège de France seminars into not being "just another man who wants to teach me something"—which also provides a connection with Lerner's treatment of the "distinguished male author" as a figure for the kind of writer he wants to avoid becoming.[87] Finally, when Barthes refers to holding forth as a form of "invested speech," he is playing in part on the psychoanalytic concept of *Besetzung* or cathexis, but more directly on the idea of holding forth as a form of speech that has been "bestow[ed] or invest[ed] with a power, an authority, through various ceremonies, one of which is to be dressed in a garment."[88] Thus for Barthes, as for Solnit and Lerner, the one who holds forth is playing the role of somebody in a position of authority, complete with costume choices—like the "distinguished male author" with his "salt-and-pepper beard"—and props—like "Mr. Very Important" with his "rugged luxury cabin at 9,000 feet complete with elk antlers, lots of kilims, and a wood-burning stove."[89] In "Men Explain Things to Me"—picking up on Barthes's emphasis on the "theatricalization" of holding forth—Solnit describes herself as having been cast "in my assigned role as ingénue" in contrast to Mr. Very Important in his role as, well, Mr. Very Important.[90]

Up to this point, I have mostly been concerned with the ways in which Barthes's investigation of holding forth corresponds with—and anticipates by two or more decades—the ways in which Solnit, Kraus, Heti, and Lerner treat the same phenomenon. Beyond its prescience, though, Barthes's analysis is also valuable for how it departs from those writers' work. Here I want to focus on one particular aspect of holding forth that Barthes explores, one that the other writers I have looked at do not explicitly discuss, but that provides insight both into their work and into the figure of the Man Who Holds Forth more generally. "We hold," Barthes claims, "we are forever holding forth *on the same topic*": this emphasis on the repetitiveness of holding forth is central to his analysis of the phenomenon.[91]

The opening session of "What Is It to Hold Forth?" begins by quoting somebody Barthes knows, who "begins each new session with his analyst with these words": "So, I was saying …."[92] This allusion to psychoanalysis foreshadows the fact that the session as a whole draws to an unusually high degree (for Barthes) on psychoanalytic language and ideas. In fact, Barthes theorizes "holding forth" as something like a manifestation of the repetition compulsion:

> We sustain one and the same discourse until death and death is the only power that can interrupt that unremitting taking of the same line [*rompre la tenue de notre discours*]. That unending discourse is never bowdlerized. It begins again, is reborn… Put differently: to begin is always, at some level of the subject: to follow on from.[93]

Only death can "rompre la tenue de notre discours": can break the holding of our discourse, can break us off from holding forth. Until death, we are stuck in the same repetitive track—our discourse "endlessly repeat[ing] itself," beginning again, getting reborn—even when we want to pretend that we have escaped.[94] Barthes asks whether it is possible for the "discourse to be abruptly broken off" by anything other than death—whether one could, for example, relinquish one's discourse and invest one's psychic energies in a different one instead: "Conversions?" he wonders. "You can be converted to another object," he answers, "but not to another discourse."[95] To translate this into the psychoanalytic terms that are implicit in this idea: our desire might alight on a new object (we might fall out of love with one person and in love with another, say), but at a more fundamental level, we are still stuck in the same cycle; we are still holding on to the same discourse.

The repetitiveness of holding forth has a social dynamic as well as the individual psychic dynamic described above:

> "Holding forth" comes down to (we'll probably come back to this later on) to repeating, in your own fashion, a discourse that's already been set out, that's already been heard a thousand times before (taking a hackneyed line), but doing so as if it were you who were inventing it, with the conviction of the first time.[96]

When holding forth, you do not just repeat *yourself*. You also repeat others—but "with the conviction of the first time," claiming ownership of the ideas you have appropriated, claiming originality. There is an echo here of Solnit's Mr. Very Important and the way that he tries to explain to her all about "the *very important* Muybridge book that came out this year," claiming expertise on the subject when in fact he is just repeating back something that he read in *The New York Times Book Review* (which he does not remember well enough to realize that it is Solnit's book he is talking about). And there is an echo too of *How Should a Person Be?* and the repetitiveness of its succession of men who hold forth: recall the first word in the phrase "another man who wants to teach me something," not to mention the repetition of the phrase itself: men who want to teach women something are everywhere in the novel, unaware of their utter un-uniqueness, of the "hackneyed line" they are taking.[97]

Barthes's analysis of the repetitiveness of holding forth is valuable: it gives us a way of understanding Men Who Hold Forth as subjects stuck in the repetition compulsion, but insistent on their own originality—their difference both from others and from past versions of themselves. It gives us a set of critical questions to ask of them, ways to defuse their claims to authority, in a manner similar to that in which Solnit's friend in "Men Explain Things to Me" interrupts Mr. Very Important "three or four times" to say "That's her book."[98] Are you actually saying anything different or new, or are you just repeating yourself, holding on to the same old discourse? Or: whose discourse are you repeating with such conviction, as if it were your own? But even though Barthes gives us critical resources for theorizing the figure of the Man Who Holds Forth, what he does not give us, as I mentioned at the beginning of this section, is any indication that he recognizes holding forth as a gendered phenomenon.

The first session of the seminar concludes with six examples of holding forth: three in which the phenomenon is purely verbal and three in which it is "complex": "verbal, gestural, behavioral."[99] The first three examples are treated relatively value-neutrally: he mentions the opening of *Robinson Crusoe*, in which Robinson's father subjects him to a "Discourse" (6–7); a scenario in which, at a social gathering of "men and their wives," one of the wives suddenly "delivers a grand discourse on dogs"; and a loquacious taxi-driver who talks at his passenger from beginning to end of the journey.[100] Barthes then gives three further "complex" examples, which vary in tone. First is a man who eats his breakfast with "force, vigor, continuity, tension, a certain theatricality": all the qualities Barthes associates with holding forth.[101] Barthes describes his attitude toward this man as "affectionate." He also describes a young man showing off on his motorbike, "wind[ing] other people up": Barthes's tone here, again, is free of annoyance; the motorcyclist, it seems, is merely indulging in youthful folly. The remaining example, though, is the longest and most detailed of the six, a description of a "young specialist nurse."[102] This example Barthes describes as "more irritating, more corrosive," and his description takes the form of a catalogue of all of the nurse's objectionable behaviors:

> On the train, a "young specialist nurse" (traveling with a secondary-school teacher who's clearly in thrall to her and whom she dominates): a succession of competing signs of affirmation: (a) a big tape player in our compartment, (b) a loud, booming voice, (c) unembarrassed discussion of all sorts of subjects, (d) lolls over two seats, (e) takes her shoes off, (f) eats an orange, (g) cuts in on my conversation with my traveling companion. In short, she holds forth.[103]

Reading this passage today, what is most striking is the way in which Barthes's "young specialist nurse" engages so unmistakably in a set of behaviors that have come to be generally coded as masculine. She "lolls over two seats"—like someone on public transport "manspreading."[104] She "cuts in on my conversation"—as in another neologism that has recently found widespread use, "manterrupting."[105] Barthes, like popular culture feminist discourse in the second decade of the twenty-first century, recognizes the connection between taking up physical space, taking up auditory space, taking up affective space, and taking up social space.[106] But he locates all of these traits in a young woman. How are we to read this?

In part, of course, the fact that Barthes does not address the genderedness of the phenomenon he describes could be explained by the context in which he was writing: the predominantly North American, Anglophone conversation about mansplaining, manspreading, etc., simply had not happened in France in 1977. We might also point toward the fact that Barthes is making a deliberate effort to define holding forth in as broad a way as possible, as something to be understood at the level of psyche, regardless of gender. It is worth pointing out that Solnit, Kraus, Heti, and Lerner all have their blind spots too: the conversation around mansplaining quickly developed to consider the ways in which the dynamic that Solnit describes—"when people explain things to me I know and they don't"[107]—is not only a gendered phenomenon but also, for example, a racialized phenomenon, leading to a number of additional neologisms using the same "-splain" suffix: whitesplain, straightsplain, cissplain, ablesplain.[108] From this point of view, a theory of holding forth that does not define itself in relation to just a single vector of power, such as gender, might ultimately be more useful. Nevertheless, the fact that Barthes does not acknowledge *any* of the vectors of power along which the phenomenon of holding forth tends to operate remains a frustrating limitation. It is a limitation that in the next section I aim not to explain away, but to contextualize within the wider history of Barthes's reception and his uneasy relationship to political commitment and to categories of identity.

3. Roland Barthes, Man Who Holds Forth?

3.1. The Charge of Apoliticism

Especially when read in comparison to Solnit, Kraus, Heti, and Lerner, Barthes's "What Is It to Hold Forth?" seems to go out of its way not to consider the question of *who it is* who holds forth, to be as noncommittal as possible. To longtime readers of Barthes, though, this lack of commitment should come as no surprise. Charges that Barthes is afraid of political commitment, that he is apolitical, or even antipolitical have been levelled repeatedly over the last several decades, both in general—by critics like Annette Lavers, who argued in her influential early monograph on Barthes that by 1973's *The Pleasure of the Text* he had abandoned any interest in "ideological commitment" and "was on the way to being fully integrated into the bourgeoisie"—and more specifically.[109]

In the following sections, I examine three particular critiques of Barthes, all of which center on the accusation that his thinking is insufficiently political, and the responses to these critiques. Each of these three critical conversations centers respectively on questions of sexuality and queer politics, orientalism and the aftermath of May 1968, and gender and authorship. And each of them, I argue, follows a particular logic. On the one hand, there are critics who, for justifiable reasons, take Barthes to task for the ways in which his thinking fails to address specific political concerns, in terms of sexuality, class and race, and gender. On the other hand, there are critics who defend Barthes, making the case that his evasiveness when it comes to politics (and the politics of identity in particular) is best understood not as a failure, but as a deliberate strategy, which in fact has a specific political value: by eluding the grammar of belonging and commitment that structures mainstream political discourse, Barthes is attempting to rethink the language of politics along broader and more liberatory lines.

My own position in each of these debates is closer to the latter. In the three sections that follow, I outline both sides of the argument: I highlight what is most urgent in the queer, anti-racist, and feminist critiques of Barthes, for—as in the context of Barthes's stubborn failure to discuss the genderedness of holding forth—his determination to avoid the language of political commitment frequently has significant drawbacks. In the final analysis, though, I tend to side with the more recent thinkers who, benefiting from having read Barthes's detailed theorization of his political evasiveness in the Collège de France seminars (in particular, *The Neutral*), are better placed to understand the political stakes of Barthes's apparent apoliticism. Via a detailed consideration of these thinkers—figures like Maggie Nelson, Nicholas de Villiers, and Diana Knight—I aim to provide an answer to the question that the previous section of the chapter set up: why is Barthes so reluctant to talk about the question of *who holds forth*? In doing so, I also hope to demonstrate why it is that, in recent years, progressive writers and thinkers, especially in feminist and queer circles, have increasingly found Barthes an enabling thinker, in ways that a previous generation of thinkers (most notably in the 1980s and 1990s) did not.

The key issue at stake in all three of the debates I focus on is the question that Barthes asks in the afterword to his highly contentious essay "So, How Was China?": "Isn't it ultimately a shabby idea of politics to think that it can only find expression in the form of a *directly* political discourse?"[110] To Barthes and his defenders, the answer is yes—and his work in the Collège de France years represents in part his sustained attempt to find expression for politics outside of "the form of a *directly* political discourse." To critics like D. A. Miller, Lisa Lowe, and Sara Ahmed, on the other hand, Barthes's flight from such discourse is a failure of nerve, a symptom of his own privileged position, or evidence of a drift toward reactionary politics. Let me illustrate this dynamic with an example, one that provides an overview of both sides of the argument: the argument in favor of Barthes's evasiveness (or what we might term his *neutrality*), and the argument in favor of direct political engagement and commitment. In *The Argonauts*, Maggie Nelson—who, as I discussed in the first chapter, is deeply influenced by Barthes's work—gives a relatively even-handed assessment of his controversial politics, bringing out both the value of his mode of thinking and its pitfalls.

About halfway through that book, Nelson describes an evening she spent with her partner Harry watching the movie *X-Men: First Class*: a movie in which two groups of mutants, led respectively by Charles Xavier (or Professor X) and Erik Lehnsherr (better known as Magneto), are in conflict over the question of whether mutants ought to seek harmony with the humans who have oppressed them or whether they ought to radically turn against their oppressors.

> Afterward we debated: assimilation vs. revolution. I'm no cheerleader for assimilation per se, but in the movie the assimilationists were advocating nonviolence and identification with the Other in that bastardized Buddhist way that gets me every time. You expressed sympathy for the revolutionaries, who argued, *Stay freaky and blow 'em up before they come for you, because*

no matter what they say, the truth is they want you dead, and you're fooling yourself if you think otherwise... We bantered good-naturedly, yet somehow allowed ourselves to get polarized into a needless binary. That's what we both hate about fiction, or at least crappy fiction—it purports to provide occasions for thinking through complex issues, but really it has predetermined the positions, stuffed a narrative full of false choices, and hooked you on them, rendering you less able to see out, to *get* out.[111]

Later in the text, when faced with another situation in which she feels suffocated by the demand to choose between what feel like a set of predetermined positions, Nelson turns to Barthes's *The Neutral* as a resource to help her "to see out, to *get* out." The Neutral, she writes, is "that which, in the face of dogmatism, the menacing pressure to take sides, offers novel responses: to flee, to escape, to demur, to shift or refuse terms, to disengage, to turn away."[112] The Neutral is a way of transcending the "shabby idea of politics" that insists on "*directly* political discourse," that insists that our options are limited to the false choice between Professor X and Magneto, meek assimilation and violent revolution. What is valuable about Barthes's way of thinking (what is valuable about his *neutrality*) is his realization—and, as I will discuss, this is a characteristically post-1968 realization—that much political discourse is just such a "crappy fiction," in Nelson's words. It eliminates any space for nuance—one of Barthes's most highly prized qualities—and it traps us in the realm of the *doxa*.

But Nelson also points out that the "novel responses" made possible by Barthes's mode of thinking—flight, escape, turning away—are not always the best ways of responding: "a studied evasiveness," she suggests, "has its own limitations."[113] In some situations, "insistence," "persistence," or "obligation" may be more appropriate or ethical; turning away may not even be an option.[114] The *X-Men* movies have often been understood as an allegory for queer politics, a connection that is also implicit in Harry's commitment to the revolutionary cause: "*Stay freaky ... the truth is they want you dead, and you're fooling yourself if you think otherwise.*" In such a life-or-death situation, a response like Barthes's risks coming across as cowardly or as the kind of response that is only viable if one is already sufficiently shielded from its consequences.

These, then, are the stakes of the debates that follow: do we value commitment, persistence, and direct political discourse, or the possibility of a break with the false choices of orthodox politics and the potential for a more nuanced approach that would expand the sphere of the political?

3.2. Barthes and Queer Politics

During his lifetime and in the couple of decades since his death, the apparent evasiveness with which Barthes treated the subject of his own homosexuality tended to frustrate queer readings of his work. Despite a number of potential points of intersection between Barthes's work and the emergent field of queer theory, the fact that Barthes avoided outspoken proclamations of his queerness at all costs put him at odds with queer thinkers such as D. A. Miller and Hervé Guibert who saw openness about one's sexuality as a key prerequisite of good queer politics and aesthetics. More recently though—and especially in the years since the publication of the Collège de France seminars—a number of queer critics (Nicholas de Villiers) and thinkers (Maggie Nelson) have been energized rather than frustrated by Barthes's cagey neutrality when it came to his sexuality. In this section, I demonstrate how and why this shift in reception has taken place, siding ultimately with the latter position, the queer defense of Barthes. From this vantage point, it is possible to see most clearly the resonances between Barthes's project and the project of queer theory: specifically, both Barthes and queer theorists are interested in theorizing politics and sexuality outside of the overbearingly identitarian and binaristic categories that structure heteronormativity.

The most widely discussed example of the first position—the queer *critique* of Barthes—is D. A. Miller's *Bringing Out Roland Barthes* (1992), which makes an argument that comes from a similar place to Harry's commitment to staying freaky. Miller has a certain degree of sympathy with Barthes's preference for refusing the terms proffered by a homophobic society: "such disappearing acts," he writes, "are not always performed homophobically," even if they are "always the effect of homophobia."[115] But ultimately, he argues, "Barthes's relation to the act of gay self-nomination proves nothing short of phobic."[116] Barthes's equivocation and elusiveness is, for Miller, complicit with heteronormativity:

> Society continues to prefer the sotto voce stammering of a homosexuality from which nothing in fact is more tolerated, more desired, than that it be *provisional* ("it's just a stage"), *revocable* ("keep your options open"), *insignificant* ("it doesn't necessarily mean"), *inessential* ("are you sure?"), and, under the cumulative weight of all these attributes, expulsively *irrelevant*.[117]

To Miller, Barthes's attempts to outplay meaning, to resist the suffocating and reductive forces of classification, and to disengage sexuality from stable categories of identity are too close for comfort to the homophobic rhetoric he quotes in this passage: "keep your options open," "it doesn't necessarily mean," "are you sure?" Precisely in his efforts to avoiding taking on "a prescribed social identity," Barthes ends up doing exactly that, by perpetuating the idea of homosexuality as the love that dare not speak its name.[118]

For the French writer Hervé Guibert—at least if we follow Ralph Sarkonak's argument in the second chapter of his monograph *Angelic Echoes*, where he traces the many allusions to Barthes in Guibert's work—Barthes's refusal to be open about his sexuality was not so much a political failure as it was an intellectual and an aesthetic one. Sarkonak reads the following passage from

Guibert's *Ghost Image* (1981) as an implicit response to Barthes's *Camera Lucida* and that book's lack of explicit engagement with homosexuality:

> It's not that I want to dissimulate it, or that I want to boast about it arrogantly. But it's the least I can do in the way of sincerity. How can you speak of photography without speaking of desire? If I mask my desire, if I deprive it of its gender, if I leave it undefined, as others have done more or less cleverly, I would feel as if I were weakening my stories, or writing carelessly. It's not even a matter of courage (I'm not militant), it has to do with the truth of writing. I don't know how to say it more simply.[119]

Sarkonak understands this passage as an "example of Guibert trying to outdo or just plain 'out' Barthes."[120] And Barthes is indeed somebody who, "more or less cleverly," masks his desire and "deprive[s] it of its gender": this is what Miller resents when he points to "the alternation of masculine and feminine pronouns in *A Lover's Discourse*."[121] On the other hand, there is something very Barthesean about Guibert's approach here, specifically in the way that Guibert locates the question of how much and how to express his sexuality in an aporia between silence and speech, between being closeted and being out: "It's not that I want to dissimulate it, or that I want to boast about it arrogantly." This double bind is precisely the kind of false choice that Barthes (and Nelson, in the *X-Men* example) wants to outplay. Barthes certainly never boasts arrogantly about his sexuality—arrogance, as should already be clear from the passages quoted from "What Is It to Hold Forth?," is a quality that Barthes abhors—but neither does he entirely dissimulate his desires, as demonstrated by the discussion of "the two H.'s: homosexuality and hashish" in *Roland Barthes by Roland Barthes*, for example.[122] He is wary about the way that adjectives and identity categories can be oppressive and constricting, but he is just as wary of the way that persistent, defiant silence around a topic can become its own form of categorization. As he writes in *The Neutral*, "Silence: becomes, willing or not, its own sign."[123] To persist too vehemently in refusing categories of identity can be to take on, against one's best intentions, the identity of the one who refuses.

In their recognition of this double bind—the way in which discussing one's sexuality comes across either as too coy and evasive or too brash or insistent—Barthes and Guibert are on the same page. They differ, though, in their response to this bind. Guibert justifies his openness as a form of sincerity, a way to be more truthful in his writing. Barthes, on the other hand, has read his Freud, Sartre, and Marx and is skeptical of the notion of sincerity, seeing it as a futile delusion based on the flawed notion that we have access to the truth about ourselves.[124] For a critic like Miller, Guibert's is the more politically admirable response. But for more recent critics, like Nicholas de Villiers, Barthes's response is not only more intellectually sophisticated; it is also more effective as a form of queer resistance.[125] Whereas Guibert, by his own admission, is "not militant," Murray Pratt suggests that Barthes is: "Barthes's militancy," he writes, "lies in his imaginative disappropriation of the aggressivity of identity, which imagines a plural space for a liberated gay erotics in both text and life."[126] De Villiers, in *Opacity and the Closet*, makes the inverse argument to Miller: whereas Miller suggests that Barthes's equivocation is complicit with homophobia, de Villiers argues that "it is Miller's response, not Barthes's, that is on the side of homophobia."[127] Homophobia, he writes, works just as much by "the sad reverse discourse whereby homosexuality can only be tolerated if it is *essential, stereotyped*, and *irrevocably* cannot be helped, rather than a *provisional* or strategic choice," and by seeking to *bring out* Barthes, Miller is complicit with this discourse.[128]

De Villiers cites Barthes's preface to Renaud Camus's queer novel *Tricks* (1979), in which Barthes writes: "To proclaim yourself is always to speak at the behest of a vengeful Other, to enter into his discourse, to argue with him, *to seek from him a scrap of identity*."[129] In Barthes's hostility toward the "vengeful Other" and his disdain for attempts to seek validation from or integration into a homophobic society, we can see resonances not only with Harry's revolutionary commitment in *The Argonauts* ("*no matter what they say, the truth is they want you dead*") but also with contemporary queer theory more generally—in its widespread disdain for the mainstream LGBTQ campaign for marriage equality, for example, which theorists like Judith Butler, Tim Dean, David Eng, and Jasbir Puar all see as problematic in the way that it seeks, in Barthes's phrase, "a scrap of identity" from the very same heteronormative neoliberal society that continues to oppress queer people.[130] The fact, therefore, that Barthes (especially in his later work) is more interested in refusing society's terms of engagement than in working within them goes some way to explaining not only his resonance with contemporary queer theory but also his current popularity among more theoretically oriented queer writers. In addition to *The Argonauts*, there is Wayne Koestenbaum, who wrote a foreword to *A Lover's Discourse*, or Edmund White, who called Barthes "a writer whose books of criticism and personal musings must be admired as serious and beautiful works of the imagination."[131] And in his 2016 essay collection *Proxies*, Brian Blanchfield discusses *How to Live Together* at length and foregrounds the fact that Barthes "is a signal influence on my conception of this very book."[132]

Barthes's relationship with queer politics has therefore been tempestuous precisely because of his refusal to engage in the kind of "*directly* political discourse" that he critiques in the passage from "So, How Was China?" quoted above. I would suggest that critics like de Villiers and writers like Nelson and Blanchfield, who have all read Barthes's Collège de France seminars, are better placed than Miller and Guibert to understand the theoretical resources that Barthes can offer to queer political thought. Barthes's late work provides an in-depth analysis of one of the key questions of queer theory: how to think politics and sexuality outside of the oppressive binaries of heteronormative society.

3.3. Barthes and Post-1968 Orientalism

If D. A. Miller was frustrated with Barthes because of his refusal to openly proclaim his sexual identity and his commitment to queer politics, Lisa Lowe—the critic with whom I begin this section—is frustrated with Barthes because of his refusal to openly proclaim his leftist identity and his commitment to left politics in the wake of the events of May 1968. She is also frustrated, though, with one specific aspect of Barthes's response to '68: his turn to the "Orient"—primarily Japan, as well as China—as a utopian space that could provide a radical decentering of the West and what Barthes perceived as its unhealthy addiction to meaning and hermeneutics. For Lowe, this turn took on (against Barthes's best intentions) a distinctly orientalist cast. There are therefore two key issues at stake here: first, under the sign of class, the question of commitment to leftist politics in post-1968 politics, and second, under the sign of race, the question of Barthes's idealization of China and Japan in 1970's *Empire of Signs* and "So, How Was China?" (an article written following his trip to China with Philippe Sollers, Julia Kristeva, and other *Tel Quel* thinkers, published in *Le Monde* in 1974, and translated in the 2015 collection *"The 'Scandal' of Marxism" and Other Writings on Politics*).[133]

Broadly speaking, I agree with the second aspect of Lowe's critique: that Barthes's work on China and Japan fails to entirely escape implication in the Western, colonial gaze that it sought to undermine. But I am less convinced by the first half of her argument, her claim that, by turning away from France and toward China and Japan, Barthes thereby abandons the sphere of the political. Rather, I see Lowe's argument as operating on an assumption that runs parallel with the assumptions that determined Miller's and Guibert's critiques: all three assume that the only viable form of political thought is one that is committed, open, and direct. I side instead with Diana Knight, who sees in Barthes's utopian figurations of China and Japan an attempt to find new, less direct but more expansive forms for political thinking.

In *Critical Terrains: French and British Orientalisms* (1991), then, Lowe puts forward two key critiques of Barthes's treatment of Japan and China in the 1970s. I agree with her argument that, even though Barthes's intention in *Empire of Signs* and "So, How Was China?" is precisely to critique predominant Western conceptions of the East and the colonial, orientalist gaze through which they operate, his project is undermined by the fact that he "deploy[s] an orientalist trope" in order to do so: the arguments that Barthes and his *Tel Quel* compatriots make "tend to contribute to the very logics they wish to criticize."[134] Barthes writes that his aim in "So, How Was China?" was "to respond to the way many Westerners hallucinate the People's Republic of China in a dogmatic, violently affirmative/negative or falsely liberal way," but Lowe sees him as failing to escape those same hallucinations in his work.[135]

Lowe's other critique is that Barthes's tendency to fetishize China in "So, How Was China?" is a dangerously escapist response to the events of 1968: for her, Barthes and the *Tel Quel* set abandon the attempt to grapple with concrete political questions in post-'68 France in favor of a fantasized and romanticized version of revolution abroad:

> The embrace of Maoism and the fetishizing of China represent more than a projection of the Orient as Other by a group of leftist intellectuals disillusioned after May 1968. It also reveals their judgment that socialist revolution could never occur in France and therefore that nothing would be sacrificed if they withdrew their political focus from France and turned their gaze toward a political utopia elsewhere. In a sense it represented a desertion of the continuing contradictions created by May 1968.[136]

In this respect, Lowe's critique finds common ground with Miller's and Guibert's: all three find Barthes wanting because of what they perceive as his lack of commitment and intellectual dishonesty. Like Miller, Lowe sees Barthes's disavowal of direct political discourse in favor of an approach that seeks to find ways of refusing meaning—for what ultimately excites Barthes about his perceptions of China and Japan is the way that they render interpretation and meaning-making impossible—as ultimately a political and theoretical failure.

For the flipside of this argument, we can turn to Diana Knight's book-length analysis of Barthes's utopianism.[137] For Knight, although Barthes's work is often complicit with orientalism (especially in his writings on Morocco), Barthes was (contra Lowe's argument) all too well aware of how his interest in Japan and China as utopian spaces could slide into apolitical escapism:

> Barthes never stopped hypothesizing and fantasizing how things might be otherwise—otherwise, that is, than in his own alienated and class-torn society. Barthes constantly worried about the extent to which an intellectual must, at the same time, take a stand on the contemporary terrain, about the extent to which utopia could never be more than a foil highlighting the shortcomings of present-day society, about the extent to which *immersion in utopia might seem an escape from historical obligations.*[138]

Knight reads Barthes's interest in utopia as a way for him to bridge "the literary and political dimensions of his work," a way for him to give a political valence to his literary criticism.[139]

Furthermore, Knight's reading is, I argue, more consistent than Lowe's with the project to which Barthes devoted himself in the final years of his life: the project of theorizing both the literary and the political stakes of utopian spaces. Though *Barthes and Utopia* predates the publication of the Collège de France seminars and lectures (with the exception of the inaugural lecture and an unauthorized transcription of the first lecture from *The Neutral*), these three volumes exemplify Knight's argument: the utopian spaces Barthes analyzes in *How to Live Together*, for example, are literary spaces—in the subtitle to the course, Barthes calls them "novelistic simulations of some everyday spaces"—but, as the first part of the title makes clear, they have a profoundly political import: Barthes employs these "simulations" as ways of thinking through the question of how to build a non-oppressive community.[140]

The example of *How to Live Together* gets at what is most politically valuable about Barthes's thought, as well as at what seems most incompatible with politics. His utopian thinking, in this volume and elsewhere, is by his own admission impossible: as he writes in a short article titled "Utopia" from 1974, "no utopia has the slightest chance of being applied as a total system," and as a result the perspective of politics "resents" the supposed "irresponsibility and triviality" of utopian thinking.[141] Nevertheless, Barthes maintains, utopian thinking's opposition to the pragmatic orientation of quotidian politics is exactly what makes it politically important:

> It is the elements, the inflections, the obscurer nooks and crannies of the utopian system that reappear in our world as flashes of desire, as thrilling possibilities. If we were more receptive to them, they would prevent Politics [*le Politique*] from congealing into a totalitarian, bureaucratic, moralistic system.[142]

In this passage, Barthes justifies the political relevance—not direct, but indirect—of his fascination with figures of utopia. Specifically, he makes the claim that, even if utopian literature does not speak the everyday, bureaucratic language of *politics*, it is nevertheless *political*. In the translation cited above from *The "Scandal" of Marxism*, Chris Turner translates "le Politique" as "Politics."[143] It might be better translated, however, as "the Political." In an interview from 1975, Barthes explains the difference between "the political" ("« *le* » *politique*") and "politics" ("« *la* » *politique*"). Whereas the former refers to the political as "a fundamental order of history," the latter refers to everyday, pragmatic political discourse: "the moment when the political changes into the same old story, the discourse of repetition."[144] The latter (politics, *la politique*) is the congealed "totalitarian, bureaucratic, moralistic system" described above, which is precisely what utopian thought prevents. Utopian thought, that is, is not on the side of "la politique," but it *is* on the side of "le politique": utopian thought is political in the proper sense, rather than being mere politics; utopian thought is precisely that which prevents the political from congealing into politics.[145]

In this sense, I would suggest that we could profitably understand Barthes's utopian writing alongside the post-1968 French political philosophers Jean-Luc Nancy and Philippe Lacoue-Labarthe, who rely on a similar distinction between *le politique* and *la politique* in the texts collected in *Retreating the Political* (1997). Although this missed encounter between Barthes and political philosophy is beyond the scope of this chapter, I want to point out that it could also encompass the work of Roberto Esposito and his theorization of what he calls the impolitical (*l'impolitico*) in *Categories of the Impolitical* (1988). As Bruno Bosteels points out, Nancy, Lacoue-Labarthe, and Esposito are all engaged in the task of rethinking (or re-treating—rather than simply retreating *from*) the political in the wake of May 1968 via a logic "of sidestepping the necessity of the alternative itself, of voiding the obligation to choose—by means of a resolute decision or a partisan commitment—either one side or the other."[146] This logic is of course precisely the logic of Barthes's Neutral: the tactic of sidestepping the false choices that characterize the discourse of politics (*la politique*) so as to reenergize and expand the field of the political (*le politique*).

I hope to have shown, then, that although Barthes's utopian thought frequently took problematic forms—indulging in the same orientalist gaze it professed to be critiquing—it is ultimately anything but escapist and apolitical. I would follow Knight in maintaining that Barthes's utopian thought represents the key point of intersection between "the literary and political dimensions of his work" and would add that his work in the Collège de France years— especially in *The Neutral*—represents a key addition to his political thought by providing a logic through which the sphere of the political can be prevented from congealing into mere politics.

3.4. Barthes and Feminism

So far, we have seen a number of critics, such as D. A. Miller and Lisa Lowe, take Barthes to task for his refusal to engage directly with political questions, and we have seen a number of other critics, such as Nicholas de Villiers and Diana Knight, defend Barthes's evasiveness, suggesting that such evasiveness is itself a valuable political strategy. In this section, I return to the question of gender. I begin by describing the stakes of the feminist conversation, at its most active in the 1980s and 1990s, that focused around "The Death of the Author" and poststructuralist anti-authorialism more generally. As mentioned above in the opening section on "Men Explain Things to Me," this conversation turned on the question of whether "The Death of the Author" deliberately and dangerously skirted over the history of the institution of authorship and the gendered and racialized exclusions on which it is based, thereby undermining feminist and postcolonial efforts to broaden the canon, or whether Barthes's essay provided feminism and other politically oriented approaches with the theoretical resources for a broader critique of (patriarchal, colonial) authority as well as (literary) authorship. The first option entails a critique of Barthes that is closely aligned with D. A. Miller's and Lisa Lowe's: it reads Barthes as problematically evasive over questions of politics where he ought to have been direct and committed. And the second option entails a *defense* of Barthes that recalls Nicholas de Villiers and Diana Knight: it reads Barthes as deliberately avoiding categories of identity so as to provide new, more expansive ways of thinking about authorship and power. The section concludes by returning once more to "What Is It to Hold Forth?" How we interpret that seminar, and its notable disregard for the question of *who* holds forth, depends on whether we side more closely with critics like Miller and Lowe (and feminist theorists like Sara Ahmed and Cheryl Walker who critiqued "The Death of the Author") or with de Villiers and Knight (and other feminist theorists like Toril Moi and Jane Gallop whose positions are closer to Barthes's). Like the first group, I think it is important to resituate Barthes's theories, bringing them into contact with the (gendered, as well as racialized and otherwise constructed) spaces of lived experience: this is why I chose to read Barthes alongside Solnit, Kraus, Heti, and Lerner. But ultimately, my position is closer to the second group: despite his shortcomings, I see Barthes, in "What Is It to Hold Forth?" and in the Collège de France lectures and seminars more broadly, as offering valuable resources for thinking through the proximity between authorship, agency, power, and privilege.

The 1980s and 1990s feminist critique of Barthes and "The Death of the Author" ought to be understood in its original context. The key figures in this debate—Toril Moi, Peggy Kamuf, Nancy K. Miller, Barbara Christian, Cheryl Walker—were writing at a time when French theory was beginning to find unprecedented popularity in the Anglo-American academy, and Barthes's widely anthologized essay was often treated as a metonym for poststructuralism and its critique of the Enlightenment subject more broadly. Of course, despite the apparent polemic rigidity of "The Death of the Author," Barthes's views on authorship and subjectivity were rarely static. In the previous chapter, I argued that inconsistency can be a theoretical virtue, and Barthes's work is arguably testament to this. From this perspective, "The Death of the Author" might best be understood not as evidence of straightforward anti-authorialism, but as the flipside of Barthes's fascination with authors, on full display in texts like *Sade, Fourier, Loyola* (1971) and *The Preparation of the Novel*. As it does in relation to so many questions, Barthes's position in relation to authorship oscillates and cannot be simply understood as either entirely critical or entirely celebratory, aggressive, or reparative.[147] Nevertheless, this critical debate is an instructive one, especially when considered alongside the previous two discussed above.

The most contentious issue at stake is the question that Barthes asks at the beginning of "The Death of the Author": when it comes to literature, who is the source of the words on the page? "Who is speaking thus?"[148] For Barthes, the answer is inaccessible and ultimately irrelevant: "We shall never know, for the good reason that writing is the destruction of every voice, of every point of origin."[149] Some feminist critics, like Toril Moi in 1985's *Sexual/Textual Politics*, agreed: "If we are to undo this patriarchal practice of *authority*," she writes, we must reject the "critical practice that relies on the author as the transcendental signified of his or her text ... and proclaim with Roland Barthes the death of the author."[150] For Moi, Barthes's theories of textuality, alongside the work of Hélène Cixous, Luce Irigaray, and Julia Kristeva, held far more theoretical potential for a radical critique of patriarchy than studies by Anglo-American feminist critics like Sandra M. Gilbert and Susan Gubar, who maintained a "belief in the true female authorial voice as the essence of all texts written by women."[151] Moi and Peggy Kamuf both side with Barthes, denouncing the kind of feminist criticism that seeks to combat a patriarchal canon primarily by switching focus from male authors to female authors. According to Kamuf, all such work serves to do is "to propose cosmetic modifications on the face of humanism and its institutions."[152] For Moi and Kamuf, the value of Barthes's work lies in his more profound break with humanism, exemplified by his contention that it does not matter "who is speaking thus."

Other feminist critics disagreed. Rita Felski summarizes their key objection as follows:

> It is no coincidence, they claimed, that at the very moment women were gaining prominence in the academy, male scholars began to disparage all talk of authorship as passé. Threatened by the dramatic upsurge of interest in writing by women, these scholars were trying to sabotage feminist criticism by discrediting one of its guiding concepts.[153]

What Moi and Kamuf saw as revolutionary, other feminist scholars saw as reactionary. Most frequently cited among these scholars is Nancy K. Miller, especially her assertion that "the postmodernist decision that the Author is Dead and the subject along with him does not ... necessarily hold for women, and prematurely forecloses the question of agency for them."[154]

Miller and Kamuf are key figures in the 1980s feminist conversations around Barthes, chiefly because of the debate between them that began in the pages of *Diacritics* in 1982 with Kamuf's "Replacing Feminist Criticism" and Miller's "The Text's Heroine: A Feminist Critic and Her Fictions" and continued in an exchange of letters in 1989.[155] In Miller's insistence in her *Diacritics* article that the answer to Barthes's question "who is speaking thus?" does indeed matter a great deal, she is closely aligned with Chris Kraus's assertion in *I Love Dick* that "the only question" that matters is "who gets to speak and why?"[156] But Miller's attitude to Barthes more generally is significantly more positive than selective quotation might indicate. Her critique of "the postmodernist decision that the Author is Dead" comes from an essay that begins by acknowledging the potential for an alliance between Barthes and feminism in terms of both his critique of "the work of art as (paternally authorized) monument" and his emphasis on the "Birth of the Reader," and ultimately argues for a position that avoids both the extreme insistence on the specificity of women's writing and the extreme insistence that language is the place where identity is lost.[157] In *Getting Personal*, her 1991 study of feminist personal criticism and its performance of the self, she also suggests that Barthes in fact "modeled the possibility" of this type of criticism.[158] Here Miller cites Jane Gallop, who attributes "the Barthes of the seventies"—with his "softer, more subjective, more bodily" stance compared to his 1960s structuralist work—with authorizing Gallop's own move toward more autobiographically inclined critical writing in 1988's *Thinking through the Body*.¹⁵⁹ If Barthes's earlier work was theoretically antithetical to much of the impetus of feminist criticism in the Anglo-American academy during the 1980s, his later work was at the same time—at least in its formal departures from the conventions of (impersonal, pseudo-scientific) literary criticism—a useful resource for many feminist critics. Furthermore, the tradition of feminist criticism that Miller examines in *Getting Personal* is a clear predecessor to the kind of work that Kraus is doing in *I Love Dick* and elsewhere, and more recently the kind of work that Kate Zambreno has done in *Heroines*: work that, in Zambreno's phrase, expresses "the urgency of not erasing the self in our criticism."¹⁶⁰ There is, then, an unexpected, indirect line of influence from Barthes, via Gallop and Miller, to Kraus and to Zambreno.

Nevertheless, the charge remains that Barthes's critique of the author is problematic in the way that it erases the particular history of the institution of authorship and the gendered and colonial exclusions on which it is based. In that sense, to insist that the author is dead is not only, as Cheryl Walker argues, "an act of oppression" in that it "erase[s] a woman poet as the author of her poems"; it is also dangerously ahistorical and complicit with patriarchy and colonialism.¹⁶¹ This is the argument that Sara Ahmed makes in her chapter on authorship in *Differences That Matter* (1998). For her, the chief defect of Barthes's critique of the author is his "detachment of writing from bodies," a rhetorical strategy that is complicit with the way in which "the universalism of the masculine perspective relies precisely on being disembodied, on lacking the contingency of a body."¹⁶² "A feminist perspective," on the other hand, "would surely emphasise the implication of writing in embodiment, in order to re-historicise this supposed universalism, to locate it, and to expose the violence of its contingency and particularity (by declaring some-body wrote this text, by asking which-body wrote this text)."¹⁶³ For Ahmed, then, the author is a "some-body" rather than a textual construct, and they are located in a particular historical and geographical context involving "the demarcation of boundaries between self and other that are implicated in both gendered and colonial histories": that is, authors achieve "access to the privilege of the authorial 'I'" through the exclusion of others: specifically, women and—in Ahmed's reading—especially Black women.¹⁶⁴ In this sense, more so even than Nancy Miller, Ahmed asks the same question as Kraus, the question that Barthes tends to ignore: "who gets to speak and why?" To follow Barthes in consigning the author and their body to the theoretical waste bin would be to gloss over and risk perpetuating this history.

It would be easy to try to counter Ahmed's critique here by pointing to the ways in which Barthes's 1970s writing *does* "emphasise the implication of writing in embodiment." As Jane Gallop reminds us, the 1970s Barthes is "more bodily" and much less inclined to detach "writing from bodies," than he was in 1967's "The Death of the Author." In her 2011 book *The Deaths of the Author: Reading and Writing in Time*, Gallop discusses at length the way that, in 1973's *The Pleasure of the Text*, Barthes figures the author as having a specifically bodily existence.[165] But the body of the author in *The Pleasure of the Text* is an erotic body, a figure desired by the reader—"I *desire* the author: I need his figure"—rather than a body subject to history and politics, a gendered and racialized body of the type with which Ahmed is concerned.[166]

In this sense, my argument with respect to "What Is It to Hold Forth?" is aligned with Ahmed's position and her urging to resituate the question of authorship in the context of the specific bodies who aspire to authorship and the specific bodies who are recognized as authors. By reading Barthes's work on holding forth alongside Solnit's, Kraus's, Heti's, and Lerner's, I have aimed to go some way toward this work of feminist rehistoricization and location, declaring with Ahmed that it is *some-body* who is holding forth in these texts and that the *some-body* in Barthes's seminar stands in uneasy opposition to the *some-bodies* in "Men Explain Things to Me," *I Love Dick*, *How Should a Person Be?*, and *10:04*.

But reading Barthes alongside these texts is also in this chapter a way of demonstrating what is valuable and useful about his work: reading the Collège de France seminars more generously, in the manner of critics like De Villiers and Knight, helps to make visible the resources Barthes's thought offers to an analysis of Men Who Hold Forth. For example, just as Knight reads Barthes's theorizations of utopia as ways of bridging the literary and political, so I read "What Is It to Hold Forth?" as an exercise in bringing out the political stakes of Barthes's work on (literary) authorship. For Barthes, analyzing the everyday phenomenon of holding forth, even in the most seemingly innocent examples (like the young nurse on the train), is a way of getting at the structures of power inherent in language that, at their most extreme, he characterizes as fascism. Indeed—and this is the claim that the next and final section of this chapter takes up—Barthes's teaching in the Collège de France years can be understood as an extended analysis of the proximity between authorship and authoritarianism and as an attempt to think through the question of how to be an author without being an authoritarian and how to be a teacher without being "just another man who wants to teach me something."[167]

3.5. Barthes as Teacher and Author

The challenge I have just described takes a form that should at this point be familiar. In Chapter 1, I analyzed the ways in which Maggie Nelson negotiates the challenge of trying to communicate with her reader without effacing the difficulties inherent in communication—difficulties that critical theorists like Barthes brought out in their work. In Chapter 2, I demonstrated how Zadie Smith and Judith Butler carve out space for (authorial) intention, despite their awareness that intentions are far from sovereign—again, an awareness that the work of critical theorists like Barthes reinforced. And here, I focus on how

Barthes attempts to be an author and a teacher—in short, a figure of agency and power—despite the critique of agency, power, and authorship to which he himself provided a key contribution. In all three of these aporias, we see writers and thinkers caught between allegiance to the insights of posthumanist theory on the one hand and on the other the desire to be an author in precisely the ways that posthumanist theory critiqued: to keep faith with language's communicative capacity, authorial intention, and, in Barthes's case, the author as "an *actor of writing*," somebody who exerts agency through language.[168]

At stake, therefore, is the following question, which has divided Barthes's critics: does Barthes's return to authorship and his desire to become an author in his late work represent a reactionary move, a betrayal of progressive theory? Or is it, in Barthes's own language, a "third turn of the screw," going forward rather than back, not *retreating from* his earlier critique of the author, but *retreating* it?[169] Jonathan Culler, writing in a special issue of *Paragraph* on the Collège de France lectures, makes the former argument, suggesting that for the most part Barthes's return to the author in *The Preparation of the Novel* is a "regression."[170] My own position is close to the latter: in his Collège de France teaching, Barthes not only skillfully stages the aporias involved in returning to the author; he also both theorizes and models ways of responding to these aporias.

Like Heti, Barthes is interested in thinking through the power structures inherent in the pedagogical situation, and from the very beginning of his tenure at the Collège de France, he grapples with the challenge of being both a critic of structures of power and somebody who has been put in a position of significant power within the structures of academia. As Lucy O'Meara points out in the most extensive work of scholarship to date on Barthes's approach to teaching at the Collège de France, his new institutional home had a "paradoxical status: it is arguably the most eminent academic institution in France, but it is not part of the mainstream university system."[171] Both the Collège and Barthes's previous employer, the École pratique des hautes études, are part of what O'Meara calls "the marginal academy in France."[172] Barthes alludes to this status in his inaugural lecture when he refers to the Collège as a "place that we can strictly term *outside the bounds of power*."[173] But this is arguably an equivocation, for there are also key differences between the EPHE and the Collège de France: not only is the Collège a more prestigious institution, conferring on Barthes an unprecedented degree of mainstream academic validation; it also required him to get used to a new style of teaching: as Andy Stafford writes, he was "no longer the hard-working seminar tutor, but the magisterial lecturer."[174] This shift gave rise to the pedagogical dilemma just described, one which Barthes begins to address in the same inaugural lecture. Having defined his own role as a critic of the plural structures of power "hidden in any discourses," Barthes ends his lecture by tentatively laying out how he plans to integrate this role into his teaching, how he plans to mitigate the significant authority conferred upon him by his new position:

What I hope to be able to renew, each of the years it is given me to teach here, is the manner of presentation of the course or seminar, in short, of "presenting" a discourse without imposing it [*de « tenir » un discours sans imposer*]: that would be the methodological stake, the *quaestio*, the point to be debated. For what can be oppressive in our teaching is not, finally, the knowledge or the culture it conveys, but the discursive forms through which we propose them. Since, as I have tried to suggest, this teaching has as its object discourse taken in the inevitability of power, method can really bear on the means of or at the least, of this only loosening, baffling, very lightening power. And I am increasingly convinced, both in writing and in teaching, that the fundamental operation of this loosening method is, if one writes, fragmentation, and, if one teaches, digression, or, to put it in a preciously ambiguous word, *excursion*.[175]

In Richard Howard's translation, Barthes describes the way he wishes to *present* a discourse, but in the original the phrase is the now familiar *tenir un discours*: to hold or sustain a discourse, to hold forth. Here, then, Barthes acknowledges the necessity as a teacher of occupying the same position—as a wielder of the force of language, of "language's *intimidating* function"—that he subjects to critique in "What Is It to Hold Forth?"[176] What he intends to do in response is to hold forth *sans imposer*, without imposing: the seeming contradiction in terms here brings out the aporia in which Barthes finds himself. Nevertheless, though, Barthes puts forward a theory as to how he can move beyond or "loosen" the aporia, both as a writer and as a teacher: "if one writes, fragmentation, and, if one teaches, digression."

We can note the similarity of Barthes's response here and Maggie Nelson's in *The Argonauts*: as I suggested in Chapter 1, fragmentation is one of the key strategies Nelson uses in order to create the space necessary for communication to take place *sans imposer*. And though Barthes's teaching does frequently display digressive tendencies—almost the entire first half of *The Preparation of the Novel* is devoted to haiku, rather than the novel Barthes is ostensibly preparing—it is fragmentation above all that characterizes both his writing—as in the subtitle of *A Lover's Discourse: Fragments*—and his teaching. Both *How to Live Together* and *The Neutral* are presented in the form of a series of figures, traits, or twinklings, arranged arbitrarily, as in *A Lover's Discourse* and *Roland Barthes by Roland Barthes*.[177] In both their arrangement and their brevity, these traits are, as Diana Leca argues, a way of encoding Barthes's "philosophy of minimal demands into his own stylistics."[178] And specifically in the context of teaching, the way that Barthes structures his courses allows him to undermine his magisterial position, making his lectures a little more seminar-like and countering the "forced monologism" that teaching at the Collège entailed: at the beginning of the third session of *How to Live Together*, Barthes describes the course as "a checkerboard of boxes" that can be filled in either by himself or by his students: "I shall try to incorporate your remarks into each lecture. A bit like exchanging letters with my audience."[179] Later in the course, Barthes returns to this image: "Boxes are put in place ... I'm the maker (the artisan) cutting out the pieces of wood. You're the players."[180] The course's fragmentary structure leaves it up to the students to assemble the fragments as they wish: Barthes is not so much an authority figure as a mere "artisan" (the craft of authorship without the authority), and the objective is not to lead the students to a certain, predetermined goal, but to create the conditions in which they are enabled to move for themselves. "There is no final painting," Barthes maintains: "at best, it would be up to you to produce one."[181]

In the same section, Barthes expands on this non-goal-oriented teaching philosophy: "Perhaps the ideal lecture course," he ventures, "would be one where the professor—the locutor—is less interesting than his audience, where what he says is of less consequence than what the lectures provoke."[182] Here, Barthes's approach recalls Rancière's well-known theorization of a teaching situation "where what [the teacher] says is of less consequence than what the lectures provoke" in *The Ignorant Schoolmaster*, which analyzes the political stakes of recasting the role of the teacher as someone who merely acts as a catalyst for students to learn for themselves as opposed to a magisterial explainer of all things.[183] For Rancière, this shift in pedagogy is a microcosm for a large-scale emancipatory democratic politics, based on the equality in intelligence and capacity of professor and student, and by extension the equality of all citizens. For Barthes, too, the effect of his attempts to cede his position of mastery is intended to be emancipatory, freeing the student from the authority of the teacher in the same way that "The Death of the Author" attempted to free the reader from the authority of the author. In *Talking Back*, bell hooks critiques the tendency of professors "who advocated radical politics" not to allow "their critique of domination and oppression to influence teaching strategies."[184] I have made the case that Barthes's politics are in some sense radical—albeit not in the committed Marxist sense that hooks is referring to here. If Barthes can be considered radical, it is in the way that he radically expands the field of the political, finding expression for politics outside of "the form of a *directly* political discourse."[185] Barthes's commitment to making visible and working against structures of power and domination wherever they appear—in the classroom, for example—makes him an exception to the rule hooks observes. His lectures at the Collège de France represent a sustained attempt to translate his "critique of domination and oppression" into "teaching strategies"—and his seminars, like "What Is It to Hold Forth?," go even further toward ceding mastery by having most of the course be led by invited speakers, including his students.[186]

Barthes's final two courses at the Collège, however, represent a shift in his pedagogy and his theory of authorship—a shift that challenges the idea of outplaying the element of holding forth in teaching via strategies of fragmentation and ceding mastery. Rather, in *The Preparation of the Novel* Barthes experiments with what it would be like to fully embrace the role of master, teacher, and author; he dives even further into the aporia described at the beginning of this section. As a first step, Barthes abandons the fragmentary and multivocal form of *How to Live Together* and *The Neutral*, announcing at the beginning of *Preparation*'s second half: "If you're agreeable, we're going to think of the Course that's beginning as a film or a book, basically as a story, the narration of which will, I think, occupy us for the ten two-hour sessions and of which, as a rule, I'll be the only narrator."[187] The dominant metaphors Barthes uses to describe his teaching philosophy have shifted: the course is no longer a game, a series of boxes, or an exchange of letters, but "a film or a book," a linear and bounded form, and one that has a single narrator, a single author: Barthes tells his audience in the same session that he will at times "speak as the *author* of the course."[188] *The Preparation of the Novel*, then, is an exercise in "the transition from the fragment to the nonfragment," an exercise in setting aside the strategies Barthes had previously employed to undercut his authority, "to keep a meaning from 'taking.'"[189] The question that arises here is: is it possible to do so without becoming "just another man who wants to teach me something," just another Man Who Holds Forth?

There are several ways of answering this question, but I want to conclude this chapter by pointing to one particular reason why, for Barthes, becoming an author is *not* necessarily synonymous with becoming the kind of bad authority figure that I have identified here with the Man Who Holds Forth. Put simply, by the end of the 1970s, Barthes had realized that there were far more powerful and dangerous authority figures than authors. His teaching during the Collège de France years, especially in *The Preparation of the Novel*, is characterized throughout by a sense of the increasing marginalization of literature and the declining prestige of the author. In part, of course, the author's declining prestige can be credited to Barthes's own work in the 1960s, and the wide reception that this work had found, both in France and (even more so) in the Anglo-American academy, to the point where Barbara Christian could argue in her 1987 essay "The Race for Theory" that French theory, with its insistence that "authors are dead," had itself "become *authoritative discourse*."[190] The death of the author only serves to make the author's killer into a new authority.[191]

This paradox—hypocrisy, even—is one that Barthes goes some way toward acknowledging in *The Preparation of the Novel*. In a passage he had intended to deliver during the session of January 19, 1980, but which ended up being cut for time, Barthes describes the way in which, during the 1960s, a certain "trend" within literary criticism had gained ascendency precisely by "repress[ing] the author" or "depriv[ing] him of consciousness."[192] "I myself," he tells us, "wrote an article, the title of which summarizes this trend: 'The Death of the Author.'"[193] By the end of the 1970s, however, Barthes had come to realize that—partly because of his own earlier work and partly because of what he understood as a more general cultural decline in interest in literature—the author was not "really all that prestigious anymore," and anti-authorialism within literary criticism was therefore misplaced: "go and ask Khomeiny, Carter, Marchais,

Giscard, or the woman I buy my chickens from (I know what she thinks because she's very chatty) what they think of Kafka!"[194] In 1980, then, Barthes seems to share Christian's sense that anti-authorial discourse had become a form of "authoritative discourse," both in literary circles and in the wider world. In Barthes's terms, it has become the *doxa*.

By 1980, it is far more plausible to understand the author as a figure *lacking* in authority than as someone brimming with it. Barthes points to two reasons for this historical shift: the hegemony of anti-authorial criticism within the academy and a perceived decline in the status of the author and of literature in Western society and culture more broadly. And if, as he suggests, Jimmy Carter cared little for Kafka, Carter's successor Ronald Reagan cared even less, showing himself to be actively hostile to the arts in policy terms by ushering in major cuts to federal arts funding.[195] In such a cultural context, it would make more sense to understand the author as a figure of *resistance to authority*—think of Rushdie and Khomeini or literary critiques of Reagan like Kushner's *Angels in America*—than as a figure of authority. I would suggest that this is also true of the Obama-era texts analyzed in the first half of this chapter—and even more so in the Trump era, when America is under the leadership of a Man Who Holds Forth par excellence, who has consistently attempted to eliminate federal arts and humanities funding.[196] In fact, it is in the work of authors like Solnit, Kraus, Heti, Lerner, and Barthes that we find some of the most enabling resources for resistance against Men Who Hold Forth: not only do these thinkers provide us with a vocabulary to understand and critique such figures. They also provide us with alternative, more dialogic and less authoritarian models for thinking, teaching, and writing.

Chapter 4

LABOR: DAVID FOSTER WALLACE, COWBOY OF INFORMATION

The secret of Labor (the labor of writing): *to bureaucratize writing.*
—Roland Barthes, *The Preparation of the Novel*

1. Introduction

1.1. Bureaucratizing Writing

The Roland Barthes I discussed in the last chapter was a theorist of authorship. He was interested in the theoretical questions—above all, the question of agency—at stake in the figure of the author. In this guise, Barthes was invested in the project that Judith Butler, as quoted in Chapter 2, referred to as the critique of the "author-subject": the critique of the author as a figure of excessive agency (exemplified in the Man Who Holds Forth) and the attempt to answer the question of how to temper the author's authoritarian tendencies.[1] This is a version of Roland Barthes that we know well at this point: it is the Barthes of "The Death of the Author," who exposed the myth of the all-powerful "Author-God," and it is the Barthes whose inaugural lecture at the Collège de France set out his intention to be a critic of the "'authorized' voices which authorize themselves to utter the discourse of all power."[2] This is Barthes the *theorist* of authorship: Barthes who understands the author as first of all a *theoretical* figure, tied up in a long history of theories of subjectivity, stretching back through Freud and Hegel all the way to Descartes.

I begin this final chapter by turning instead to a different Roland Barthes. This is not Barthes the *theorist* of authorship, but Barthes the *practitioner* of authorship: a version of Barthes who is interested in the author not as a figure for the Enlightenment subject, but as an actual human being, sitting down at a desk with pencil and paper and trying to write. This is the Barthes of *The Preparation of the Novel*.

Because this distinction between the theoretical and practical aspects of authorship forms the premise of this chapter, it is useful at this point to introduce terms to help maintain the distinction. There are a number of possible precedents to follow here, but for the sake of clarity, the terms I will use in the following pages are *author* and *writer*. By *author*, I mean the *theoretical* figure: the author whose death Barthes declared in 1967, Butler's "author-subject." And with the term *writer*, I refer to the *practical* side: the *writer* is the actual person, the one who writes. This is by no means a perfect distinction. On the one hand, the two can all too easily slide into one another (they share a proper name—Roland Barthes, David Foster Wallace—after all); on the other hand, using *only* these two terms necessitates collapsing many different possible referents into only two possible words: the single term *author*, for example, has to encompass the author as theoretical construct, the author as legal entity, the author as public figure, etc. Nevertheless, the author-writer distinction is one that will be useful for this chapter's purposes.

In *The Preparation of the Novel*, Barthes is interested in the *writer* rather than the *author*. The terminology he uses to indicate this distinction is different from mine, but helpful for the way it illuminates the distinction's complexities. Unlike the *author/writer* binary, Barthes draws a fourfold division. In a description of Proustian "Life Writing," he lays out a "typology of roles" that "are woven into, shimmer in the writing that we read":

a. *Persona*: the everyday, empirical, private individual who "lives," without writing.
b. *Scriptor*: the writer as social image, the one who gets talked about, who gets discussed, who gets classified according to school, or genre, in manuals, etc.
c. *Auctor*: the *I* who considers himself the *guarantor* of what he writes; father of the book, accepting his responsibilities; the *I* who, socially or mystically, considers himself to be a writer.
d. *Scribens*: the *I* who's engaged in the practice of writing, who's in the process of writing, who lives writing everyday.[3]

Barthes's *persona* and *scribens* signify two different aspects of what I'm calling the *writer*: the *persona* is the writer when they are living rather than writing, and the *scribens* is that same individual when they are actively engaged in the activity of writing. *Scriptor* and *auctor*, on the other hand, bring out different valences of the *author*. Barthes's focus in "The Death of the Author" was almost entirely confined to the second two: what he critiques in that essay is "the image of the Author" (that is, what he calls in *Preparation* the *scriptor*) and the idea of an Author who, like *Preparation*'s *auctor*, exists "in the same relation of antecedence to his work as a father to his child."[4] In *The Preparation of the Novel*, though, Barthes is much more interested in both the *persona* and the *scribens*. He is interested in "the practice of writing," the everyday, empirical activity that is involved in producing a novel; his focus is on the individual *writer*, not only during the actual process of writing (the *scribens*) but at other times too, during the "life" that may or may not become material about which to write (the *persona*).

What are the consequences of this shift in focus? How does Barthes's treatment of authorship change when his interest is no longer so much in the theoretical issues at stake, but rather in the lived experience of writing—when his interest is no longer in the author, but in the writer? What new insights about authorship does he gain by switching levels, from the theoretical to the practical? The most important consequence of this realignment of focus is the following realization, expressed in Barthes's inimitable, epigrammatic prose: "You can 'think' by dint of inspiration; you can only write by dint of *labor*."[5] "The writer's labor," Barthes finds, is "somehow *unsinkable*": if you want to produce a "monumental work," there is no getting around the fact that you are going to have put in the hours, "in health, in discomfort, in affective misery."[6] We are a long way now from either Plato's divinely inspired poet of the *Ion* or the nourishing father and all-powerful "Author-God" derided in "The Death of the Author." If the author has tended to be understood as having divine qualities, the writer on the other hand is all too human: merely a "good workman."[7] And worse, he is an office drone. "The secret of Labor (the labor of writing)," Barthes suggests, is "*to bureaucratize writing*. Kafka found the Office draining? Switch things around: make the Desk into an Office, somewhere to go and work at regular times."[8]

The writer as office worker: in what follows, I proceed from the premise that this stubbornly unromantic metaphor is one that is worth taking seriously. Furthermore, I argue that it is a metaphor that David Foster Wallace takes seriously in *The Pale King* (2011), his posthumously published, unfinished novel about a group of accountants, mostly examiners of tax returns, working at the IRS's Peoria Regional Examination Center in the mid-1980s. I began this chapter with a discussion of Barthes's *The Preparation of the Novel*, then, for two reasons: first, because it helps narrate the transition that takes place at this point in *Authorship's Wake*, from a theoretical conversation about the author to a practical consideration of the writer; and, second, because the image Barthes uses to describe the practice of writing—bureaucratic labor—coincides productively with Wallace's metaphorical terrain in *The Pale King*. If Barthes helps us to begin to see the ways in which writing is like office work, Wallace can tell us what exactly is at stake in this comparison. *The Pale King* helps us to think through not just the quantitative similarities between the work of the writer and the work of the bureaucrat (long hours spent at a desk, poor pay), but also the qualitative similarities: *The Pale King*, I argue, posits a similarity between writing and accountancy at the level of the qualitative nature of the activity each profession involves.[9]

Therefore, I devote the body of this chapter to a discussion of *The Pale King* for (at least) two reasons. First, because *The Pale King*, in terms of its content, shares with this chapter an overarching concern with labor: both the labor of writing and labor in postwar America more broadly. It is a book about the everyday drudgery that goes into maintaining an effective system of taxation and a functioning democracy and—both literally and figuratively—about the everyday drudgery that goes into writing. Second, I focus on *The Pale King* because it is a book that exists because of an unusually large amount of labor—and furthermore, because (conveniently) much of the evidence of that labor has been available to view since September 2012 in the University of Texas at Austin's Harry Ransom Center, in the series of *Pale King* materials in their David Foster Wallace papers.

Looking over box after box of drafts, notes, research, and correspondence in the Ransom Center reading room—as I did over the course of three weeks in December 2016—it is difficult to avoid a heightened awareness of both the sheer amount of work that goes into producing a novel and how little of this work is visible in the published version. As Adorno—quoted in one of Benjamin's more avowedly Marxist moments in *The Arcades Project*—notes, "the autonomy of art has its origin in the concealment of labor."[10] This disproportion between the amount of labor that goes into a novel and the amount of that work that is visible in the commodity form it takes when published is an attribute of any novel—of any supposedly autonomous work of art, if we follow the Frankfurt School. But this disparity is especially important to *The Pale King*, a novel that, in its paratexts (Editor's Note, a selection of Wallace's Notes and Asides, four deleted scenes), does a lot to undo the concealment of authorial and editorial labor, but that also exists as a result of over ten years of research, writing, rewriting, and editing: more visible labor, but also much more concealed labor, labor that is only visible in the archives. As David Hering lays out in his "detailed genetic history of the novel's composition" in *David Foster Wallace: Fiction and Form*, *The Pale King* went through a number of incarnations as Wallace worked on it between 1997 and 2007, and it required still more work by Wallace's editor Michael Pietsch in order to render it into publishable form—not to mention the work that this difficult, fragmentary novel demands of its readers.[11] In *The Preparation of the Novel*, Barthes points out that

> all the "great writers"—those who produced a monumental work (a whole work or fragments of a work)—were animated by or endowed with an *unfailing will* (in the most flatly psychological sense of the term): will for labor, for corrections, for copying out that functions in all possible conditions: in health, in discomfort, in affective misery, a veritable bodily energy.[12]

Nowhere is this more evident than in the case of *The Pale King*.

This chapter makes the argument that Wallace's depiction of the inner workings of the IRS Regional Examination Center in Peoria, Illinois, can tell us as much about the labor of authorship as it can about attention, boredom, neoliberalism, and the other themes through which critics have tended to read *The Pale King*. At the center of this argument is the claim that writing in the novel can best be understood as a form of *information work*: work characterized by the activity of surveying large quantities of information, and from this body of data selecting a small amount, excluding the rest, and manipulating the chosen set into a coherent form.

Part 2 introduces and contextualizes this claim via a discussion of Amy Hungerford's *Making Literature Now* (2016). Hungerford's concern with contemporary literary production is one that this chapter shares, but her approach differs importantly from mine in that, whereas I take Wallace's novel as my key case study, her book explicitly makes a case for refusing to read Wallace's work altogether: she argues that Wallace's art cannot easily be separated from the way he treated women in his life and that his biographical misogyny goes hand in hand with the fact that he has nothing worthwhile to say about gender and sexuality. Against Hungerford's refusal, I suggest that *The Pale King* would in fact be an especially helpful resource in answering the questions she explores in *Making Literature Now*: Hungerford and Wallace, I argue, are both trying to propose ways of dealing with overwhelming quantities of information.

Sections 2.2 and 2.3 expand on Wallace's treatment of this issue. Fleshing out Barthes's comparison between the writer and the bureaucrat, I read *The Pale King* as countering dominant imaginaries of authorial labor by focusing less on *creation* and more on *selection*. The selective aspect of artistic labor, though familiar in the context of other forms and genres, from photography to nonfiction prose, is less widely acknowledged in the context of the novel—an occlusion that this chapter counters. Drawing in particular on Sianne Ngai's theorization of the *interesting* as "an aesthetic mode of difference as information" in *Our Aesthetic Categories*, I connect Wallace's treatment of information work in *The Pale King* to the novel's formal qualities (its tendency toward seriality rather than linear narrative) and to its unfinished status.[13]

The final section of Part 2 switches from one metaphor of labor to another: whereas Sections 2.2 and 2.3 focus on the connection the novel draws between accountants and writers, Section 2.4 considers Wallace's several references to cowboys. *The Pale King* uses the cowboy as a metaphor for the IRS employee not only to give humble tax accountants a gleam of authority and prestige but also to emphasize the frequent instability and itinerancy involved in working for the Service.

In Part 3, my focus widens, connecting the novel's aesthetics more explicitly to its political and economic context. I argue that Wallace's treatment of accountancy and writing as forms of information work is a vital part of the novel's analysis of contemporary forms of labor more broadly. By experimenting with these metaphors of labor, *The Pale King* engages in what McKenzie Wark identifies as a strategy of "low theory": employing and extending metaphors drawn from particular forms of labor in order to create new ways of thinking about a bigger picture—here, the bigger picture that critics have tended to refer to as "neoliberalism." Whereas the reception of *The Pale King* has tended to treat the novel's analysis of information, attention, and boredom on the one hand and its narration of the mid-1980s shift toward neoliberalism on the other as relatively independent, focusing on one thread at the expense of the other, I argue that what is most important about the novel is the fact that it draws a connection between these two threads: specifically, it understands that the phenomenon that Wendy Brown and many others call "neoliberalism" has its genesis in the postwar shift in North America toward an economy based on *information* as a form of property and as an object of labor.

Connecting Ngai's argument about the politics of the interesting to work by Wark and Jasper Bernes on the importance of information work in postwar America—in terms of both economics and aesthetics—I argue that Wallace's novel not only attempts to redefine authorship as a form of information work; it also demonstrates how the characteristics of information work have been central to the development of contemporary neoliberalism and its relations of production. The chapter closes by returning to a larger concern of the project as a whole: the relationship between theory and literature. Specifically, I suggest that *The Pale King* can be understood as a form of "low theory." This term, which I trace via Wark back through the work of Jack Halberstam, Stuart Hall, and Antonio Gramsci, names a possibility that I argue is fulfilled in the work of writers like Wallace, Maggie Nelson, Zadie Smith, Chris Kraus, Sheila Heti, Ben Lerner and many more: that writing does not have to be published under the sign of "theory" to do theoretical work.

2. Accountants, Writers, and Cowboys

2.1. On Amy Hungerford Not Reading DFW

Of the existing scholarship on David Foster Wallace and authorship, the majority focuses more on theory than on practice; in the terms I introduced at the beginning of this chapter, it has been more interested in the author than the writer. The title of Adam Kelly's early state-of-the-field essay from 2010 is instructive: "David Foster Wallace: The Death of the Author and the Birth of a Discipline." "The Death of the Author" here refers of course both to Wallace's actual death in 2008 and to Barthes's essay, which Wallace wrote about in "Greatly Exaggerated," a review of H. L. Hix's *Morte d'Author: An Autopsy* (1990).[14] This review, in which Wallace ultimately positions himself—like Zadie Smith in "Rereading Barthes and Nabokov"—as "anti-death," has been an important point of reference for Wallace scholars interested in questions of authorship, from Marshall Boswell in *Understanding David Foster Wallace* (2009) to David Hering in *David Foster Wallace: Fiction and Form* (2016).[15] Hering argues that Wallace's fiction can be read as "an ongoing attempt to establish an author-persona that interacts dialogically with the text" rather than monologically claiming authority and mastery over text and reader alike.[16] Hering's argument is therefore parallel to the one I made in the previous chapter about Barthes and Lerner, though it takes its theoretical framework from Bakhtin rather than Barthes. There, I argued that Barthes and Lerner both seek out a way of writing without holding forth, of being authors without being authoritarians—in the Bakhtinian terms that Hering employs, they seek to be dialogic rather than monologic.

So as to avoid reproducing this kind of argument about the theoretical figure of the author, I focus in this chapter on the practical, lived experience of writerly labor: a topic that has so far been relatively underserved by Wallace scholars. The strand of criticism that Hering calls the "'archival turn' in Wallace Studies"—of which his own book is perhaps the foremost example, especially with respect to *The Pale King*—has gone some way in redressing this shortcoming.[17] But Hering's account of Wallace's compositional labor ultimately circles back to the (theoretical) author rather than the (practical) writer: in the end, his archival work functions to support an argument about the tension between monologism and dialogism in Wallace's work. Here, I draw on archival material with a different goal in mind: a more materially oriented analysis of writerly labor and of contemporary forms of work more broadly.

This is a chapter, then, about the everyday practice and the lived experience of *making literature now*—which is also to say that this is a chapter that shares its primary concern with Amy Hungerford's 2016 *Making Literature Now*. The primary goal of Hungerford's book, as her title indicates, is to provide new ways of mapping the terrain of contemporary literary production, with an emphasis on "the daily labor" that goes into that production.[18] The scope of her research includes not only the labor of individual authors but also the work of readers, reviewers, teachers, publishers, booksellers, and more: the sum total of "the institutions and relationships that organize and shape [literary] work."[19] *Making Literature Now*—part of the influential book series edited by the Post45 collective, of which Hungerford is a founding member—is, by virtue of both its research concerns and its status in the field of postwar American literary studies, an important intertext for this chapter. But in my engagement with the book, I also need to grapple with one notable difference between Hungerford's approach and my own: whereas *Making Literature Now* closes with a chapter, titled "On Not Reading DFW," explaining Hungerford's decision not to read the work of David Foster Wallace, this chapter centers on a reading of Wallace's *The Pale King*.[20] In this section, therefore, I address both what is useful about Hungerford's work and why I have chosen to part ways from her method, focusing on the one writer whom Hungerford explicitly and emphatically refuses to read.

The first point of connection between our respective projects is a shared interest in the specific kinds of labor that go into literary production. But the value of Hungerford's book has as much to do with its method as with its subject. The key methodological question underlying her project is this: faced with vast quantities of potential objects and sources, how does the scholar of contemporary literature decide what to pay attention to? How does one approach a prodigious volume of information, much of it of little discernible relevance or interest, and make from it something coherent, relevant, and interesting? This question emerges for Hungerford in two particular contexts.

The first is the choice of which literary texts to focus on—a choice that is especially fraught for a scholar of contemporary literature simply because so much literature is published every year. There is no getting around what Hungerford calls "the undeniable fact of literary overproduction."[21] Franco Moretti famously described literary history as a "slaughterhouse": "if we set the canon of nineteenth-century British novels at two hundred titles," he observes, then that means that about 99.5 percent of the total number of novels published in that period (around 40,000) have "disappear[ed] forever."[22] Today, as Hungerford points out, the numbers of literary texts going to slaughter— in Margaret Cohen's phrase, "the great unread"[23]—are even greater. The consequences of this fact shape all six of *Making Literature Now*'s chapters: throughout, she is interested in the question of why certain works escape the slaughterhouse and others do not and in the possibility of reshaping the boundaries between the read and the unread. She does so by paying attention to writers who have been accorded relatively little scholarly attention (chapters one through four), and by interrogating the conditions under which certain writers *do* come to receive critical acclaim (chapters five and six).

The problem of how to decide what is worth paying attention to returns for Hungerford in a second context, as a function of her theoretical framework. Whereas Moretti deals with the vast disparity between the tiny canon and the great unread by abandoning "the very close reading of very few texts" in favor of the computerized distant reading of very many, Hungerford deals with the same dilemma by going in the opposite direction, zooming in rather than out.[24] She draws in particular on Bruno Latour's Actor Network Theory: a way of reconceiving research that focuses on the micro- and macro-scale actions of human and nonhuman actors in a complex network of interrelations. Employing Latour's methods, for Hungerford, means ultra-fine-grain research that renders visible the intricate webs of social action entailed in any object of study. "The method," she writes, "calls to mind versions of study that are daunting and tedious and threaten to devolve into what one colleague called 'a heap of facts.'"[25] The researcher's task, then, is doubly hard: not only must one consider and then exclude a vast number of books from one's canon of texts to be studied, but one must also consider and then exclude a vast number of the actors, details, and facts encountered in one's study of each text that makes the cut. Hence the centrality of the problem of attention to *Making Literature Now*.

The reason why I find Hungerford's treatment of this problem simultaneously valuable and frustrating is this: what she describes throughout *Making Literature Now* as a central dilemma for scholars of contemporary literature—the excessive amounts of information we are faced with and the consequent challenge of making sense of it all—is precisely the same dilemma that Wallace analyzes as a problem for accountants, for writers, and for contemporary information workers more generally. Her approach to her topic coincides in important ways with Wallace's project in *The Pale King*—but because she refuses to read Wallace, she cannot draw on the resources that his work offers. This chapter takes up *Making Literature Now*'s questions, aiming to arrive at some different answers by turning to that book's self-imposed blind spot.

How, then, does Hungerford justify her decision not to read Wallace? Her reasoning operates at two levels. At the general level, she aims to destigmatize the idea of refusing to read a book: precisely because so much literature is published, "all of us, especially scholars of literature, refuse to read books every day."[26] "Is it ever acceptable," she asks, "to refuse the culture's rising call to attend to a literary work?"[27] Hungerford's answer is yes: we do so all the time. But she also makes the case that Wallace's works *in particular* are not worth attending to. Ultimately, this comes down to the fact that they are really long but not especially insightful about the topics they are interested in. Hungerford focuses in particular on Wallace's treatment of gender, misogyny, and the "erotics of reading."[28] On the basis of the evidence she has—which she readily admits is far from complete, as is the nature of all decisions to not-read—she concludes that, while Wallace is interested in good questions, he does not produce any good answers, a result not unconnected to the fact that he often behaved in a misogynist manner himself.[29] While some scholars would respond that the fact that Wallace does not propose obvious solutions to the problem of contemporary gender relations is part of a larger "drive to stage rather than resolve philosophical conflicts in his fiction," the question of misogyny in Wallace's work, including as it relates to his biography, remains an important one.[30] For one response to Hungerford's charge, see David Hering's short article, "Thinking about David Foster Wallace, Misogyny and Scholarship," which emphasizes the importance of "a more diverse conversation on Wallace" but maintains that his work, including as it engages (sometimes problematically) with questions of gender, is nevertheless worthy of attention.[31]

In this chapter, my response is slightly less direct: rather than arguing that Wallace does have worthwhile things to say about gender and misogyny, I am suggesting simply that he also has worthwhile things to say about other questions—in particular, the same question that Hungerford is interested in: what ought we to pay attention to and why? The problem of how to manage an unwieldy "heap of facts" is at the center of *The Pale King*'s characterization of labor: the work of information management that Hungerford sees as the key aspect of contemporary scholarly labor is for Wallace the key aspect of contemporary labor more broadly, from tax accounting to writing and beyond. For Hungerford, *writing about* literature now is a task of managing a crisis of excess information. For Wallace, managing a crisis of excess information is the task that defines *making* literature now.[32] In Sections 2.2 and 2.3, I expand on this claim.

2.2. Accountants

I want to anchor the analysis that follows around a passage from the second section (§2, as it is labelled) of *The Pale King*. In it, an early-career tax accountant named Claude Sylvanshine takes a flight from Chicago to Peoria. As the plane nears its destination, Sylvanshine watches the landscape beneath him and reflects on the contrast between his tendency to be overwhelmed by massive quantities of information and the way that his colleague Reynolds is able to winnow large data sets down so that only the relevant points remain:

> Their descent was mainly a heightening of the specificity of what lay below—fields revealed as plowed and perpendicularly furrowed and silos as adjoined by canted chutes and belts and an industrial park as individual buildings with reflective windows and complicated clumps of cars in the parking lots. Each car not only parked by a different human individual but conceived, designed, assembled from parts each one of which was designed and made, transported, sold, financed, purchased, and insured by human individuals, each with life stories and self-concepts that all fit together into a larger pattern of facts. Reynolds's dictum was that reality was a fact-pattern the bulk of which was entropic and random. The trick was homing in on which facts were important—Reynolds was a rifle to Sylvanshine's shotgun.[33]

This passage describes two opposing processes or shifts in perception. The first, occasioned by the plane's descent, is characterized by "a heightening of the specificity of what lay below": an increase in the amount of information Sylvanshine perceives. To nouns—"fields"—are appended adjectives—"plowed"—and then, adding more detail, adverbially modified adjectives—"perpendicularly furrowed." Wallace's word order here—noun, adjective, adverb-plus-adjective—renders the gradually increasing resolution of the picture. The closer to the ground Sylvanshine gets, the more information he registers. A few pages before this passage, the novel's first section—a similarly detailed description of the Midwestern landscape—had closed with the exhortation: "Read these."[34] Here, Sylvanshine does exactly that: as his plane descends, the landscape becomes more and more legible, yielding information about the land itself, then the material objects (silos, buildings, cars) that populate it, and then even the histories of human labor (design, production, transportation, sales, financing, insurance) immanent in each object.

This kind of moment of expanding apprehension of the material world is, I would suggest, a characteristic trope of contemporary fictions of capitalism. We see something similar in Ben Lerner's *10:04*, when the narrator picks up a package of instant coffee and is awestruck on perceiving the "organization of time and space and fuel and labor becoming visible in the commodity itself."[35] This perception prompts him to list, like Wallace, the stages of production the commodity has undergone: growth, harvest, roasting, grinding, soaking, dehydrating, packaging, transportation. Lerner's vocabulary—"labor," "commodity"—clues us into the fact that one way to read these moments would be as Marxist acts of interpretation, as attempts to reveal the labor that, as Adorno and Benjamin knew, is hidden in the putatively autonomous commodity form. Certainly such a reading would fit well with my argument here about writerly labor: we could see Sylvanshine's cars and Lerner's instant coffee as stand-ins for *The Pale King* and *10:04* themselves, in that novels, like commodities, contain vast quantities of concealed labor. Another way to understand them would be as moments of the Latourian Actor Network analysis I referred to above: what initially appears as a simple object (a matter of fact) turns out on further inspection to be composed of a complex gathering of actors—what Latour calls a matter of concern—and each actor in the gathering is as complex and multifarious as the gathering itself.[36] These would both work as effective explanations of Lerner's grocery store epiphany. But as far as *The Pale King* is concerned, neither a Marxist nor a Latourian approach is an especially useful way of considering the *second* perceptual shift that takes place in this passage.

This second and opposing movement is described in the final sentence above: "The trick was homing in on which facts were important." This is crucial: to be an effective accountant, one does not just have to acquire massive quantities of data (to heighten the specificity of one's perceptions, as Sylvanshine does so well); one also has to decide which pieces of data to discard and which to "hom[e] in on." Here, the similarities between Sylvanshine's dilemma and Hungerford's in *Making Literature Now* become clearer. Recall Hungerford's gloss of her Latourian method as "call[ing] to mind versions of study that are daunting and tedious and threaten to devolve into what one colleague called 'a heap of facts.'"[37] Similarly, as Sylvanshine's plane descends and he gathers more data, the description he assembles risks collapsing into an "entropic and random" "fact-pattern." What Reynolds refers to (in the language of the accountancy classes Wallace took as research and of professional programs more generally) as a "fact-pattern" is the same thing that Hungerford's colleague calls "a heap of facts" and what Latour refers to as a "sheer flood of information."[38] In all three cases, the bigger challenge is not the work of collecting all of the facts about all of the actors, but the selective labor of sorting through them and "homing in on which facts were important."

This selective labor, the work of choosing what to pay attention to, has been one of the key points of focus in scholarship on *The Pale King*. It corresponds to the first of the two "broad arcs" of the novel that Wallace himself summarized in his notes (included as an appendix to the published novel) as follows:

1. Paying attention, boredom, ADD, Machines vs. people at performing mindless jobs.
2. Being individual vs. being part of larger things—paying taxes, being "lone gun" in IRS vs. team player.[39]

In Part 3 of this chapter, I will focus on the connection between these two threads, but here I am mostly concerned with the first. Wallace scholars have provided an array of interpretations of the novel's concern with attention and the ways in which its characters deal with information. Conley Wouters (in his contribution to *David Foster Wallace and "The Long Thing"* from 2014) reads *The Pale King* as Wallace's attempt to negotiate the terrain of a world characterized by "informational avalanches": faced with prodigious amounts of information to process, the novel's accountants find themselves positioned uneasily between their humanity and the necessity of acting like a "sentient computer."[40] In the same volume, Stephen J. Burn posits that, in their attempts to deal with this condition of overwhelming immersion in swathes of mostly irrelevant data, Wallace's accountants stand for the workings of human consciousness in general.[41]

There is good archival evidence for this argument: Burn points out that, while working on *The Pale King*, Wallace read Timothy Wilson's *Strangers to Ourselves: Discovering the Adaptive Unconscious* (2002), which (drawing on research in psychology) demonstrates the vast disparity between the huge amount of information humans perceive at any given moment and the tiny proportion of that data that can be consciously processed by the mind—thereby establishing the importance of filtering out the irrelevant excess (the vast majority) and "homing in on which facts were important." For Wilson, this is the task that the adaptive unconscious performs. In the same period, Wallace also read *The User Illusion: Cutting Consciousness Down to Size* (1991) by Tor Nørretranders, a popular science book that likewise argues for the importance to human consciousness of a nonconscious process of "getting rid of information in which you are not interested."[42] Jeffrey Severs, in *David Foster Wallace's Balancing Books: Fictions of Value* (2017), points out how Wallace more or less lifts wholesale a passage from *The User Illusion* as the basis for a key scene in *The Pale King*.[43] For him, though, Wallace's interest in "information sorting" is not—as Wouters argues—about the porous-seeming boundaries between human and machine, nor is it about—as Burn suggests—Wallace's attempts to ground his fiction in neuroscientific accounts of the mind.[44] For Severs, *The Pale King*'s focus on information gets at a whole host of larger issues, from economics, to aesthetics, to morality. Severs argues that, throughout his oeuvre, Wallace repeatedly enlists the reader in scenes of "cognitive labor" that involve comparing and evaluating different pieces of information, and that the question of how to make successful comparative evaluations—economic evaluations, aesthetic evaluations, and moral evaluations—is the fundamental question of Wallace's career.[45] Hence Severs's title, *David Foster Wallace's Balancing Books*: Wallace's books, Severs argues, are ultimately about balancing competing factors against one another, so as to move toward a more manageable way of existing in a profoundly imbalanced world.

My own approach in this chapter has the most in common with Severs: I focus primarily on the economic and the aesthetic dimensions of *The Pale King*'s concern with attention and information. In Part 3, I discuss the economic; for now, my focus will predominantly be on the aesthetic. My claim is this: that Wallace's interest in accountants as information workers is not just about "machines vs. people" or neuroscience and psychology—it is about writing.

2.3. Writers

At the heart of my reading of Sylvanshine's descent was the claim that being an effective accountant is not only about acquiring as much information as possible but also about discarding most of it so as to be left with what is important. In this section, I suggest that the same applies to writing. To put this another way, writing a novel—and in particular, a novel like *The Pale King*—does not just involve *writing*: it also, crucially, involves a whole host of other less obviously creative or generative forms of work: editing, deletion, reordering. To put this another way, via the words of Teju Cole in his essay "Far Away from Here": "Authorship ... is not only what is created but also what is selected."[46]

Making this argument, however, entails a departure from the claims that Wallace himself made about the writing process. Here, I want to explain my reasons for reading *The Pale King* in a manner that directly contradicts the theory of fiction and nonfiction writing that Wallace puts forward in "Deciderization 2007: A Special Report," his introduction to the 2007 volume of *Best American Essays*, which he wrote at the same time that he was working on *The Pale King*. In that essay, Wallace draws a distinction between fiction and nonfiction as follows:

> Writing-wise, fiction is scarier, but nonfiction is harder—because nonfiction's based in reality, and today's felt reality is overwhelmingly, circuit-blowingly huge and complex. Whereas fiction comes out of nothing. Actually, so wait: the truth is that both genres are scary; both feel like they're executed on tightropes, over abysses—it's the abysses that are different. Fiction's abyss is silence, *nada*. Whereas nonfiction's abyss is Total Noise, the seething static of every particular thing and experience, and one's total freedom of infinite choice about what to choose to attend to and represent and connect, and how, and why, etc.[47]

Here, Wallace sets up a binary: with nonfiction, you start with "Total Noise," with everything, with information overload, and the writer's labor consists in paying attention, selecting the right bits, and connecting and explaining them. Good nonfiction essays, he says later on, "serve as models and guides for how large and complex sets of facts can be sifted, culled, and arranged in meaningful ways."[48] With fiction, though, you start with silence, with nothing, and, with just the power of your imagination, you build something brand new, from the ground up. So if Teju Cole says that authorship is about creation and selection, Wallace splits this statement into two, saying that yes, authorship is about creation and selection, but we can be more specific than that and say instead that nonfictional authorship is about selection, and fictional authorship is about creation.

It is safe to say that I do not buy Wallace's claim here—and more importantly, that I do not buy that Wallace really buys it either: most importantly, because all available evidence—both in the archive and in the text of the published version—points to a characterization of *fiction* writing that sounds much closer to "Deciderization"'s description of *nonfiction*. Insofar as it is a useful guide to reading *The Pale King*, we are better off ignoring what "Deciderization" has to say about fiction writing's abyss of silence and turning instead to its account of nonfiction and its abyss of noise. If "Deciderization" follows commonsense dogma and says that, sure, fiction-writing involves some selective labor (research, revising) but its underlying quality is creation from scratch, then *The Pale King*, as I read it, says something close to the inverse: sure, fiction-writing involves some creating from scratch, but the majority of the labor that undergirds it is not creative but selective.

When he makes the claim that authorship is about both creation and selection, Teju Cole is not directly talking about writing. He is talking about photography—or rather, about photography via a comparison with writing:

> I let go of some "good" photos, the way you strike out pretty sentences from a draft, and I learned how a number of tightly argued photos should be followed by one or two that are simpler and more ventilated. Authorship, after all, is not only what is created but also what is selected.[49]

The comparison between media is revealing. Photography, among all art forms, is perhaps the one in which creation and selection are most inextricably and controversially intertwined—not just in Cole's sense of "let[ting] go of some 'good' photos" when putting together a sequence, but in the very process of making the photograph in the first place. This is the point that Rosalind Krauss makes in the second part of "Notes on the Index: Seventies Art in America": the photograph literally depends for existence on a process of "*selection* from the natural array by means of cropping": it is defined as much by the choice of what to exclude from the frame as by the choice of what to include.[50] What is most arresting about Cole's claim, then, is not what it says about photography—a form that we are used to understanding as involving a mix of both creation and selection, or perhaps, in a more Kraussian vein, as involving *only* selection. What is arresting is that he makes this claim about writing. Sure, the fact that writing involves "strik[ing] out pretty sentences from a draft" is an undisputable fact, but the notion of giving relatively equal weight to the selective and creative labor involved in writing is nevertheless one that unsettles our dominant (creation-oriented) ways of talking about authorship: the old metaphors of divine inspiration, of invention out of nothing, of birth and parenthood—the same metaphors that Wallace employs in "Deciderization."

At the same time, it is worth clarifying that I am not trying here to emphasize the selective aspects of writerly work to such an extent that the creative elements disappear. One way to understand Wallace's privileging of the creation-ex-nihilo aspect of fiction-writing would be as part of the "anti-death" of the author position that Wallace had staked out in "Greatly Exaggerated"—since Barthes, in that essay, had sought to strip literature of all creative mystique precisely by *replacing* creation in favor of selection as the sole mode of composition. When he argues that the text is "a tissue of quotations"—as in, a combination of preexisting materials that the writer merely selects and reassembles—that sounds like a fairly accurate description of conceptual poetry.[51] For the *nouveaux romans* that Barthes had in mind, or, say, a Kathy Acker book, this characterization may be hyperbolic but still contains a degree of truth. As a description of *The Pale King*—which, for all its fragmentation and occasional formal experimentation, nevertheless hews closely to the realist mode for long chunks at a time—"a tissue of quotations" seems inadequate.[52] Thus, my position here is somewhere in between "The Death of the Author" and "Deciderization," in that—although I am ultimately *more* interested in thinking the place of selective than creative labor—I nevertheless want to retain a place for both. In this respect, my orientation is closest to Barthes's in his late 1970s work rather than in "The Death of the Author." In *The Preparation of the Novel*, he characterizes the critical "tendency to erase the author" and his creative capacity as a "trend" from which he has long moved on.[53] The hypothetical work that he "should like, either to write, or to see written today" is one that necessarily involves both creation and selection: "you have to transpose the writing of the past, fine like an old wine, and yet be willing to slip some new words, some new metaphors in between the lines."[54] If in "The Death of the Author" Barthes insisted that the writer's "only power is to mix writings," to select from a "ready-formed dictionary," in *The Preparation of the Novel* his position is closer to Cole's claim that authorship involves both creation and selection and therefore also to my own argument regarding *The Pale King*.[55]

This kind of position is also visible in some of the scholarship on the novel. For an archival-turn version of the claim, we can turn to David Hering, who suggests that, especially in the period from 2005 to 2007, a key part of Wallace's work consisted in taking on a "curatorial role over the mass of data he [had] accumulated"—that is, having spent years amassing hundreds of pages of notes and drafts, Wallace now found himself staring into something like "nonfiction's abyss [of] Total Noise."[56] In a note to self from June 2005 (which Hering also discusses at length), Wallace emphasizes on several occasions what Barthes in *The Preparation of the Novel* calls the "*unsinkable*" fact of writerly labor, telling himself that "the key here is time and effort. There is no substitute" and that "all I have to do is stick with it. Not give up. Do the footwork."[57] This work is not *only* selective—none of the "promising nuggets in this old stuff ... can just be re-used per se"—but this phase in the novel's composition nevertheless exemplifies Cole's claim about authorship entailing both creative and selective labor—and not, crucially, Wallace's own claim about fiction-writing taking place over an abyss of silence.[58]

It is also important to note that neither of the two most detailed archival reconstructions of *The Pale King*—in Hering's *Fiction and Form* and in Toon Staes's "Work in Process: A Genesis for *The Pale King*"—devotes much discussion to the final stage in the novel's composition, under the hand of Wallace's longtime editor Michael Pietsch, whose "heroic work … on the rough manuscripts," Staes suggests, might well accord him the title of "co-author."[59] Looking at the twenty-nine-page spreadsheet Pietsch put together, logging 474 separate documents and attempting to gather together and date all the various versions of each section, it is hard not to concur. Importantly, though, that "heroic" coauthorial work is, at least in the literal sense, entirely selective: it is work that would in most circumstances be done by the author, or collaboratively by author and editor, but qualitatively speaking, it involves working with ready-made pieces rather than adding new material: making decisions about which sections to include, which version of each section, what order to put them in.[60]

If archival research reveals that the writerly labor (performed by both Wallace and Pietsch) that went into *The Pale King* was characterized as much by selection as by creation (by working against "Total Noise" as well as against "silence"), an approach that focuses on the aesthetics of the published novel demonstrates that Wallace's readers too are faced with a daunting amount of selective labor and that selective labor is in some sense the novel's topic. A number of critics have commented on the way that the novel's narrative style demands that readers make careful choices regarding what to attend to when faced with a panoply of details that can easily start to resemble "Total Noise" or a "heap of facts." Jeffrey Severs and Andrew Warren both explicitly connect *The Pale King*'s tendency toward information overload to Wallace's description of the abyss of "seething static" in "Deciderization."[61] For Severs, this tendency connects once again to Wallace's concern with acts of evaluation.[62] For Warren, it is part of a kind of sublime aesthetic of "the data mass's implicit"—and horrifying—"infinitude."[63]

But the most convincing interpretation of Wallace's aesthetic strategy does not come via the long-established category of the sublime, nor even via a reading of *The Pale King*, but rather via Sianne Ngai's theorization in *Our Aesthetic Categories* (2012) of the *interesting*. For Ngai, the interesting is an aesthetic in which selection is central. In its postwar form, which she observes at work across media and genres from conceptual art to (crucially) the novel, the interesting is "an aesthetic of difference as information": it functions by presenting the viewer with some information and asking them to pay attention to the differences that make one piece of information stand out from the rest.[64] Though Severs does not cite Ngai, her notion of the interesting is thus closely connected to the argument that he makes about Wallace's aesthetics of readerly evaluation. Ngai, in fact, does briefly cite Wallace as one of several twentieth-century and contemporary writers of "sprawling, encyclopedic works often explicitly about seriality or ongoingness" in which "the authors seem to have deliberately increased the proportion of boredom in the ratio of boredom to interest, as if engaging in an experimental quest to discover what the absolute minimal condition of 'interesting' might be."[65] When Ngai mentions Wallace here, she is referring to *Infinite Jest* rather than *The Pale King*, which had not been published when she wrote the first version of this passage in an article for *Critical Inquiry*.[66] But I would suggest that it works even better as a description of Wallace's fragmentary posthumous novel about the boring and repetitive work of tax accountants.

"The authors seem to have deliberately increased the proportion of boredom in the ratio of boredom to interest": that is, rather than simply keeping the exciting stuff and cutting the rest, Wallace and Pietsch have—for a variety of reasons, including Pietsch's stated desire to edit the novel "only lightly" in Wallace's absence—left the boring, apparently extraneous material in.[67] And they have done so, if we follow Ngai's argument, "as if engaging in an experimental quest to discover what the absolute minimal condition of 'interesting' might be."[68] Pietsch interprets Wallace's choice of subject matter as unavoidably entangling *The Pale King* in just such a tightrope act, a challenge to retain the reader's attention despite the odds of stultifying dullness: "If anyone could make taxes *interesting*," he writes, "it was [Wallace]."[69] And his editorial choices raise the stakes of this challenge, as does Wallace's own tendency to include vast amounts of detail, despite the apparent importance accorded in the novel to the act of winnowing away the useless excess.[70] The 2012 edition, which adds an extra twenty-three pages of previously deleted scenes, goes even further in this direction.

The Pale King's "interesting" aesthetic, then, is a function of properties of the novel that both predate and postdate Wallace's death: characteristics attributable primarily to Wallace and characteristics attributable primarily to Pietsch. This claim has two consequences: first, that there is a degree of aesthetic consistency between the work of Wallace and that of Pietsch, and, second, that there is a connection between *The Pale King*'s unfinished, coauthored status and its "interesting" aesthetic mode. The second consequence—the connection between unfinishedness and the interesting—is one that Ngai (via Schlegel and David Hockney) also notes, arguing that "whereas beautiful is 'final,' interesting is in medias res, 'on its way' to a 'there' whose actual destination is uncertain."[71] This might be a way of making sense of the first consequence: the aesthetic consistency between the material Wallace wrote and the way that Pietsch dealt with the novel's unfinished status. Understanding *The Pale King* via the framework of an aesthetic mode of which unfinishedness is a key characteristic clearly makes sense when we are talking about Pietsch's coauthorial work on the novel. But if *The Pale King* was *interesting* from the beginning, then Ngai's argument would imply that it may also have been in some sense *unfinished*— even *unfinishable*—from the beginning. Completeness would in some sense have fundamentally undermined the aesthetic project in which Wallace was engaged. This is not to say that the nature of *The Pale King*'s aesthetic project is the sole reason why the novel remained unfinished: Wallace's suicide cannot help but loom large over the reception of the book. I do not wish to draw Wallace's death too closely into the sphere of the novel's aesthetics; rather, I am suggesting that there is something about the book's project and its aesthetic mode—its attempt to think through the difficulties of dealing with massive quantities of information via the aesthetic of the interesting—that made closure and completeness especially difficult, which might go some way to explaining why, after ten years of work, *The Pale King* remained unfinished.

From archival evidence, it seems as if Wallace had come to a similar understanding as early as 1999, when, in an "embryonic outline" of the novel, he described it not as a coherent whole, unified by the causal, centripetal logic of narrative, but as "a series of set-ups for stuff happening."[72] Crucially, however, "nothing actually happens."[73] The word "series" is important here: *The Pale King* operates more by a logic of seriality than of causality, in a "series of set-ups" with no end in sight. Mark McGurl helpfully connects the novel's aesthetic of "serial self-expression" to the ideal of "everyone 'finding his voice' and having his or her say in turn" shared by Alcoholics Anonymous and MFA creative writing workshops.[74] What I would emphasize in turn is the connection between seriality and unfinishedness. Like the work of recovery (one day at a time), the work of storytelling undertaken by *The Pale King*'s multiple narrators has no endpoint in mind—it works precisely to delay the endpoint (relapse; silence) as long as possible. Hence, perhaps, a chapter like §25, which consists of a long, repetitive list of actions taking place in an examinations room: "'Irrelevant' Chris Fogle turns a page. Howard Cardwell turns a page. Ken Wax turns a page …."[75] One page at a time. This series of dull, rote descriptions of dull, rote tasks has no climax, and it does not lead anywhere. It ends pretty much where it begins: "Ken Wax turns a page. Joe Biron-Maint turns a page. Ann Williams turns a page."[76] Paying attention is rewarded not with the teleological pleasures of plot—"nothing actually happens"—but with the sheer accretive effect of action followed by unconnected action (Ken Wax turning a page does not cause Joe Biron-Maint to turn a page) and the occasional oddly affecting non-sequitur buried among the rest: between "Jay Landauer feels absently at his face" and "Ryne Hobratschk turns a page," we read "Every love story is a ghost story": the line that D. T. Max selected as a title to his 2012 biography of Wallace.[77] This chapter works precisely in the way that Ngai describes. To get to a single "Every love story is a ghost story," the reader has to wade through dozens of sentences along the lines of "Ryne Hobratschk turns a page": the ratio of boring to interesting has been ratcheted up beyond all reasonable expectations. §33 ends with a paragraph that notes how the word "bore" actually predates the word "interesting" by two years—as if, as Ngai suggests, the interesting is a fundamentally relative category, which exists only as a result of a comparison with the boring: "what is interesting is never inherently interesting but only so in comparison with something else."[78] A passage like §25 is good evidence to support her claim.

Ngai's theorization of the interesting—specifically, the way she links postwar American "interesting" art to its particular economic context—will return in Section 3.1 of this chapter. For now, what is important to note is this: reading Ngai and Wallace together helps make sense of *The Pale King*'s unfinished status as something more significant than a by-product of Wallace's premature death. It is not just that the novel's unfinishedness conveniently correlates with its interest in seriality (in the sense that seriality undermines aesthetic completion): rather, the novel's seriality and its unfinishedness can both be understood as effects of its larger aesthetic project—that is, to think about the ways in which humans (whether they are accountants, writers, or, like the character David Wallace, both) attempt to make sense of overwhelming quantities of information. By making visible the unfinished nature of the novel and enlisting the reader into the work of making sense of it, in all its overwhelming and potentially boring volume of information, Pietsch's light-touch editorial work takes exactly the right approach.

2.4. Cowboys

Up to this point, my argument about the way in which Wallace uses the work of the accountant as a metaphor for the work of writing has focused primarily on one aspect of that work—its emphasis on selection over creation—and secondarily on the ways in which *The Pale King*, in form and content, both enacts and demands this kind of work. In this final section of Part 2, I want to go into more detail regarding Wallace's use of the accountant-writer metaphor—specifically, via a second metaphor of the accountant as *cowboy*. For Wallace, a writer is like an accountant. But an accountant is also like a cowboy. How? And in what sense, therefore, is a *writer* like a cowboy? In the pages that follow, I argue that the comparison drawn between the accountant and the cowboy does a very particular type of work: as well as emphasizing the centrality of selective labor already discussed, the cowboy metaphor functions to give the labor of accountants an aura of romantic prestige, while also implicitly justifying aspects of their working conditions that would otherwise be undesirable.

The earliest appearance of the cowboy metaphor in the *Pale King* archives comes in the notes Wallace made during the first of three undergraduate accounting classes he audited at Illinois State University in Bloomington-Normal (where he taught at the time) between fall 1996 and spring 1998. In his notes for Accounting 131 with Patty Hudson from September 10, 1996, there appears (in block capitals spread across the bottom of the page) the phrase "ACCOUNTANTS ARE COWBOYS OF INFORMATION."[79] This phrase comes to Wallace remarkably early in the composition process of what became *The Pale King* (only seven months after the publication of *Infinite Jest*, and almost fifteen years before *The Pale King* was finally made available), and it seems to strike him forcefully, given the idea's reappearance at the climactic moment of the novella-length §22: the section that Pietsch chooses to place at the novel's center, in which Chris Fogle describes the events that led to him joining the Service. This moment—the rhetorical culmination of a mysterious substitute accounting professor's final exhortation to a class Fogle attends by mistake in the winter of 1978—is worth quoting from at length:

> I wish to inform you that the accounting profession to which you aspire is, in, fact, heroic ... True heroism is *a priori* incompatible with audience or applause or even the bare notice of the common run of man. In fact ... the less conventionally heroic or exciting or adverting or even interesting or engaging a labor appears to be, the greater its potential as an arena for actual heroism ... Yesterday's hero pushed back at bounds and frontiers—he penetrated, tamed, hewed, shaped, made, brought things into being. Yesterday's society's heroes generated facts ... In today's world, boundaries are fixed, and most significant facts have been generated. Gentlemen, the heroic frontier now lies in the ordering and deployment of those facts. Classification, organization, presentation. To put it another way, the pie has been made—the contest is now in the slicing ... You have wondered, perhaps, why all real accountants wear hats? They are today's cowboys. As you will be. Riding the American range. Riding herd on the unending torrent of financial data. The eddies, cataracts, arranged variations, fractious minutiae. You order the data, shepherd it, direct its flow, lead it where it's needed, in the codified form in which it's apposite.[80]

It is difficult to know exactly how seriously to take this speech. Even though it has an indisputably life-changing effect on Fogle, who leaves the classroom no longer a "wastoid" slacker and newly intent on a career in tax accounting, he nevertheless voices some skepticism of the teacher's "jumbled" metaphors of "cowboys and pies," to which the class responds with the "terrible sound" of the applause of "only a few scattered hands."[81] The text is unclear on how much stock we should put in Fogle: a few pages later, David Wallace dismisses Fogle's account of his conversion as mostly "self-indulgence and ... hand-wringing."[82] An earlier draft of §22 suggests that Fogle's narrative, which takes place within the frame of a series of interviews, was intended at one point to include marginalia indicating the interviewers' increasing frustration and boredom at Fogle's verbosity.[83] This makes it more difficult still to assess the status of his dramatic conversion and the speech that crowns it: do we read it as sincere or ironic? Liam Connell, in *Precarious Labour and the Contemporary Novel* (2017), leans toward the latter, reading the scene as "largely a case of the [substitute professor] over-extending his rhetoric" and arguing that the main significance of the cowboy metaphor is its anachronism: the metaphor works by *not working*, signaling "a rupture or incompatibility" between "the way that work is currently conducted"—as in the IRS—and "the way that the nation has traditionally been imagined" via the imagery of cowboys and the American West.[84] My reading, though, proceeds from the premise that the accountant-cowboy metaphor is worth taking seriously—in part because the speech's overall thrust regarding the quiet heroism of dull, selective labor aligns more closely with the novel's overall argument and tone than Fogle's skepticism or David Wallace's snark and in part because the cowboy comparison is surprisingly useful in helping us gain a more specific understanding of *The Pale King*'s characterization of labor.

The teacher's address begins with a claim about the value of ordinary, seemingly boring work. The kind of "heroism" he describes is inversely proportional to the degree of its recognition and to the promise of excitement it holds. Marshall Boswell, Clare Hayes-Brady, and Liam Connell have all connected this way of thinking about work to Wallace's engagement with American Pragmatism, especially William James, Richard Rorty, and Stanley Cavell.[85] It is a different thinker from that tradition, though, whose work is especially relevant to Wallace's characterization of the heroism of ordinary labor, even though Wallace did not (as far as the archive suggests) read his work. This thinker is Richard Sennett, whose body of writing on the philosophy of work argues for the importance of craftsmanship—defined as "the desire to do a job well for its own sake"—in a manner that converges with the substitute professor's praise of the honor and commitment of those who devote themselves "to the care of others' money."[86] Sennett's argument that the "working human animal can be enriched by the skills and dignified by the spirit of craftsmanship" shares with *The Pale King* a sense of nostalgia for a specific imaginary of labor, one that, as Sennett acknowledges in *The Craftsman* (2008), has tended historically to be marked in terms of gender, as well as race, class, and other factors.[87] Making the connection between Wallace and Sennett therefore does not just alert us to *The Pale King*'s philosophical underpinnings in American Pragmatism; it also makes visible some of the limiting particularities of the vision Wallace and Sennett share.

In *Be Creative* (2016), Angela McRobbie critically examines the maleness of Sennett's conception of craft, which "remains too closely tied to the image of the solitary male worker, engrossed in the task at hand, which entails an object" to be able to speak usefully to the specificities of women's work.[88] As she notes, the workers Sennett writes about often seem "to have walked right out of a novel by John Updike or Philip Roth": that is, they are mostly white men, often "conservative" and "patriarchal."[89] Similarly, Fogle notes in this section of *The Pale King* that, as far as he remembers, "nearly everyone" in the classroom was male.[90] "A handful," he notes, "were also oriental"—which means, presumably, that *all but* a handful of the "forty-eight" students in the room (and the one white teacher) were white.[91]

In addition (and perhaps connected) to its white, male particularity, the vision of labor that Wallace and Sennett both seem to valorize is one that is unabashedly hierarchical. Sennett begins *The Craftsman* by considering medieval workshops "in which masters and apprentices work together but as unequals" and ultimately makes a case for the value—not so much the commercial as (surprisingly) the *ethical* value—of a workplace structured by hierarchical power relations between a skilled authority figure and his obedient subordinates.[92] Resisting what he understands as a peculiarly "modern" worry about "paying obeisance to authority"—a concern that was at the heart of my previous chapter and which characterizes much of contemporary critical theory, from the Frankfurt School to feminism—Sennett instead argues that embedding authority in a particular skilled human being is "infinitely preferable" to placing one's trust in "a lifeless, static code of practice."[93] In the context of a North American political sphere newly attuned to the dangers of fascism, it is hard not to read this as unsettlingly close to a defense of authoritarianism and a dismissal of the rule of law.

Indeed, Fogle sees in the charismatic substitute not only a powerful emanation of "authority" (a word that appears six times in eight lines in a description of him) but also something that is explicitly *not* "democratic."[94] The substitute, he says, "may have been the first genuine authority figure I ever met," and he prompts in Fogle a realization "that a real authority was not the same as a friend or someone who cared about you, but nevertheless could be good for you."[95] What this suggests is something more specific about Wallace's figure of the accountant than just the emphasis on selective rather than creative labor: the accountant in *The Pale King*—and by analogy, the author in *The Pale King*—is someone whose work philosophy is tinged with a patriarchal, authoritarian streak. Up to this point, I have tended toward a generous reading of the novel's emphasis on the unglamorous labor of selection, suggesting that it undermines the hegemonic image of the author-as-creative-genius. Fogle's identification of the substitute accounting professor's unabashed *authority*, though, starts to suggest that the accountant-author comparison is rather more ambivalent and that the old figure of the overly agentic author(itarian)—the Man Who Holds Forth—can all too easily creep back in.

Mark McGurl claims in "The Institution of Nothing: David Foster Wallace in the Program" that "decoding the politics of [*The Pale King*] is not that hard."[96] In his reading, the novel's position can be easily reduced to a set of axioms: "rampant marketization and social irresponsibility" are bad, while "civic responsibility" and paying more taxes are good.[97] *The Pale King*'s faith in the "traditional morality" of the pre-neoliberal, civic-minded IRS is, for McGurl, a symptom of "the conservatism of Wallace's embrace of institutional authority."[98] The point I just made—that Wallace's valorization of unglamorous, craftsman-like work contains an implicit authoritarian streak—is consistent with McGurl's argument. But I'm not quite convinced that *The Pale King*'s politics are as easy to decode as McGurl suggests. Paying close attention to the way in which Wallace employs the cowboy comparison reveals how difficult it can be to pin down his political commitments. It's easy to read the cowboy as a vehicle for a conservative politics—to understand the use of this symbol as a way of privileging white, patriarchal authority—but I want to suggest that Wallace's employment of the cowboy is considerably more ambivalent. In addition to the connotations of institutional authority, settler colonialism, and hypermasculinity, the figure of the cowboy also carries less conservative implications, including ultimately a critique of precarious labor.

The cowboy is a capacious vehicle for metaphor: in this speech, he symbolizes both creative and selective labor. "Yesterday's hero"—the classic cowboy—is a figure of creation, "generat[ing] facts" and expanding the frontiers of the nation.[99] "In today's world," on the other hand, the cowboy of *information* performs primarily selective labor, corralling data as a ranch hand would drive cattle to market: "Riding herd on the unending torrent of financial data."[100] This is what Wallace meant in his class notes from 1996: as a herd of cattle is to a cowboy, so a "torrent of financial data" is to an accountant. The cowboy is faced with an overwhelming mass of preexisting material (a herd of cattle spread across a giant ranch), and through a process of selective labor (herding and driving), he turns it into something of financial value (a delivery of cows to market and, ultimately, the meat-packing plant). Similarly, the accountant is faced with an overwhelming mass (of tax returns), and through his careful selective labor (scanning the fact-pattern for relevant data), he eventually produces something of financial value—in this case, a figure expressing an individual or corporation's tax liability.

As important as the type of work a cowboy does, though, is the set of cultural associations in which he is enmeshed, especially in the context of a novel set in the United States in the late 1970s and early 1980s. The way in which Wallace alludes to the cowboy here and throughout *The Pale King* draws on a number of these associations—both those that emphasize the cowboy's grandiose, quintessentially American virility and those that undermine his seeming authority. In order to draw out the complexities of the cowboy's array of connotations in the novel, it helps to turn to a number of critics that we can group together under the heading of Cowboy Studies. As a kind of microfield, Cowboy Studies, which overlaps with strands of masculinity studies, cinema studies, and studies of the American West, has done a great deal to add nuance to the received idea of (in Daniel Worden's phrase) "cowboy masculinity."[101] By studying representations of cowboys from the nineteenth century through the present day (by writers and artists who were themselves cowboys, and by writers and artists who were not), critics like Worden, Jane Tompkins, Blake Allmendinger, and Lydia Cooper have showed that cowboys (represented and real) are, to cite Eve Sedgwick, both "kinda hegemonic" and "kinda subversive."[102] As close an association as they have with patriarchal and imperialist traits, they are also in many ways figures of resistance to hierarchies of gender, race, and class, and often as much victims as agents of oppression.[103] In *The Pale King*, both of these sides to the cowboy are visible, and it is the interplay between them that makes him such an important figure.

As Fogle experiences, the cowboy holds an immense attraction in the (white, male) American psyche. The novel shows that this attraction is one that can be manipulated for all sorts of ends, from recruiting new IRS employees (as in the case of Fogle) to electing a president. In §19, a long conversation about political economy, taxation, and civics held in a stalled elevator, one character makes a prediction about the 1980 elections (in which Ronald Reagan first won the presidency): "Look for us to elect someone who can cast himself as a Rebel, *maybe even a cowboy*, but who deep down we'll know is a bureaucratic creature who'll operate inside the government mechanism instead of naively bang his head against it the way we've watched poor Jimmy [Carter] do for four years."[104] This prediction is of course partially accurate: Ronald Reagan certainly did "cast himself" (the thespian language here is telling, given Reagan's prior career in Hollywood) as a cowboy. Another participant in the elevator conversation makes a similar point, predicting "a Bush-Reagan ticket" with "Reagan for symbolism, the Cowboy, Bush the quiet insider, doing the unsexy work of actual management."[105] In reality, the 1980 Republican ticket was Reagan-Bush rather than the other way round, but what is most important to note here is the way that, in both of these quotations, Wallace figures the presidency as having two sides: a glamorous cowboy side and an "unsexy," "bureaucratic" side that sounds a lot like the way that the substitute describes the quiet heroism of IRS accountants near the beginning of his speech. Thus, the presidency shares with accountancy a double-sided nature: the glamorous symbolism embodied by the cowboy and the dull, everyday labor of the bureaucrat. That this bifurcation echoes the way I described the *author* (via Barthes) at the beginning of this chapter, as theoretical *author* (a powerful figure of authority) and practical *writer* (for Barthes, a humble office worker), is no accident. The ambivalence of Wallace's representation of the accountant, I am arguing, reflects the ambivalence inherent in the author/writer, as simultaneously powerful and ordinary, rebellious and anti-rebellious. This last pair of terms derives both from the quotation above ("Look for use to elect someone who can cast himself as a Rebel") and from the famous ending of Wallace's 1993 essay "E Unibus Pluram: Television and U.S. Fiction," where he suggested that the next artistic avant-garde might be a set of "literary 'rebels'" who rebel precisely by being a "weird bunch of '*anti*-rebels,'" rejecting the radical posturing of the "old postmodern insurgents."[106] The vocabulary of rebellion and its opposite shared between these two passages—a commonality noted by critics like Marshall Boswell—emphasizes the connection in Wallace's writing between literary labor and other forms of work: the work done by accountants, by cowboys, and even by presidents.[107] In each, there is a notable double-sidedness: a glamorous symbolic sheen and quieter, unsexy reality.

In the case of the cowboy, this unsexy reality—which a study like Blake Allmendinger's *The Cowboy: Representations of Labor in an American Work Culture* (1992) usefully details—manifests in a number of aspects that tend to be glossed over in glamorous depictions of hegemonic cowboy masculinity like the substitute professor's: "Riding the American range ... *man*[*ning*] the walls" of the nation.[108] Most relevant in the context of *The Pale King* is the cowboy's economic subordination to the rancher who employs him: "Hired in the spring to brand and castrate the stock, in the summer to graze the meandering herds, and in the fall to drive them to market, cowboys were then dismissed in the winter by ranchers who had no more use for a cheap and expendable labor force that had, in effect, worked itself out of a job."[109] As in the case of the explicitly "unequal" relationship between the authority-imbued substitute professor and the subordinate accounting students (or between master and apprentice in a medieval workshop), the cowboy is subject to a rigidly hierarchical power structure—more specifically, though, this subordination leaves him alternating seasonally between hard labor on the ranch and long periods of unemployment. This, for Allmendinger, is the flipside of what he refers to as the "drifting myth" of cowboy work culture: the popular idea, perpetuated in cowboy literature, of "the drifting cowboy's continuing desire to move," to remain unmoored from the fetters of polite, sedentary society.[110] Thus, the glamorous image of the lone ranger has as its ugly underside a reality of precarious employment made even less bearable by the fact that their intense rural work when employed left cowboys "geographically isolated and socially cut off" and prevented them "from engaging in relations with women for great lengths of time."[111]

The Pale King's overwhelmingly male (and straight) accountants share with cowboys some significant obstacles against settling down with a wife. "It's hard to meet women in the Service," one worker complains: not only because of the IRS's reputation ("It's not the most popular") but also because it values a flexible labor force that it can move from one rural or suburban location to another with minimal friction.[112] Like nineteenth-century ranchers who "hired only unmarried cowboys," the IRS prizes single men, who can be reposted easily: whereas reposting an entire family is expensive and time-consuming, if you are a single male employee, "you stop even unpacking."[113] Importantly, Wallace explicitly draws this connection between itinerant IRS utility examiners and cowboys:

> There is a certain prestige or romance to the UTEX [utility examiner] lifestyle, but part of this is married or elsewise dug-in employees' romanticization of the unattached lifestyle of somebody who goes from Post to Post at the institutional whim of the Service, *like a cowboy or mercenary.*[114]

This passage gets to the heart of the importance of the cowboy metaphor: simply put, it is a way of giving a romantic sheen to something otherwise unappealing. The utility examiners are poorly paid, since they move from post to post too quickly to develop rapport with a manager who would recommend them for a promotion. They are socially isolated, constantly on the move, and stuck doing the most rote examinations work. Comparing them to cowboys—who were also poorly paid, socially isolated, itinerant workers who performed grueling selective labor—seems at one level to give their lifestyle "a certain prestige or romance," but it also unwittingly brings out what the two professions share in terms of undesirable working conditions.

This section began by asking two questions: first, in what sense is an accountant like a cowboy? And second, in what sense is a *writer* therefore like a cowboy? I have suggested that accountants share with cowboys not only a form of labor that is in large part selective rather than creative but also working conditions that lead to an isolated and itinerant lifestyle. Much of this description could also apply to writers, whose work, as I have argued, entails a great deal of selective labor and whose employment status, as McRobbie argues in *Be Creative*, conventionally lacks the stability associated with careers outside of the creative industries. The artist, she suggests, "has historically embodied a kind of free spirit, an unbridled freedom of movement as he or she roams about in search of the ideas that will inform the next piece of work."[115] If this sounds rather like Blake Allmendinger's characterization of the drifting cowboy and his "continuing desire to move," it is no coincidence: I want to close this section by developing (via a return to McRobbie, whose critique of Richard Sennett I previously cited) the claim made above that the author/writer shares with a cowboy a double-sided nature characterized by a romantic image and a less than romantic lived experience. In fact, the argument that McRobbie makes in *Be Creative* about the figure of the artist coincides neatly with the argument I am making here about the figure of the cowboy: both are figures that can be employed insidiously to convince people to accept and even enjoy inferior labor conditions.

McRobbie focuses on the creative industries in the UK in the 1990s and 2000s. She argues that, during this period, Tony Blair's New Labour government employed the figure of the artist as part of a "call to be creative" that functioned as "a potent and highly appealing mode of new governmentality directed to the young in the educational environment, whose main effect [was] to do away with the idea of welfare rights in work by means of eclipsing normal employment altogether."[116] Labour's policy co-opted "the myth of the romantic artist or creative genius," because the artist-subject is a subject trained to see themselves as human capital and ready to accept a "flexible" (that is, precarious) career because making art is "historically associated with the social good, with enjoyment, entertainment and education."[117] Thus, the artist became a metaphorical means—circulated primarily through the university and its newly renamed "Centres for Creative Economy"—by which to undermine unionized labor and hasten the spread of an exploitative and precarious form of labor that we have since come to associate with neoliberalism.[118] In *The Pale King*, I argue, the cowboy serves the same function. As I have already discussed, it is the association between the cowboy and "a certain prestige or romance" of free movement that Wallace offers as an explanation of why utility examiners end up accepting poor pay and social isolation. And it is the cowboy, in the substitute professor's charismatic exhortation ("directed," as in McRobbie's argument, "to the young in the educational environment"), who functions as a recruitment tool for IRS examiners in the Carter-era United States, on the cusp of the arrival of Reaganite neoliberal policies.

What a close consideration of the cowboy-accountant metaphor in *The Pale King* reveals is that the cowboy's double-sidedness (romantic image, unsexy reality) serves a very particular function. Just as the romantic image of the author or artist can function as symbolic compensation for the poorly paid and precarious reality of a creative career, so the cowboy's glamor gives a career in the IRS an attractive symbolic sheen: as the cowboy is to the accountant, the (romantic, prestigious) author or artist is to the (humble, bureaucratic) writer. More specifically, the romance of the author or of the cowboy can be *weaponized* so as to render these kinds of employment circumstances as conditions to be relished rather than resisted. Another name for these kinds of employment conditions—a lack of stability or unionization and the pressure to behave as an entrepreneur of oneself—is neoliberalism. It is this that the final section of this chapter addresses.

3. Two Broad Arcs

3.1. Neoliberalism and Information Work

In Section 2.2, I quoted Wallace's description of the two "broad arcs" of *The Pale King*: "Paying attention, boredom, ADD, Machines vs. people at performing mindless jobs" and "being individual vs. being part of larger things—paying taxes, being 'lone gun' in IRS vs. team player"; the information arc and the neoliberalism arc; or, the cognitive arc and the political arc.[119] Whereas in Part 2 I concentrated primarily on the first of these, in Part 3 my aim is to explain how these two seemingly separate threads are connected. There is a clue to this connection in the metaphor Wallace employs in his description of the second thread: the "lone gun." This image clearly connects to the analysis above of the cowboy drifter. It sets up a tension between the figure of the cowboy, understood as a predominantly solitary (itinerant and isolated) figure, and the communality of "being part of larger things" or being a "team player." The *cowboy of information* is therefore a figure who spans both of *The Pale King's* major arcs: he is somebody whose work involves rote, selective labor (examining tax returns), but he is also somebody who, in his isolated individualism, connects to the novel's political argument.

Much of the body of criticism on *The Pale King* can be understood as taking up one of the two arcs that Wallace describes. For the (generally earlier) wave of critics who concentrate on the first thread, the importance of tax accountancy lies in the nature of the labor it entails: accountants pay attention, they deal with often extreme levels of boredom, and they perform rote, repetitive tasks that draw comparison with (and potential competition from) automated processes. Let us refer to this as the *information* thread within Wallace criticism: criticism that takes as its focus the ways in which *The Pale King*'s accountants deal with information. In this vein, we can turn to critics cited above such as Conley Wouters and Stephen Burn, both of whom focus on the question of how to deal with overwhelming quantities of information.

Marshall Boswell, on the other hand, attends to the novel's second arc, reading *The Pale King* as an explicitly political book, and its focus on IRS accountants during the Reagan years as a way of critiquing the neoliberal erosion of civic responsibility evident in the transformation in the public perception of the IRS from an institution that forms an essential link between citizen and state to "the national symbol of the government as repressive parent that individualist Americans need to defy."[120] Boswell's essay presaged a second thread of *Pale King* criticism, which we can group together under the heading of *neoliberalism*: a term that is of course highly contested and difficult to pin down, but one that for these critics stands for a number of ideas, from individualism (the "lone gun"), to economic rationality and self-entrepreneurship, to the decline of organized labor and the rise of precarious jobs. In this vein, we can turn to Stephen Shapiro on the novel's exploration of "the simultaneous, but heterogeneous temporalities within capitalism," to David Hering on Wallace's shifting opinions regarding Ronald Reagan, or to Liam Connell on *The Pale King* as a critique of neoliberalism's forms of precarious and nonproductive labor.[121]

Thus, in the *information* thread, critics have analyzed tax accountants in terms of the material on which they work and the particular form that work takes. And in the *neoliberalism* thread, critics have moved from the micro- to the macro-level, analyzing accountants instead in terms of the diachronic shift in the political-economic relations under which they work: broadly speaking, from a postwar welfare state dependent on taxation as a means of redistribution to a post-Reagan neoliberal form of government, in which the IRS is understood as a corporation with the duty to maximize profits, and the state functions above all to prop up the functioning of the free market.[122] The point that critical work in both threads miss, however, is this: what is most important about *The Pale King* is not simply one arc or the other, but the relationship between them. The shift to what has come to be termed neoliberalism is not independent of the increase in importance of information-based work: it is the virtue of *The Pale King* that it makes the connection between these two developments, and it is the limitation of the bulk of the novel's criticism that it tends to focus on one development at the expense of the other. Why does *The Pale King* take accountants as its subject? Because it is accountants whose labor *and* political symbolism are paradigmatic of the historical moment whose origins Wallace traces in *The Pale King*, a historical moment characterized both by two related developments: the predominance of information-based work and the rise of neoliberalism.

What precisely is the nature of this connection between neoliberalism and information work? And why has this connection tended to be overlooked by critics of the novel? Wallace scholars are by no means alone in this tendency to read neoliberalism as primarily a question of ideology rather than of labor: that is, as a development characterized above all not by shifts in the relations and forces of production, but by the predominance of a free-market mindset, determining the operations of both the state and the individual subject, who, in the words of Wendy Brown, is cast "as human capital who must constantly tend to their own present and future value."[123] Brown's understanding of neoliberalism as a "governing rationality" centered on the sovereignty of the market draws largely on Foucault's widely influential series of lectures on *The Birth of Biopolitics*.[124] This is a common approach, and it is one that fits well with a reading of *The Pale King* that emphasizes the novel's tracing of the IRS's transformation from a bureaucratic organ of civic binding—what Wallace (cited above) called "being part of larger things"—to a quasi-corporation intent on "only one overriding operational question: Which returns are most profitable to audit, and how are those returns most efficiently to be found?"[125] However, my contention is that this kind of reading—of *The Pale King* and of neoliberalism—is a limited one, specifically insofar as it occludes the vital importance of a shift in the forms and organization of labor toward work based on *information* as inherently connected to—even formative of—the shift in "governing rationality" on which Brown focuses.

Rather than Brown's Foucauldian approach, I draw here on the work of scholars such as McKenzie Wark, Jasper Bernes, and Sianne Ngai, and (in Wallace Studies) Jeffrey Severs, and Richard Godden and Michael Szalay—scholars who are as attentive to developments in *techne* and in labor as they are to shifts in aesthetics and in ideology or, put more simply (though Bernes rejects such a simplified distinction), as attentive to base as to superstructure.[126] For Wark, the problem with Brown's Foucauldian approach is that it names neoliberalism as a phenomenon at the level of ideas—the market as "governing rationality"— without asking about the relationship between this ideal phenomenon and the material conditions under which it arose. In her critique of Foucault and Brown in *General Intellects*, she provides the following as "a sketch that makes sense of neoliberalism as effect rather than cause":

> It is no accident that neoliberalism has its moment in the postwar period, when the infrastructure of command and control through *information* that had developed during the war for managing complex systems was extended out of the military industrial complex into civilian industry ... The developed world became the overdeveloped world. Commodification ran up against the limits of what it could claim to organize efficiently or effectively. Whole chunks of social life had to be hacked off and fed into the flames to keep the steam up. Commodification moved on from land to things to *information*. A whole infrastructure grew, of information vectors, backed up by the growth of "intellectual property" into a comprehensive set of full private property rights.[127]

As far as Wark is concerned, Foucault's mistake is essentially the same as the mistake of those readers of *The Pale King* who focus on the neoliberalism thread while ignoring the information thread: both fail to apprehend the fact that neoliberalism is precisely a function of an economy based around information as the central commodity form.

In *A Hacker Manifesto* (2004), Wark puts forward an alternative story to Foucault's, one that focuses on development at the level of the material—in terms of property forms, class antagonisms, and labor—rather than the ideal. She sees the postwar economy of the Global North (to which she refers above, following Paul Gilroy, as "the overdeveloped world") as being characterized above all by a new dominant property form.[128] As she summarizes in the passage above: "Commodification moved on from land"—as in agrarian feudalism—"to things"—as in industrial capitalism—"to *information*." To this property form corresponds a new form of class struggle: *vectoralists*, rather than capitalists, control the means of production (the vectors of information: the material supports that "move information," from fiber optic cables to satellites) and exploit the productive labor of the *hacker* class.[129] And in this shift, the forms that labor takes too are subject to change. If the Fordist factory worker was the exemplary laborer of industrial capitalism, then in the new "vectoral economy," it is the computer hacker whose form of labor is paradigmatic.[130] And whereas the Fordist factory worker was engaged in a series of repetitive, assembly-line, physical actions that ultimately produced a material commodity—a car—Wark's hacker is someone whose labor, though it relies on material infrastructure and involves particular kinds of physical actions and tolerances, produces primarily immaterial forms: "the names and numbers," "relations, and relations of relations," "knowledge" and "distinctions."[131] The hacker's labor—information labor—looks less like factory labor and more like the labor of Wallace's accountants: dealing with massive quantities of data, assessing for relevance, and producing coherent and usable patterns of facts.

For Wark, it is only against this background that we can gain an adequate understanding of what has come to be termed neoliberalism. Neoliberalism for her is merely "a catch-all term for a collection of symptoms" of the fact that, as part of the developments described above, most professions in the overdeveloped world "have been redefined as kinds of information-work."[132] The material conditions that, from a Foucauldian perspective, could be read as effects of the ascendancy of a market-based rationality—flexible, precarious jobs and the decline of organized labor; increasing automation; massive corporate deregulation—are better understood, according to Wark, as the characteristics of a mode of production in which the central form of property is information.

In *The Work of Art in the Age of Deindustrialization* (2017), Jasper Bernes narrates the complex interplay between neoliberalism and information in slightly more detail and with particular attention to the role that art and literature play in this dynamic. For him, the best way of describing what Wark referred to as a shift in dominant property forms from capital to information is *deindustrialization*: a turn "from work based on making things or objects to work oriented around the performance of administrative and technical processes or the provision of services to customers."[133] Despite differences of terminology, though, Bernes and Wark share a great deal of common ground. Importantly, they both see "neoliberalism" (a word from which they both keep a degree of critical distance) as having its origins in the postwar shift toward (in Bernes's words) "intellectual work or symbol-based work," or what Wark calls information work.[134] Bernes understands this form of labor as taking symbols or language as its raw materials and applying to them "a series of techniques or processes: rearranging, sorting, cataloguing, parsing, transcribing, excerpting."[135] In an information economy, workers are asked "to treat written signs as a kind of *material* to be manipulated, processed, extracted, shaped, collated, cut and pasted, and transcribed, irrespective of its referential content."[136] What all of these verbs have in common, crucially, is that they are not *creative* in the standard sense of the term, but *selective*. They do not produce new things from scratch but rather manipulate existing things. And even more importantly, for our purposes, Bernes sees art during the same period as engaging in the same non-creative techniques—and doing so precisely in a dialectical relationship with these changes in the form of labor in general. That is to say, Bernes sees art as *responding* to changing conditions of labor, but he also sees labor as responding to art: it is postwar art, for him, that "provided tropes, motifs, and forms of articulation for a dissatisfaction" within the workplace and thereby helped consolidate a "qualitative critique" of labor conditions.[137] This critique, however—and here Bernes's argument coincides with Luc Boltanski and Eve Chiapello's in *The New Spirit of Capitalism* (1999)—ended up being co-opted by industry, thereby laying the groundwork for the kinds of restructuring (flexible jobs, for example) that come under the sign of neoliberalism.[138] To give one example, if 1960s art offered intellectual resources for labor activists, helping them to articulate their critique of centralized, hierarchical working structures, corporations responded not by resisting demands for self-directed work, but by acceding in such a way as to reduce their own administrative costs: "Self-managing workers who participate in managerial decisions require fewer supervisors, as long as one can find mechanisms to keep the productivity of such workers high."[139] For Bernes, therefore, art is not only conditioned by transformations in "the kinds of things people do for work."[140] It is also complicit in those transformations.

In this respect, Bernes's argument coincides with Sianne Ngai's in *Our Aesthetic Categories*. As discussed in Section 2.3, Ngai theorizes the *interesting* as "an aesthetic of difference as information," which emphasizes selection over creation.[141] What I did not explicitly address in that discussion, though, was Ngai's argument about the relationship between *interesting* art and its economic context. For her, the interesting is an aesthetic that is closely tied to the "information-saturated … conditions of late capitalism."[142] It is an artistic mode of response to economic conditions characterized by a rapid increase in the speed and volume in which information was being circulated: 1960s conceptual art, Ngai argues, was not only "increasingly information-based"; it "was both an instance of and an art about" the blurring of the lines between productive (creative) labor and circulatory (selective) labor (or what Wark calls information work).[143] Her characterization of conceptual art corresponds closely to Bernes's analysis of the same movement, as well as his description of the project of contemporary conceptual poetry as "a set of formal techniques for the management, indexing, and filtration of the unwieldy torrents of information we encounter each day."[144]

As should by now be clear, the arguments that Wark, Bernes, and Ngai make clearly echo the way in which Wallace, in *The Pale King*, characterizes the work of his accountants and the work of writing: all four thinkers are interested in information work, rather than (say) industrial work. And Wark, Bernes, and Ngai—the three theorists—all clearly share an understanding of the close connection between neoliberalism and information work—specifically, the idea that the phenomenon Brown and many others call "neoliberalism" has its genesis in the postwar shift toward an economy based on information as a form of property and as an object of labor. What I am arguing here is that, put simply, *The Pale King* gets this too—even if the body of criticism on the novel has tended to emphasize neoliberalism at the expense of information work or vice versa and has thereby obscured the fact that Wallace is interested precisely in the *connection between* these two phenomena. *The Pale King* understands that a good theory of neoliberalism must also address the question of the form of labor on which neoliberalism is based—which is also, then, to make another claim: that *The Pale King* is a *theory* of neoliberalism. In what sense can a novel be a theory?

3.2. Low Theory

The idea that a novel (or another literary form, such as Maggie Nelson's autotheoretical *The Argonauts*) can do the same kind of work as a text that explicitly claims the status of theory has been a key tenet of this study, in which I have read texts across multiple generic affiliations as contributing to the same theoretical debate about authorship, extending its wake over time and space. Returning to this idea here therefore makes for a fitting conclusion to the project.

In the case of *The Pale King*, I want to locate that methodological precept in relation to a specific intellectual genealogy, one that runs from Antonio Gramsci to Stuart Hall, and from there to Jack Halberstam and McKenzie Wark (which is also to say across Marxism, cultural studies, queer theory, and media theory). In a very particular sense, the kind of theoretical work that *The Pale King* does is, I want to suggest, the work of what Wark—following Halberstam, Hall, and Gramsci—calls *low theory*.

4. Labor

Perhaps more so even than "neoliberalism," "low theory" is a term that resists all-encompassing definitions. It emerges negatively, in opposition to high theory, but the distinction between the two can at times appear mostly rhetorical. Individual texts can flit between low and high modes (think of the stylistic ensemble of Black radical aesthetics and canonical poststructuralist texts in Fred Moten's *In the Break*, for example), and certain thinkers—Derrida, for example—are subject to competing claims: while for many he is an archetype of high theory, for others (like Moten) he is part of an altogether more radical, less elitist, and less white philosophical tradition.[145] But low theory's resistance to definitional enclosure is a productive one, rooted in low theory's wider commitment to openness. What Hall identifies as "low" in Gramsci's work is a conceptual orientation toward "the lower levels of historical concreteness" as opposed to the "exalted level" of abstract generality at which "high" theoretical concepts work.[146] For Hall and for Halberstam, this is a virtue: Gramsci "was aiming low in order to hit a broader target."[147] "Broader" here refers not so much to his concepts' *applicability*—high theory preserves its prestige in part by being so widely applicable, by "claiming to legislate for other domains of thought and practice"—as to their "accessibility."[148] Low theory aims at a "broader target" *readership* rather than at a broader range of objects to analyze. Where high theory as Halberstam characterizes it is rigorous, teleological, and large-scale, low theory is "adaptable," "open to unpredictable outcomes," and "antimonumental."[149] Low theory emerges in unexpected places, from "the 'silly' archives of animated film" that Halberstam mines in *The Queer Art of Failure* to the public toilet outside of which Wark recalls receiving a "soiled photocopy of a typescript" in "'pirate' translation, made by a self-described 'nasty street queen'"—her first introduction to the work of Foucault.[150] It refuses to engage in a pretense of impersonality, instead foregrounding its embeddedness in the lived experience of the body writing. This physicality connects low theory to a feminist tradition of theoretical writing that aims, in Sara Ahmed's words, to "do more" by getting "closer ... to the skin"—a tradition that spans not only the forebears whom Ahmed cites (bell hooks, Audre Lorde, and Gloria Anzaldúa) but also a number of Ahmed's contemporaries, such as Paul B. Preciado and Maggie Nelson.[151] Importantly (and as the examples of Anzaldúa and Nelson indicate), it often takes up practices that are explicitly aesthetic—thus opening up the possibility that a novel could be a vehicle for low theory.

The particular low-theoretical aesthetic tactic on which I want to focus here is one that Wark describes as follows: low theory "experimentally plays between metaphorical extensions from various forms of labor and science as they relate to the world right now"; it tests out these metaphors "as ways of understanding the big picture."[152] What is specifically *low* about this procedure is not merely the fact that it employs metaphor—in that sense, high theory too is prone to adopting aesthetic strategies. Rather, it is the specific manner in which such metaphors are employed: not so as to "subordinate all labors, particularly new and advanced kinds" under the master-signifier of one unchanging metaphor of labor (recall high theory's tendency to want to "legislate for other domains of thought and practice"), but proceeding "experimentally," playing with multiple metaphors at once, combining them in new and unexpected ways so as to open up new paths of thought and action.[153] Another way of putting this might be to say that low theory proceeds in the mode of *fiction*. (Recall Adam Phillips's characterization of Freud's and Winnicott's theories, quoted in Chapter 1: "useful fictions," which produce for the reader the possibility of a wider field of usefulness when read in excess of their literal meaning.[154])

Given the particular focus on metaphors of *labor*, it makes sense that most of the texts that adopt this particular low-theoretical strategy operate somewhere within what Wark refers to as the "Marx-field."[155] Michael Hardt and Antonio Negri, in fact, identify the practice with Marx himself, suggesting in *Multitude* (2004) that his focus on industrial labor is best understood as a way of drawing on a relatively new and at that point not yet quantitatively dominant form of work in order to shed light on the big picture of capitalism.[156] In their own work too, Hardt and Negri reject the idea of any "political priority among the forms of labor": no single metaphor legislates over all the rest.[157] Paul B. Preciado, who cites this same passage from *Multitude* in *Testo Junkie: Sex, Drugs, and Biopolitics in the Pharmacopornographic Era* (2008), makes a similar move, looking to the contemporary pornographic and pharmaceutical industries as two new forms of labor from which to extract fresh metaphors for understanding post-Fordist forces and relations of production.[158] And Wark, in both *A Hacker Manifesto* and *Gamer Theory* (2007), looks outside of the scope of activities traditionally designated as labor—to computer hacking and gaming—as further new metaphorical resources, in part so as to suggest that the form of activity that characterizes contemporary production might not even be best described under the sign of "labor" anymore.[159]

I want to close this chapter by reframing the argument I have made about *The Pale King* in relation to the central methodological principle of *Authorship's Wake*: the idea that theoretical arguments are not the exclusive domain of texts that would be categorized under the heading of "Critical Theory" or "Theory and Criticism" in a bookstore or course syllabus. In this chapter, I have argued that, in *The Pale King*, accountants, cowboys, and writers are three figures, operating at three different metaphorical levels and connecting with each other in multiple ways, which provide the basis for the novel's theory of the "big picture"—whether we call that big picture *neoliberalism* (Brown), the *vectoral economy* (Wark), *empire* (Hardt and Negri), the *pharmacopornographic era* (Preciado), or something else entirely. *The Pale King*, that is, is a work of *low theory*—or at least has as much claim to that title as Wark's *A Hacker Manifesto* or Preciado's *Testo Junkie*. That it is also a novel, a work of fiction, does not weaken that claim: fictionality, as Adam Phillips tells us, is a characteristic of much work that lacks the legal disclaimer that "the characters and events in this book are fictitious."[160] *The*

Pale King, in fact, includes that disclaimer only to explicitly deny it, claiming nonfictional status.[161] Wallace's (and Pietsch's) book is marked by a crisis of genre: its title page calls it an "unfinished novel," its putative author addresses the reader in §9 to tell them that "*The Pale King* is, in point of fact, more like a memoir than any kind of made-up story," and its critics have called it "an almanac, or a narrative compendium," or even an "antinovel."[162] Far from solving this crisis, this chapter has sought to make an additional claim: that *The Pale King* is also a work of theory.

CONCLUSION: STUDY GROUPS

Authorship's Wake has argued that the critical conversation about what it means to be an author, far from fading away, is more vital than ever—at least if we know where to look. I have sought to demonstrate that, even as "The Death of the Author" passes its fiftieth birthday, authorship remains a central issue in the work of contemporary writers who read Barthes's essay as students and then went on to grapple with its legacy in their work. In other words, the best contemporary theorists of authorship are writers who are primarily known as authors, rather than as theorists. Maggie Nelson is not only the author of a genre-queering nonfiction account of contemporary family-making; she is also a theorist of writing's fraught communicative ability. Zadie Smith is a theorist of the complexities of intentionality. Chris Kraus, Sheila Heti, and Ben Lerner are theorists of the relationship between authorship, gender, and political agency. David Foster Wallace is a theorist of writerly work and of labor more broadly. At the same time, I have argued that writer-thinkers whose work falls under the heading of "theory"—Roland Barthes, Judith Butler—can be most insightful when their writing least looks like theory: at its most anecdotal (Butler's story of a faculty meeting in *Precarious Life*), at its most inconsistent (Barthes's change of heart between his 1960s critique of the author and the Collège de France seminars at the end of the 1970s), at its most literary and novelistic.

The last chapter ended with an analysis of this proximity between literature and theory via the concept of "low theory," as it appears in the resolutely unconventional work of Antonio Gramsci, Stuart Hall, Jack Halberstam, and McKenzie Wark. There, I claimed that one particular attribute that affiliates *The Pale King* with the low theoretical tradition is the way it employs a particular form of work (for Wallace, accounting) as a metaphorical tactic for getting at a bigger picture of contemporary political economy. Here, I want to extend the claim I made at the close of that chapter: that all of the writers I have worked with in this study are best understood as doing something like low theory. Specifically, I want to focus on one further aspect that Wark and others have identified as a distinctive characteristic of low theory: its profoundly *collective* status. Whereas high theory, despite its anti-authorial rhetoric, can often end up reinforcing the myth of a singular authorial voice—the voice of the theorist himself, as a kind of Man Who Holds Forth in obscure yet deeply stylish prose—low theory emphasizes the embeddedness of theoretical knowledge in the social spaces of everyday life.[1]

In *Authorship's Wake*, my loyalties lie with the low over the high. This allegiance has informed my argument that theoretical knowledge can emerge from unanticipated sources and especially from close contact with lived experience: the experience of making a family in Chapter 1, or the experiences of running up against everyday patriarchy in Chapter 3, for example. But the arguments I have made in these chapters have also testified to the fact that the "sole author" leaves a long wake, one from which it is hard to remove oneself entirely. Even in an investigation of the contemporary echoes of a critique of the monotheistic doctrine of the singular author, I have for the most part retained an approach that focuses on singular authors. What I want to bring out here is what that kind of approach can all too easily elide: that truism of acknowledgments sections, that despite the single name on the title page, these books exist as a result of the work of the many, not just the one. Not (in Zadie Smith's words) "the sole author" so much as—in a phrase that I will spend some time unpacking—the *study group*.[2]

The way that I use the term "study" here comes primarily from Stefano Harney and Fred Moten's exploration of the term in *The Undercommons* (2013), though it also takes inspiration from work by thinkers such as Robin Kelley, Sara Ahmed, and Maggie Nelson. For Harney and Moten, "study" is a way of reorienting the way we think about intellectual activity. At one level, it is a way of refusing the university's exclusive claim over such activity. To think about study after Harney and Moten is to recognize that there is a whole lot of "common intellectual practice" taking place outside of (or perhaps under) the rigorously codified structures of university teaching.[3] Some of this is happening within the physical space of the university—which makes sense, because the university gathers together an enormous amount of intellectual and social resources in a single place—but it doesn't just happen during lectures and seminars, and it doesn't just take place in classrooms.[4] Study is inimical to the kinds of rigid hierarchical structures inherent in the teacher-student dynamic—the kinds of structures that Barthes, in Chapter 3, had such difficulty with. In a place of study, people might "take turns doing things for each other or for the others" rather than deferring to one person's authority.[5] The study group is no place for the figure that haunts Sheila Heti in *How Should a Person Be?*: the "man who wants to teach me something."[6]

"When I think of study," Harney says, "I'm as likely to think about nurses in the smoking room as I am about the university."[7] We could equally think of the picket line or the mass demonstration. Robin Kelley (whose thinking, like Moten's, has roots in a Black Studies tradition in the lineage of their teacher Cedric Robinson) argues that "social movements generate new knowledge, new theories, new questions."[8] That is, knowledge is generated not primarily within academic spaces as a theory to then be applied to life; rather, the theory springs from lived experience. Study, then, is a mode of living as much as a mode of thinking.

This sense of theory's rootedness in life is shared by Sara Ahmed. In *Living a Feminist Life* (2017), Ahmed takes inspiration from "writing in which an embodied experience of power provides the basis of knowledge": "texts by black feminists and feminists of color including Audre Lorde, bell hooks, and Gloria Anzaldúa."[9] Like other critics in this tradition—Saidiya Hartman, Christina Sharpe—Ahmed aims to "bring theory back to life" by getting "closer ... to the skin" rather than moving toward abstraction.[10] This is part of the reason why she suggests that "to become a feminist is to stay a *student*."[11] Feminist study for Ahmed—like Black study for Harney and Moten—means studious activity, but studious activity, crucially, that recognizes that knowledge is generated as much from everyday "embodied experience" and from conversations (Ahmed mentions the communications she has received from students via her blog, *Feminist Killjoys*) as from books and classrooms.[12]

To refer not just to study but to the study *group* is a way of emphasizing the sociality inherent to study—a way of emphasizing that, as Moten puts it, "study is what you do with other people."[13] It is important to point out here that those "other people" do not necessarily have to be there in the room with you. When Moten talks about study groups—as, for example, in the Acknowledgments to *In the Break*—he refers to the friends and comrades with whom he gets together in person—a "Jazz Study Group" based at Columbia University—but he also refers to those others with whom he shares a "sense of working together on a collective project," across disciplinary lines (Black Studies, performance studies, queer theory, film studies, English, sociology).[14] A study group could also include one's intellectual forebears, alive and dead—it could be understood, along the lines of Maggie Nelson's project in *The Argonauts*, as a form of queer family-making.[15] Nelson, adopting a phrase from the poet Dana Ward, refers to "the many gendered-mothers of my heart": a way of tracing a queer genealogy or even "cosmology" for oneself.[16] A study group could be a way of forming an "invisible community" when one lacks a tangible one: "Minus a community," Kate Zambreno writes in *Heroines* (2012), "I invented one": an invisible community full of "paper soulmates."[17] Writing can be social, even when one is entirely alone.

To call it a "study group" is also to attest to a level of informality, a degree of separation from institutional structures: it is a study group, among students, outside of class time, rather than a scheduled seminar with an (under)paid discussion leader. This is what Jack Halberstam gets at, in the preface to *The Undercommons*, when he describes study as "a mode of thinking with others separate from the thinking that the institution requires of you."[18] And study is therefore unconstrained by the institutionally policed borders between different spheres of knowledge. As McKenzie Wark says of the bibliography of Paul B. Preciado's low-/auto-theoretical *Testo Junkie*, "the reading list is determined by a need to live rather than disciplinary boundary keeping."[19] Hence, the study group does not—or should not—look anything like the "boring study groups on Jacques Lacan" that Chris says put her off "experimental film world feminism" in *I Love Dick*.[20] But it might look more like the "political study group" that was Robin Kelley's "lifeblood" as a student, which made him realize that it was possible (albeit difficult) to form "intellectual communities held together by principle and love" rather than performances of mastery and petty competitiveness.[21]

This brief overview has tried to communicate something of the vitality that results when one thinks about intellectual activity not in terms of sole authorship but in terms of group study. To some extent, this study has tried to adopt such an approach. "Study" consists partly in the recognition that theorizing is a practice that does not just take place inside the covers of an academic monograph, and by arguing that the best contemporary theories of authorship can be found in unexpected places like novels, creative nonfiction, and anecdotes, *Authorship's Wake* has proceeded from precisely this recognition. Moreover, by furthering the dialogue between Nelson and the many gendered-mothers of her heart, Chapter 1 sought to make visible the fact that writing is in a very real sense a "common intellectual practice."[22] This collective aspect to cultural production also makes its presence felt in the Wallace archives at the Harry Ransom Center, which I discussed in Chapter 4.

But I want to close by emphasizing how much more work remains in order truly to be able to think about cultural production as something that emerges from the social, sub-institutional intellectual activity of study groups, rather than springing fully formed from the mind of an Author-God. A number of recent books would form the beginning of a syllabus for such a project: not only *The Undercommons* and *Living a Feminist Life* but also Mark McGurl's literary history of creative writing programs in *The Program Era*, Chad Harbach's edited volume *MFA vs NYC* (written partly in response to McGurl), Amy Hungerford's Latourian study of the networks of literary production in *Making Literature Now*, and Angela McRobbie's critique of the creative economy in *Be Creative*. Such a syllabus might also venture further away from the canon of Western, contemporary post–death of the author writing to think about medieval theories of *auctoritas* as a version of authority derived divinely, collective and anonymous forms of authorship in Victorian England, or the community-based "storywork" of North American indigenous oral narrative practices.[23] What all of the above scholarship attests to, and what *Authorship's Wake* has confirmed, is this: the sole author continues to leave a vigorous and often violent wake behind him, but within that wake, there is a lot of intellectual activity going on—collective, informal, embodied, critical, vital, and awake.

ACKNOWLEDGMENTS

This study concludes with an attempt to think about intellectual activity not in terms of sole authorship but via the idea of the *study group*, a term I'm borrowing primarily from Fred Moten and Stefano Harney. *Authorship's Wake* is the result of many hours of solitary reading and writing (and among many things I owe Mari Ruti—mentorship, friendship, intellectual inspiration, travel plans, a great deal of time and funding—is the reminder that that's important too). But it also owes its existence to many intersecting study groups: formal and informal gatherings of different scales, formed of connections of many textures and with many types of co-students—from those I've only encountered in books, to those I've shared a classroom with, to the closest of personal ties. My thanks to the following study groups:

An incredible dissertation committee, smarter and more supportive than I could have hoped: my supervisor Mari Ruti, Michael Cobb, and Andrew DuBois.

A writing (and friendship) group worth holding on to: Joel Faber, Katherine Shwetz, and Adie Todd.

Reading groups across the University of Toronto (at the Department of English, the Mark S. Bonham Centre for Sexual Diversity Studies, the Centre for Comparative Literature, and the Department of Classics), especially the Contemporary Literature Reading Group: thanks in particular to Henry Ivry, Thom Dancer, Rijuta Mehta, and Avery Slater.

Classes that I've learned from, as instructor (gratitude to the students of Wild Theory in Summer 2017), as TA (every incarnation of Literature for Our Time: massive thanks to Denise Cruz, Nick Mount, and Miriam Novick), and as student.

The University of Toronto's English Department, which is too large for me to be able to name everyone in the department to whom I owe gratitude—friends, colleagues, mentors, administrative staff. Tremendous gratitude to everyone who has made it materially possible to be a graduate student in the humanities. For me, this has meant funding from the Ontario Trillium Scholarship, the Ontario Graduate Scholarship, the University of Toronto Fellowship, the Doctoral Completion Award, and more, as well as from RA work for Mari Ruti, Denise Cruz, Sara Salih, and Siobhan O'Flynn.

Massey College, for the home, conversation, and fellowship for three years and more.

Coworkers in Unit 1 of the Canadian Union of Public Employees branch 3902. Solidarity to everyone who participated in the 2015 Unit 1 strike.

The School of Criticism and Theory (SCT) at Cornell University's 2016 session, especially the participants in Renata Salecl's seminar. My thanks to the University of Toronto's Department of English for sponsoring my place at SCT.

Everyone who made possible the time I spent with the Harry Ransom Center's David Foster Wallace archives in December 2016. A Harry Ransom Center Dissertation Fellowship, supported by the Creekmore and Adele Fath Charitable Foundation and the University of Texas at Austin Office of Graduate Studies, provided funding for my research, as did the University of Toronto's Centre for the Study of the United States (special thanks to Alexandra Rahr) and School of Graduate Studies.

The conferences where I've presented early versions of many of the ideas that appear here, including the American Comparative Literature Association (thanks in particular to the participants in the 2018 panel on autotheory), LACK, OzWallace 2017, and the 2017 UWM Center for 21st Century Studies Conference. I am grateful for the various bodies that have helped fund travel to these conferences, including the Department of English, the School of Graduate Studies, the Mark S. Bonham Centre for Sexual Diversity Studies, and Massey College.

The scholars with whom I've worked as an editor since defending in 2018, especially Kevin Lewis O'Neill and Benjamin Fogarty-Valenzuela.

The editorial and production staff at Bloomsbury Academic as well as those who gave feedback on the manuscript during the process of turning this project from a dissertation into a book.

The thinkers, teachers, and writers whose words and ideas have formed my particular manner of thinking, whether they know it or not: Abdurraqib, Ahmed, Barthes, Batuman, Bukhari, Butler, Chariandy, Cole, Heti, Hudson, Kraus, Lacan, Lerner, Moten, Nelson, Ngai, Ruti, Sharpe, Smith, Solnit, Wallace, Wark.

Globe-spanning friendships with Paul Coulter, Mélissa Gelinas, Amanda Hsieh, Diana Leca, Ted Parker, Chiara Graf, and the Fitzwilliam/Ginsberg diaspora.

Globe-spanning family—above all, my parents.

The best partner in study and life: Tajja Isen.

NOTES

Introduction

1. Zadie Smith, *NW* (Toronto: Penguin, 2012), 3.
2. Smith, *NW*, 4.
3. Smith, *NW*, 3.
4. Smith, *NW*, 178.
5. Smith, *NW*, 209.
6. Smith, *NW*, 221.
7. Smith, *NW*, 212.
8. Smith, *NW*, 212.
9. Smith, *NW*, 332.
10. Smith, *NW*, 332.
11. Zadie Smith, *Changing My Mind: Occasional Essays* (London: Penguin, 2009), 42–57.
12. Judith Ryan, *The Novel after Theory* (New York: Columbia University Press, 2012), 23–49.
13. Benjamin Widiss, *Obscure Invitations: The Persistence of the Author in Twentieth-Century American Literature* (Stanford, CA: Stanford University Press, 2011), 110.
14. Nicholas Dames, "The Theory Generation," *n+1*, Summer 2012, 163.
15. Dames, "Theory Generation," 157.
16. Mitchum Huehls, "The Post-Theory Theory Novel," *Contemporary Literature* 56, no. 2 (2015): 283, https://doi.org/10.3368/cl.56.2.280.
17. Huehls, "Post-Theory Theory Novel," 286.
18. Huehls, "Post-Theory Theory Novel," 288.
19. Roland Barthes, *Image Music Text*, trans. Stephen Heath (London: Fontana Press, 1977), 143.
20. Barthes, *Image Music Text*, 146.
21. Widiss, *Obscure Invitations*, 5.
22. For example, Dames points out that "the realist novel … has comfortably swallowed [a] motley and daunting" list of ideas: "Associationist psychology (*Tristram Shandy*); evolutionary biology (*Middlemarch*, *Tess of the D'Urbervilles*); finance capitalism (*The Way We Live Now*, *JR*); psychoanalysis (*Confessions of Zeno*); post-Newtonian physics (*The Crying of Lot 49*)"; see Dames, "Theory Generation," 160.
23. Ryan, *Novel after Theory*, 7.
24. Mark McGurl, *The Program Era: Postwar Fiction and the Rise of Creative Writing* (Cambridge, MA: Harvard University Press, 2009), ix.
25. Lee Konstantinou also points out this absence in McGurl's book, with reference to Judith Ryan and Nicholas Dames, in *Cool Characters: Irony and American Fiction* (Cambridge, MA: Harvard University Press, 2016), 5. Though Konstantinou's

book focuses on irony rather than authorship, and it maintains the literature/theory distinction that I lay aside here, *Cool Characters* can be understood as engaged in a project complementary to my own. See also John Guillory, *Cultural Capital: The Problem of Literary Canon Formation* (Chicago: University of Chicago Press, 1993), 176–265; Theodore Martin, "Contemporary, Inc.," *Representations* 142, no. 1 (2018): 124–44, https://doi.org/10.1525/rep.2018.142.1.124.

26 Maggie Nelson, "CS671: Wild Theory," CalArts School of Critical Studies Course Catalog, Fall 2013, https://catalog.calarts.edu/Documents/School%20of%20Critical%20Studies%20-%20Fall%202013.pdf.

27 Katie R. Muth, "Postmodern Fiction as Poststructuralist Theory: Kathy Acker's *Blood and Guts in High School*," *Narrative* 19, no. 1 (2011): 104, https://doi.org/10.1353/nar.2011.0000. Muth's article, in a similar spirit to this study's project, argues for the importance of understanding Acker's novel as itself "an act of theorizing."

28 Barthes, *Image Music Text*, 142–8; Michel Foucault, "What Is an Author?" trans. Josué V. Harari, in *The Foucault Reader*, ed. Paul Rabinow (New York: Vintage Books, 2010), 101–20. For acknowledgments of these texts' centrality, see Andrew Bennett, *The Author* (London: Routledge, 2005), 11; Rebecca Moore Howard, "Foreword," in *Authorship Contested: Cultural Challenges to the Authentic, Autonomous Author*, ed. Amy E. Robillard and Ron Fortune (New York: Routledge, 2016), x; Sonja Longolius, *Performing Authorship: Strategies of "Becoming an Author" in the Works of Paul Auster, Candice Breitz, Sophie Calle, and Jonathan Safran Foer* (Bielefeld: Transcript, 2016), 20; Mark Rose, *Authors and Owners: The Invention of Copyright* (Cambridge, MA: Harvard University Press, 1993), 1.

29 On Barthes and Foucault, see Jane Gallop, *The Deaths of the Author: Reading and Writing in Time* (Durham, NC: Duke University Press, 2004), 2–4; Miriam Hannah Novick, "Impostures: Subjectivity, Memory, and Untruth in the Contemporary Memoir" (PhD dissertation, University of Toronto, 2015), 47–56; Widiss, *Obscure Invitations*, 3–12. On legal and book history approaches to authorship studies, see Rose, *Authors and Owners*; Martha Woodmansee, *The Author, Art, and the Market: Rereading the History of Aesthetics* (New York: Columbia University Press, 1994); Lior Zemer, *The Idea of Authorship in Copyright* (Abingdon, UK: Routledge, 2016).

30 For detailed readings of *Sade Fourier Loyola* and other 1970s work by Barthes in relation to "The Death of the Author," see Seán Burke, *The Death and Return of the Author: Criticism and Subjectivity in Barthes, Foucault and Derrida*, 3rd ed. (Edinburgh: Edinburgh University Press, 2008), 29–41, and Gallop, *Deaths of the Author*, 35–49. For a reading of *The Pleasure of the Text*'s representation of authorship, see Widiss, *Obscure Invitations*, 9–11.

31 As discussed in Chapter 4, *The Preparation of the Novel* refers to "The Death of the Author" as a symptom of a 1960s structuralist "tendency to erase the author in favor of the *Text*": see Roland Barthes, *The Preparation of the Novel: Lecture Courses and Seminars at the Collège de France (1978–1979 and 1979–1980)*, ed. Nathalie Léger, trans. Kate Briggs (New York: Columbia University Press, 2011), 208. For more on Barthes and nuance, see Philip Sayers, "Roland Barthes and the Urgency of Nuance," *Los Angeles Review of Books*, November 4, 2018, https://lareviewofbooks.org/article/roland-barthes-and-the-urgency-of-nuance/.

32 On literature's capacity for critique, see Anna Kornbluh, "We Have Never Been Critical: Toward the Novel as Critique," *Novel: A Forum on Fiction* 50, no. 3 (2017): 406–7, https://doi.org/10.1215/00295132-4195016.
33 David Marcus, for example, argues that "*NW* seeks to render not only the cognitive disorder of postmodern experience but also the social and psychological disorders of postmodern—that is, post-welfare state—capitalism"; see David Marcus, "Post-Hysterics: Zadie Smith and the Fiction of Austerity," *Dissent* 60, no. 2 (2013): 70, https://doi.org/10.1353/dss.2013.0035. For further political readings of *NW* see Tammy Amiel Houser, "Zadie Smith's NW: Unsettling the Promise of Empathy," *Contemporary Literature* 58, no. 1 (2017): 116–48; James Arnett, "Neoliberalism and False Consciousness before and after Brexit in Zadie Smith's NW," *The Explicator* 76, no. 1 (2018): 1–7, https://doi.org/10.1080/00144940.2017.1416329.
34 Zadie Smith, *Feel Free: Essays* (New York: Hamish Hamilton, 2018), 250.
35 Philip Hensher's review of *NW* for *The Daily Telegraph* cites Thatcher's assertion: "'There is no such thing as society,' Mrs Thatcher said. 'There are individual men and women, and there are families.' There is such a thing as society in *NW*, but it's the result of millions of individual lives, and the individual's responsibility to take charge." Philip Hensher, "NW by Zadie Smith: Review," *The Daily Telegraph*, September 3, 2012, https://www.telegraph.co.uk/culture/books/9508844/NW-by-Zadie-Smith-review.html.
36 Ato Quayson, *Postcolonialism: Theory, Practice or Process?* (Cambridge: Polity Press, 2000), 9.
37 Elizabeth Freeman, *Time Binds: Queer Temporalities, Queer Histories* (Durham, NC: Duke University Press, 2010), 3.
38 Lee Edelman, *No Future: Queer Theory and the Death Drive* (Durham, NC: Duke University Press, 2004), 2.
39 Saidiya Hartman, *Lose Your Mother: A Journey along the Atlantic Slave Route* (New York: Farrar, Straus and Giroux, 2007), 6.
40 Dionne Brand, *A Map to the Door of No Return: Notes to Belonging* (Toronto: Vintage Canada, 2001), 25.
41 Fred Moten, *In the Break: The Aesthetics of the Black Radical Tradition* (Minneapolis: University of Minnesota Press, 2003), 99.
42 Jedediah Purdy, *After Nature: A Politics for the Anthropocene* (Cambridge, MA: Harvard University Press, 2015), 6, 3. With the phrase "we have never been postcolonial," I allude to another influential work of contemporary theory that troubles normative chronology: Bruno Latour, *We Have Never Been Modern*, trans. Catherine Porter (Cambridge, MA: Harvard University Press, 1993). Anthropologist Akhil Gupta draws the same connection: "One could, borrowing a formulation from Bruno Latour, argue that *we have never been postcolonial*: poverty has not been eradicated because the state has continued to function much as the colonial one did, and neoliberalism has succeeded only in bringing to India new forms of empire and neocolonialism"; see Akhil Gupta, *Red Tape: Bureaucracy, Structural Violence, and Poverty in India* (Durham, NC: Duke University Press, 2012), 23; emphasis added. Latour's argument that the distinction between nature and culture is untenable is also echoed to some extent in *After Nature* and in Anthropocene scholarship more broadly.

43 Jeffrey T. Nealon, *Post-Postmodernism: Or, the Cultural Logic of Just-in-Time Capitalism* (Stanford, CA: Stanford University Press, 2012), x–xi.
44 Stephen J. Burn, *Jonathan Franzen at the End of Postmodernism* (London: Bloomsbury Academic, 2008), 19–26. For overviews of the after postmodernism conversation, see Mary K. Holland, *Succeeding Postmodernism: Language and Humanism in Contemporary American Literature* (New York: Bloomsbury Academic, 2013), 11–15; Adam Kelly, *American Fiction in Transition: Observer-Hero Narrative, the 1990s, and Postmodernism* (New York: Bloomsbury Academic, 2013), 4–7; Wolfgang Funk, *The Literature of Reconstruction: Authentic Fiction in the New Millennium* (London: Bloomsbury Academic, 2015), 3.
45 Holland, *Succeeding Postmodernism*, 16.
46 Jane Elliott, "The Return of the Referent in Recent North American Fiction: Neoliberalism and Narratives of Extreme Oppression," *Novel: A Forum on Fiction* 42, no. 2 (2009): 351, https://doi.org/10.1215/00295132-2009-026; Jeffrey T. Nealon, "Realisms Redux; or, Against Affective Capitalism," in *Neoliberalism and Contemporary Literary Culture*, ed. Mitchum Huehls and Rachel Greenwald Smith (Baltimore: Johns Hopkins University Press, 2017), 77. Elliott's formulation is one possible choice among several. She cites Rey Chow's expression "the bracketing of referentiality" as one name for the same approach (Elliott, "Return of the Referent," 350–1). Jeffrey Nealon draws on the thinking of language poet Lyn Hejinian and mentions her phrase "the rejection of closure" as another (Nealon, "Realisms Redux," 75).
47 Nealon, "Realisms Redux," 75.
48 For another literary instance, see Nealon: "Think, for example, of Charlie Altieri's sense, in his 1970s essays on postmodern poetry, that an emphasis on the local, the idiomatic, and the affective was taken up by poets as a kind of critique of capitalism, which by extension wants to flatten out complexity and thereby standardize, rationalize, and commodify our lives" ("Realisms Redux," 75).
49 Elliott, "Return of the Referent," 352.
50 Nealon, "Realisms Redux," 72.
51 Mitchum Huehls, *After Critique: Twenty-First-Century Fiction in a Neoliberal Age* (New York: Oxford University Press, 2016), 31.
52 Nealon, "Realisms Redux," 77–9. For a related argument, see Walter Benn Michaels, who argues in *The Beauty of a Social Problem* (2015) that art that celebrates its own indeterminacy and the irrelevance of authorial intention is especially vulnerable to capitalist commodification; see Walter Benn Michaels, *The Beauty of a Social Problem: Photography, Autonomy, Economy* (Chicago: University of Chicago Press, 2015), 100–3. For Michaels, the most politically effective art being made today rejects the twentieth-century critique of intention and autonomy and insists instead on its own aesthetic meaningfulness (xi–xii).
53 Jason Potts and Daniel Stout, eds., *Theory Aside* (Durham, NC: Duke University Press, 2014), 8, 13.
54 Potts and Stout, eds., *Theory Aside*, 13.
55 Janet Halley and Andrew Parker, eds., *After Sex? On Writing since Queer Theory* (Durham, NC: Duke University Press, 2011), 4.
56 Halley and Parker, eds., *After Sex?* 49.
57 Halley and Parker, eds., *After Sex?* 80.

58 Halley and Parker, eds., *After Sex?* 80.
59 The title of this introduction—"Words Streaming in Your Wake"—is a quotation from Maggie Nelson, *The Argonauts* (Minneapolis, MN: Graywolf Press, 2015). It is from a passage in which Nelson addresses her partner Harry: "And you—whatever you argued, you never mimed a constricted throat. In fact you ran at least a lap ahead of me, words streaming in your wake. How could I ever catch up (by which I mean, *how could you want me?*)" (4; emphasis in original). The primary sense of the word "wake" that is at play here is the first—a disturbance spreading behind a moving object—but Nelson here also gets at the connection between afterness and desire, and indeed the connection between writing and the wake.
60 Barbara Johnson, *The Wake of Deconstruction* (Oxford: Blackwell, 1994), 102.
61 Christina Sharpe, *In the Wake: On Blackness and Being* (Durham, NC: Duke University Press, 2016), 14, 19.
62 Sharpe, *In the Wake*, 14, 115. For further dissections of the multiple senses of the word "wake," see Colin Davis, *After Poststructuralism: Reading, Stories, Theory* (London: Routledge, 2004), 172–3; Srinivas Aravamudan, "In the Wake of the Novel: The Oriental Tale as National Allegory," *Novel* 33, no. 1 (1999): 5–6, https://doi.org/10.2307/1346025.
63 Johnson, *Wake of Deconstruction*, 102.
64 At the beginning of the introduction to *Testo Junkie*, Paul B. Preciado writes: "This book is not a memoir. This book is a testosterone-based, voluntary intoxication protocol, which concerns the body and affects of BP [*Beatriz Preciado*]. A body-essay. Fiction, actually. If things must be pushed to the extreme, this is a somato-political fiction, a theory of the self, or self-theory [*autoteoría*]"; see Paul B. Preciado, *Testo Junkie: Sex, Drugs, and Biopolitics in the Pharmacopornographic Era*, trans. Bruce Benderson (New York: The Feminist Press, 2013), 11. Nelson cited this passage in interviews around the release of *The Argonauts*; see Maggie Nelson, "Riding the Blinds," interview by Micah McCrary, *The Los Angeles Review of Books*, April 26, 2015, https://lareviewofbooks.org/interview/riding-the-blinds/; Maggie Nelson, "Bookforum talks with Maggie Nelson," interview by Sarah Nicole Prickett, *Bookforum*, May 29, 2015, http://www.bookforum.com/interview/14663. The term "autotheory" has since come to be widely adopted to refer to an array of (especially queer and feminist) texts that blend the autobiographical and the theoretical; see Robyn Wiegman, "In the Margins with *The Argonauts*," *Angelaki* 23, no. 1 (2018): 209–13, https://doi.org/10.1080/0969725X.2018.1435403; Mari Ruti, *Penis Envy and Other Bad Feelings: The Emotional Costs of Everyday Life* (New York: Columbia University Press, 2018), xxxi; Jordan Alexander Stein, "Jordan Alexander Stein in Conversation with Jordy Rosenberg," *Social Text Online*, July 3, 2018, https://socialtextjournal.org/jordan-alexander-stein-in-conversation-with-jordy-rosenberg/.
65 Barthes, *Image Music Text*, 148, 146.
66 For the most comprehensive selection of theories of authorship, see Seán Burke, ed., *Authorship: From Plato to the Postmodern: A Reader* (Edinburgh: Edinburgh University Press, 1995).
67 Barthes, *Image Music Text*, 146.
68 Johnson, Wake of Deconstruction, 17.

69 Smith, *Changing My Mind*, 56
70 Nelson, *The Argonauts*, 97.
71 Adam Phillips, *Winnicott* (London: Penguin, 2007), x.
72 Smith, *Changing My Mind*, xi.

Chapter 1

Epigraph: Zadie Smith, *Changing My Mind: Occasional Essays* (London: Penguin, 2009), 56.

1   Smith, *Changing My Mind*, 43, 56.
2   Smith, *Changing My Mind*, 56.
3   Phillips, *Winnicott*, x.
4   Maggie Nelson, *Bluets* (Seattle, WA: Wave Books, 2009), 41.
5   Janet Gurkin Altman, *Epistolarity: Approaches to a Form* (Columbus, OH: Ohio State University Press, 1982), 4.
6   See Linda S. Kauffman, *Special Delivery: Epistolary Modes in Modern Fiction* (Chicago: University of Chicago Press, 1992).
7   Altman, *Epistolarity*, 117. For more detailed overviews of the most frequently discussed characteristics of the epistolary mode, see Liz Stanley, "The Epistolary Gift, the Editorial Third-Party, Counter-Epistolaria: Rethinking the Epistolarium," *Life Writing* 8, no. 2 (2011): 135–6; David Barton and Nigel Hall, *Letter Writing as a Social Practice* (Philadelphia: John Benjamin, 1999), 6.
8   Jacques Derrida, *The Post Card: From Socrates to Freud and Beyond*, trans. Alan Bass (Chicago: University of Chicago Press, 1987).
9   Stanley, "The Epistolary Gift," 136; Margaretta Jolly, *In Love and Struggle* (New York: Columbia University Press, 2008), 3.
10 Jolly, *In Love and Struggle*, 79.
11 Jolly, *In Love and Struggle*, 84–5. Relationality in *The Argonauts* is not figured as specifically feminine. This has partly to do with the book's subject matter—specifically, its focus on the fluidity of gender—and partly to do with Nelson's intellectual context. She engages frequently with Butler, whose theorization of relationality as a fundamental condition of the human subject regardless of (and prior to) gender she cites: "we are for *another or* by virtue of *another*, not in a single instance, but from the start and always"; see Nelson, *Argonauts*, 60. Nelson is quoting from Judith Butler, *Precarious Life: The Powers of Mourning and Violence* (London: Verso, 2004), 24.
12 Nelson, *Bluets*, 71.
13 Smith, *Changing My Mind*, 56.
14 See William Merrill Decker, *Epistolary Practices: Letter Writing in America before Telecommunications* (Chapel Hill: University of North Carolina Press, 1998), 4; Jolly, *In Love and Struggle*, 6.
15 This is an idea Altman alludes to at the very end of her study, writing that "there is a very real sense in which [epistolary literature] metaphorically 'represents' literature as a whole" (*Epistolarity*, 212).
16 Kauffman, *Special Delivery*, xiii.

17 See Maggie Nelson, "Riding the Blinds," interview by Micah McCrary, *The Los Angeles Review of Books*, April 26, 2015, https://lareviewofbooks.org/interview/riding-the-blinds/; Maggie Nelson, "Bookforum Talks with Maggie Nelson," interview by Sarah Nicole Prickett, *Bookforum*, May 29, 2015, http://www.bookforum.com/interview/14663.
18 Nancy K. Miller, *Getting Personal: Feminist Occasions and Other Autobiographical Acts* (New York: Routledge, 1991), 1. Nelson thanks Miller in the acknowledgments of her 2009 critical work *Women, The New York School, and Other True Abstractions* (Iowa City: University of Iowa Press, 2007), vii.
19 Maggie Nelson, "CS671: Wild Theory," CalArts School of Critical Studies Course Catalog, Fall 2013, https://catalog.calarts.edu/Documents/School%20of%20Critical%20Studies%20-%20Fall%202013.pdf.
20 Nelson, "Riding the Blinds."
21 In an interview with *Guernica* magazine, Nelson says: "I think of the unit of this book as anecdote": see Ariel Lewiton, "Inflections Forever New," *Guernica*, March 16, 2015, https://www.guernicamag.com/interviews/inflections-forever-new/.
22 Miller, *Getting Personal*, 7.
23 Miller, *Getting Personal*, 14; emphasis added. See also Elizabeth Goldsmith, *Writing the Female Voice: Essays on Epistolary Literature* (Boston, MA: Northeastern University Press, 1989), x.
24 Nelson, *Argonauts*, 60.
25 Barthes, *Image Music Text*, 142.
26 Chloe Caldwell, "Author Maggie Nelson on Fielding Nosy Questions about Queer Families: 'You Have to Be Tough and Foxy,'" *Salon*, May 8, 2015, http://www.salon.com/2015/05/08/author_maggie_nelson_on_fielding_nosy_questions_about_queer_families_you_have_to_be_tough_and_foxy%e2%80%9d/.
27 Judith Butler, *Senses of the Subject* (New York: Fordham University Press, 2015), 12.
28 Luce Irigaray, *To Be Two*, trans. Monique M. Rhodes and Marco F. Cocito-Monoc (New York: Routledge, 2001), 9–10.
29 Altman, *Epistolarity*, 117.
30 Coates draws formal inspiration from James Baldwin's *The Fire Next Time* (1963), which begins with a letter to the writer's nephew. The question of audience has drawn particular attention in the reception of *Between the World and Me*. Coates held the book's release event at Baltimore's Union Baptist Church, telling *The New York Times*, "It was very, very important, as far as I was concerned, that the book be launched in an African-American space … I wanted to be very clear about who the book was written for": that is, not just Samori specifically, but (metonymically) African-Americans generally; see Jennifer Schuessler, "Ta-Nehisi Coates's 'Visceral' Take on Being Black in America," *The New York Times*, July 17, 2015, http://www.nytimes.com/2015/07/18/books/ta-nehisi-coatess-visceral-take-on-being-black-in-america.html. In a widely criticized opinion piece, David Brooks expressed his discomfort at "Listening to Ta-Nehisi Coates While White"—at reading a text figured as a letter addressed to someone other than him and written for a racial group other than his own; see David Brooks, "Listening to Ta-Nehisi Coates While White," *The New York Times*, July 17, 2015, https://www.nytimes.com/2015/07/17/opinion/listening-to-ta-nehisi-coates-while-white.html; David Palumbo-Liu, "The Cult of White Liberal Race-Deniers:

David Brooks, Sandra Bland and Race Denying at Its Worst," *Salon*, July 21, 2015, http://www.salon.com/2015/07/21/the_cult_of_white_liberal_race_deniers_david_brooks_letter_to_ta_nehisi_coates_shows_race_denying_at_its_worst/; Emily M. Keeler, "Dear David Brooks," *National Post*, July 22, 2015, http://news.nationalpost.com/arts/books/dear-david-brooks. For an extended consideration of how *Between the World and Me* (alongside Elena Ferrante's Neapolitan series) deals with the difficulties of communication, see Jedediah Purdy's "Maybe Connect," which argues (along similar lines to my own argument in this chapter) that "to connect by enumerating all that makes connecting difficult, leaving the reader still frightened and baffled, but less alone for understanding it … is to succeed at writing"; *The Los Angeles Review of Books*, October 4, 2015, https://lareviewofbooks.org/essay/maybe-connect/.

31 Stanley, "The Epistolary Gift," 144.
32 There are, of course, exceptions. As discussed in Chapter 2, social media today makes dialogue between reader and author a very real possibility, just as nineteenth-century writers from George Eliot to George Sand corresponded at length with their readers; see Smith, *Changing My Mind*, 33; Walter Benjamin, *The Arcades Project*, ed. Rolf Tiedemann, trans. Howard Eiland and Kevin McLaughlin (Cambridge, MA: Belknap Press, 2002), 758. In literary scenes throughout history (the Beats, for example), writers have maintained a dialogue with each other in their published work. And in the context of queer feminist personal criticism, Eve Sedgwick—discussed frequently in *The Argonauts*—has talked about her wish for her writing to provoke written responses; see Miller, *Getting Personal*, 24. For discussions of Sedgwick, see Nelson, *Argonauts*, 28–30, 62, 74, 80, 84, 87, 93, 102–5, 111–14, 116, 122–3.
33 Caldwell, "Author Maggie Nelson"; Gillian Beer, "The Reader as Author," *Authorship* 3, no. 1 (2014): 3.
34 Nelson, *Bluets*, 71.
35 See Burke, *Death and Return*, 286.
36 Nelson, *Argonauts*, v, 3.
37 Nelson, *Argonauts*, 142–3.
38 Nelson, *Argonauts*, 129–34.
39 Nelson, *Argonauts*, 76. See André Breton, *Mad Love*, trans. Mary Ann Caws (Lincoln: University of Nebraska Press, 1987), 111, 112.
40 Nelson, *Argonauts*, 142.
41 Nelson, *Argonauts*, 76.
42 Nelson, *Argonauts*, 76. For examples of Breton's "hetero romanticism," see his description of "the eternal power of woman" as "the only power I have ever submitted to"; Breton, *Mad Love*, 112.
43 Breton, *Mad Love*, 111.
44 Nelson, *Argonauts*, 141.
45 Nelson, *Argonauts*, 37. On holding as an act of care, see also 33, 45, 46, 64, 92, 142.
46 Nelson, *Argonauts*, 141.
47 Nelson, *Argonauts*, 5.
48 Roland Barthes, "Lecture in Inauguration of the Chair of Literary Semiology, Collège de France, January 7, 1977," trans. Richard Howard, *October* 8 (1979): 5; emphasis added.
49 Barthes, "Lecture," 5; emphasis added.

50 Barthes, "Lecture," 5. See also Nicholas De Villiers, "A Great Pedagogy of Nuance: Roland Barthes's The Neutral," *Theory & Event* 8, no. 4 (2005); Andy Stafford, *Roland Barthes*, Critical Lives (London: Reaktion Books, 2015), 124–5.
51 See Louis Althusser, "Ideology and Ideological State Apparatuses (Notes towards an Investigation)," in *Lenin and Philosophy and Other Essays*, trans. Ben Brewster (New York: Monthly Review Press, 2001), 85–126. My characterization of Althusser's argument here draws—as, I think, does Nelson's—on Judith Butler; see Judith Butler, *The Psychic Life of Power: Theories in Subjection* (Stanford, CA: Stanford University Press, 1997), 106–31. Butler is an important interlocutor in *The Argonauts*: see 14–15, 53–4, 59–60, 102.
52 Nelson, *Argonauts*, 95.
53 Butler, *Psychic Life of Power*, 117.
54 Roland Barthes, *The Neutral: Lecture Course at the Collège de France (1977–1978)*, ed. Thomas Clerc and Éric Marty, trans. Rosalind E. Krauss and Denis Hollier (New York: Columbia University Press, 2005), 41–2. *The Neutral* is another key point of reference for Nelson: see Nelson, *Argonauts*, 112; *The Art of Cruelty: A Reckoning* (New York: W. W. Norton, 2011), 13–14.
55 Nelson, *Argonauts*, 48.
56 See also Slavoj Žižek, *The Parallax View* (Cambridge, MA: MIT Press, 2006), 381–5.
57 Christina Luckyj, *"A Moving Rhetoricke": Gender and Silence in Early Modern England* (Manchester: Manchester University Press, 2002), 95; Barthes, "Lecture," 5. Ahmed is another of Nelson's interlocutors in *The Argonauts* (17, 18). *Willful Subjects* analyzes figures (usually coded feminine) who, like Cordelia, do not comply with authority and whose refusal to do so compromises their "capacity … to survive"; Sara Ahmed, *Willful Subjects* (Durham, NC: Duke University Press, 2014), 1. Luckyj, on the other hand, reads Cordelia's non-compliance as a claim "to silent masculine agency" that "trigger's Lear's fears" (*Moving Rhetoricke*, 99).
58 Lisa Jardine, *Still Harping on Daughters: Women and Drama in the Age of Shakespeare* (Brighton, UK: The Harvester Press, 1983), 108.
59 Nelson, *Argonauts*, 105.
60 Eve Kosofsky Sedgwick, *Touching Feeling: Affect, Pedagogy, Performativity* (Durham, NC: Duke University Press, 2003), 130.
61 Sedgwick, *Touching Feeling*, 146.
62 Sedgwick, *Touching Feeling*, 146.
63 Luckyj, *Moving Rhetoricke*, 97. See Cordelia's aside in line 59 of the Folio: "What shall Cordelia *speak*? Love and be silent"; William Shakespeare, "The Tragedy of King Lear: The Folio Text," in *The Norton Shakespeare Based on the Oxford Edition*, ed. Stephen Greenblatt et al. (New York: W. W. Norton, 1997), I.I.59; emphasis added.
64 See also Barthes, *Neutral*, 69: "Silence: becomes, willing or not, its own sign."
65 Lewiton, "Inflections Forever New."
66 Nelson, *Argonauts*, 3.
67 Paul Engelmann, *Letters from Ludwig Wittgenstein with a Memoir*, ed. B. F. McGuinness, trans. L. Furtmüller (Oxford: Basil Blackwell, 1967), 7.
68 Ludwig Wittgenstein, "Tractatus Logico-Philosophicus," in *Major Works: Selected Philosophical Writings*, trans. C. K. Ogden (New York: Harper Perennial, 2009), section 7.

69   Wittgenstein, "Tractatus," Preface.
70   Wittgenstein, "Tractatus," 6.54.
71   Wittgenstein, "Tractatus," 4.111–12.
72   Engelmann, *Letters from Ludwig Wittgenstein*, 7; italics in original, underlining added.
73   Engelmann, *Letters from Ludwig Wittgenstein*, 84n1.
74   Engelmann, *Letters from Ludwig Wittgenstein*, 83n1.
75   Wittgenstein, "Tractatus," 2.202.
76   Wittgenstein, "Tractatus," 2.22.
77   Wittgenstein, "Tractatus," Preface.
78   Wittgenstein, "Tractatus," 1.1.
79   Wittgenstein, "Tractatus," 4.024.
80   Phillips, *Winnicott*, x. See also Nelson, *Women and the New York School*, 193; *Art of Cruelty*, 267–8.
81   Adam Phillips, *Darwin's Worms: On Life Stories and Death Stories* (New York: Basic Books, 2000), 74; *Terrors and Experts* (Cambridge, MA: Harvard University Press, 1995), 34.
82   Wittgenstein, "Tractatus," 1.1.
83   Wittgenstein, "Tractatus," 6.37.
84   Phillips, *Winnicott*, ix.
85   Phillips, *Winnicott*, x.
86   Smith, *Changing My Mind*, 56.
87   Wittgenstein, "Tractatus," 6.53.
88   Wittgenstein, "Tractatus," 6.53.
89   Engelmann, *Letters from Ludwig Wittgenstein*, 7.
90   Wittgenstein, "Tractatus," 6.54.
91   Wittgenstein, "Tractatus," 6.53.
92   In a letter to his publisher, Wittgenstein wrote that "the sense of the book is an ethical one"; see Alfred Nordmann, *Wittgenstein's Tractatus: An Introduction* (Cambridge: Cambridge University Press, 2005), 48. The fact that Wittgenstein has had such a wide influence in both literature—David Markson's *Wittgenstein's Mistress* (1988) being perhaps the most famous example; Wittgenstein is also a major presence in Wallace's first novel, *The Broom of the System*, published a year earlier—and other media (see Derek Jarman's 1993 film *Wittgenstein*) is one indicator of his work's aesthetic resonances. Marjorie Perloff has also written on the literariness of Wittgenstein's writing itself; see *Wittgenstein's Ladder: Poetic Language and the Strangeness of the Ordinary* (Chicago: University of Chicago Press, 1999).
93   See Nordmann, *Wittgenstein's Tractatus*, 212.
94   Nelson, *Argonauts*, 76.
95   Nelson, *Argonauts*, 3.
96   Nelson, *Art of Cruelty*, 105–6.
97   Smith, *Changing My Mind*, 56.
98   Barthes, *Neutral*, 18.
99   Barthes, *Neutral*, 108.
100 Nelson, *Art of Cruelty*, 109.
101 Barthes, *Neutral*, 18.
102 Nelson, *Argonauts*, 76.

103 Irigaray, *To Be Two*, 4.
104 Irigaray, *To Be Two*, 9.
105 Irigaray, *To Be Two*, 17, 35, 42; emphasis added.
106 Irigaray, *To Be Two*, 49.
107 Judith Butler, *Frames of War: When Is Life Grievable?* (London: Verso, 2009), 77.
108 Irigaray, *To Be Two*, 9.
109 Irigaray, *To Be Two*, 116.
110 In the final chapter of *Entre Nous*, Levinas, discussing Vasily Grossman's *Life and Fate* (1959), suggests that "the face can assume meaning on what is the 'opposite of the face'": in the case of a passage from Grossman's novel, "the nape of the person in front of [one]"; see Emmanuel Levinas, *Entre Nous: On Thinking-of-the-Other*, trans. Michael B. Smith and Barbara Harshav (New York: Columbia University Press, 1998), 232.
111 Irigaray, *To Be Two*, 49.
112 Nelson, *Art of Cruelty*, 105–6; Barthes, *Neutral*, 18; Irigaray, *To Be Two*, 27; Smith, *Changing My Mind*, 43.
113 Smith, *Changing My Mind*, 56.
114 Nelson, *Art of Cruelty*, 109; Smith, *Changing My Mind*, 56.
115 Adam Phillips, *Missing Out: In Praise of the Unlived Life* (New York: Picador, 2012), 61; emphasis added.
116 Andrew DuBois explores how the readers of Ashbery's poetry are "faced with a crisis of attention" in *Ashbery's Forms of Attention* (Tuscaloosa: The University of Alabama Press, 2006), xvi. In a different context—his novel *Leaving the Atocha Station*—Ben Lerner also considers the way in which "Ashbery's poems allow you to attend to your attention"; see *Leaving the Atocha Station* (Minneapolis, MN: Coffee House Press, 2011), 91. What DuBois and Lerner both suggest is that Ashbery's difficulty shifts the burden of understanding on to the reader, in a manner that can have the effect of thematizing the reader's attention, but can also risk losing it.
117 Nelson, *Argonauts*, 47.
118 Nelson, *Art of Cruelty*, 107.
119 Nelson, *Argonauts*, 45–7.
120 Nelson, *Art of Cruelty*, 146–7.
121 Nelson, *Argonauts*, 97.
122 Nelson, *Argonauts*, 102.
123 Nordmann, *Wittgenstein's Tractatus*, 200; emphasis added.
124 Ben Segal, "The Fragment as a Unit of Prose Composition: An Introduction," *Continent* 1, no. 3 (2011): 160–1.
125 Nelson, *Argonauts*, 52.
126 Nelson, *Argonauts*, 97–8.
127 Nelson, *Argonauts*, 98; Roland Barthes, *Roland Barthes by Roland Barthes*, trans. Richard Howard (New York: Hill and Wang, 2010), 48.
128 Barthes, *Roland Barthes*, 148.
129 Michael Silverblatt, "Maggie Nelson: The Argonauts," *KCRW's Bookworm*, June 10, 2015.
130 Nelson, *Argonauts*, 72.
131 Silverblatt, "Maggie Nelson."
132 Nelson, *Argonauts*, 57.

133 See also Katie Collins, "The Morbidity of Maternity: Radical Receptivity in Maggie Nelson's The Argonauts," *Criticism* 6, no. 3 (2019): 311–34, https://doi.org/10.13110/criticism.61.3.0311; Mollie Ann Kervick, "Embracing Maternal Eroticism: Queer Experiences of Pleasure in Maggie Nelson's The Argonauts," *Feminist Encounters: A Journal of Critical Studies in Culture and Politics* 3, no. 1–2 (2019): 1–10, https://doi.org/10.20897/femenc/5914.

134 Nelson, *Argonauts*, 100. On maternity and art and theory, see 41–2, 71; on maternity and radical queer politics, see 13, 75.

135 Nelson, *Argonauts*, 37.

136 Nelson, *Argonauts*, 99.

137 Nelson, *Argonauts*, 3.

138 Breton, *Mad Love*, 119; lineation added; Nelson, *Argonauts*, 142; underlined sections indicate the words Nelson takes from Breton.

139 Nelson, *Argonauts*, 76.

140 Nelson, *Argonauts*, 76.

Chapter 2

Epigraph: Zadie Smith, *Changing My Mind: Occasional Essays* (London: Penguin, 2009), 56.

1 Teju Cole, *Every Day Is for the Thief* (New York: Random House, 2014); Teju Cole, *Known and Strange Things: Essays* (New York: Random House, 2016), 89. For the reception of Cole's short story "Hafiz"—published on Twitter via collaboration in January 2014—see Isaac Fitzgerald, "Twitter Fiction: 'No Constraints, No Joy,'" *BuzzFeed*, February 24, 2014, http://www.buzzfeed.com/isaacfitzgerald/no-constraints-no-joy; David Vecsey, "Teju Cole Puts Story-Telling to the Twitter Test," *The 6th Floor Blog*, September 1, 2014, http://6thfloor.blogs.nytimes.com/2014/01/09/teju-cole-puts-story-telling-to-the-twitter-test/.

2 Teju Cole, "Teju Cole—Open City (Excerpt)," *Genius*, accessed August 17, 2016, http://genius.com/Teju-cole-open-city-excerpt-annotated.

3 F. Scott Fitzgerald, *The Great Gatsby*, ed. Ruth Prigozy (Oxford: Oxford University Press, 1998), 8, 16.

4 Teju Cole, *Open City* (New York: Random House, 2011), 3.

5 Teju (@tejucole) Cole, "On Rap Genius, All the Allusions on the First Page of Open City. Http://Poetry.Rapgenius.Com/Teju-Cole-Open-City-Excerpt-Lyrics … (Shoutout to @TalibKweli)," Twitter, June 7, 2013, https://twitter.com/tejucole/status/343054819327619072.

6 W. K. Wimsatt Jr. and Monroe C. Beardsley, "The Intentional Fallacy," in *The Verbal Icon: Studies in the Meaning of Poetry* (Lexington: University of Kentucky Press, 1954), 18.

7 Wimsatt and Beardsley, "Intentional Fallacy," 18.

8 Teju (@tejucole) Cole, "@philipsayers Intense. Thanks. (I Didn't Have Gatsby in Mind, No.)," microblog, Twitter, March 20, 2014, https://twitter.com/tejucole/status/343054819327619072.

9 For more on the appeal and lasting influence of "The Intentional Fallacy," see Joshua Gang, "'No Symbols Where None Intended,'" *PMLA* 130, no. 3 (2015):

680–1, https://doi.org/10.1632/pmla.2015.130.3.679; Michaels, *Beauty*, 48–9. Gang observes that contemporary literary criticism across the Anglophone world, including approaches seemingly far removed from New Criticism such as surface reading and affect theory, remains eager to avoid discussions of authorial intention.
10 Seán Burke, ed., *Authorship: From Plato to the Postmodern: A Reader* (Edinburgh: Edinburgh University Press, 1995), 65.
11 Barthes, *Image Music Text*, 148.
12 E. D. Hirsch Jr., *Validity in Interpretation* (New Haven, CT: Yale University Press, 1967), 1, 8.
13 Steven Knapp and Walter Benn Michaels, "Against Theory," *Critical Inquiry* 8, no. 4 (1982): 731.
14 Knapp and Michaels, "Against Theory," 723. For one representative and recent example, see Gang, "'No Symbols Where None Intended.'" For more on the twentieth-century debate over authorial intention kick-started by "The Intentional Fallacy," see Burke, ed., *Authorship*, 65–71; Burke, *Death and Return*, 138–53; Kaye Mitchell, *Intention and Text: Towards an Intentionality of Literary Form* (London: Continuum, 2008), 1–21.
15 Burke, *Death and Return*, 76–86; Fredric Jameson, *Postmodernism, or, the Cultural Logic of Late Capitalism* (London: Verso, 1991), 306.
16 Butler, *Precarious Life*, 129.
17 Paul Ricoeur, *Freud and Philosophy: An Essay on Interpretation*, trans. Denis Savage (New Haven, CT: Yale University Press, 1970), 33.
18 See also Eve Kosofsky Sedgwick, "Paranoid Reading and Reparative Reading, or, You're So Paranoid, You Probably Think This Essay Is about You," in *Touching Feeling: Affect, Pedagogy, Performativity* (Durham, NC: Duke University Press, 2003), 123–52; Bruno Latour, "Why Has Critique Run out of Steam? From Matters of Fact to Matters of Concern," *Critical Inquiry* 30, no. 2 (2004): 225–48; Stephen Best and Sharon Marcus, "Surface Reading: An Introduction," *Representations*, no. 108 (2009): 1–21.
19 Other key texts discussed as part of the turn to beauty include Denis Donoghue, *Speaking of Beauty* (New Haven, CT: Yale University Press, 2003); and Alexander Nehamas, *Only a Promise of Happiness: The Place of Beauty in a World of Art* (Princeton, NJ: Princeton University Press, 2007). One might also understand Walter Benn Michaels's analysis of works of literature and photography that assert their beauty in *The Beauty of a Social Problem* as another instance of this critical move. For a wider consideration of the "new aestheticism," see John J. Joughin and Simon Malpas, eds., *The New Aestheticism* (Manchester: Manchester University Press, 2003).
20 Gang, "No Symbols," 680.
21 My argument in this chapter is indebted to Ruti's analysis of the inconsistencies in Butler's work. What I refer to here as Butler's inconsistent anti-intentionalism and what Ruti analyzes as Butler's "reluctant universalism" could both be understood as symptoms of the tension between Butler's allegiance to the critique of the author-subject on the one hand and her political and ethical positions on the other; see Mari Ruti, *Between Levinas and Lacan: Self, Other, Ethics* (New York: Bloomsbury Academic, 2015), 39.

22 Talal Asad et al., *Is Critique Secular?: Blasphemy, Injury, and Free Speech* (New York: Fordham University Press, 2013); Judith Butler, "'Philosophy Has Become Worldly': Marx on Ruthless Critique," *PMLA* 131, no. 2 (2016): 460–8, https://doi.org/10.1632/pmla.2016.131.2.460.
23 Mari Ruti, "The Bad Habits of Critical Theory," *The Comparatist*, no. 40 (2016): 9.
24 Anette Pankratz, "'Nothing That Is Worth Knowing Can Be Taught': Artists and Academia in Novels by A.S. Byatt, David Lodge and Zadie Smith," in *Portraits of the Artists as a Young Thing in British, Irish and Canadian Fiction after 1945*, ed. Anette Pankratz and Barbara Puschmann-Nalenz (Heidelberg, Germany: Universitätsverlag Winter, 2012), 274; Dorothy J. Hale, "On Beauty as Beautiful? The Problem of Novelistic Aesthetics by Way of Zadie Smith," *Contemporary Literature* 53, no. 4 (2012): 820.
25 Zadie Smith, *On Beauty* (Toronto: Penguin Canada, 2005), Acknowledgments, n.p.
26 Elaine Scarry, *On Beauty and Being Just* (Princeton, NJ: Princeton University Press, 1999), 31; Barthes, *Preparation of the Novel*, 80.
27 Scarry, *On Beauty*, 67.
28 This is a conversation that continues apace. For one article that remains relevant in its critique of the omnipresent rhetoric of the over-sensitive, demanding student, see Sara Ahmed, "Against Students," *The New Inquiry*, June 29, 2015, http://thenewinquiry.com/essays/against-students/.
29 Smith, *Changing My Mind*, 301.
30 See Philip Tew, ed., *Reading Zadie Smith: The First Decade and Beyond* (London: Bloomsbury Academic, 2013), 95.
31 Eleanor Wachtel, "25th Anniversary Panel Interview," *Writers & Company* (Toronto: CBC Radio, August 11, 2015). For more on Smith's relationship to New Criticism, see *Changing My* Mind, 11–12.
32 Smith, *Changing My Mind*, 49.
33 Smith, *Changing My Mind*, 49.
34 Roland Barthes, *S/Z*, trans. Richard Miller (New York: Hill and Wang, 1974), 4; *Image Music Text*, 162. This is not to say that the distinction between the two is entirely rigid: in *S/Z* Barthes deliberately chooses to focus on "a classic, readerly" work—Balzac's "Sarrasine"—but to read it in such a way as to affirm the plurality (the textuality, the writerliness) of the "stereographic space of writing"; see Barthes, *S/Z*, 15.
35 Barthes, *Image Music Text*, 162.
36 Smith, *Changing My Mind*, 43; emphasis added.
37 Smith, *Changing My Mind*, 49.
38 Smith, *Changing My Mind*, 43, 49, 48. Here Smith is actually quoting (without citation) Michel A. Moos's description of Barthes's project in *S/Z*, in a commentary essay on Marshall McLuhan: see Marshall McLuhan, *Media Research: Technology, Art and Communication*, ed. Michel Moos (New York: Routledge, 2013), 143.
39 Michaels, *Beauty*, xi; emphasis added.
40 Michaels, *Beauty*, 59–63, 100.
41 For more detail on the Smith-Forster connection, see Frank Kermode, "Here She Is," *London Review of Books*, October 6, 2005; Jonathan Derbyshire, "Truths and Beauty," *Financial Times*, September 16, 2005, https://www.ft.com/content/52a1036a-25a7-11da-a4a7-00000e2511c8; Nick Bentley, Nick Hubble,

and Leigh Wilson, eds., *The 2000s: A Decade of Contemporary British Fiction* (London: Bloomsbury Academic, 2015), 19; Lawrence Driscoll, *Evading Class in Contemporary British Literature* (New York: Palgrave Macmillan, 2009), 62–83; Fiona Tolan, "Zadie Smith's Forsterian Ethics: White Teeth, The Autograph Man, On Beauty," *Critique: Studies in Contemporary Fiction* 54, no. 2 (2013): 135–46, https://doi.org/10.1080/00111619.2010.550340. See also Smith's own essay on Forster, "E. M. Forster: Middle Manager," in *Changing My Mind*, 14–27.

42 Smith, *Changing My Mind*, 43.
43 Smith, *On Beauty*, 252.
44 Smith, *On Beauty*, 330.
45 See Pankratz, "Nothing That Is Worth Knowing," 263 Tew, ed., *Reading Zadie Smith*, 92–5, 133–4; Gemma Lopez, "After Theory: Academia and the Death of Aesthetic Relish In," *Critique: Studies in Contemporary Fiction* 51, no. 4 (2010): 350–65, https://doi.org/10.1080/00111610903380030.
46 Smith, *On Beauty*, 145.
47 For more critical response to Katie Armstrong, see Kathleen Wall, "Ethics, Knowledge, and the Need for Beauty: Zadie Smith's On Beauty and Ian McEwan's Saturday," *University of Toronto Quarterly* 77, no. 2 (2008): 767–8, https://doi.org/10.1353/utq.0.0281; Alexander Dick and Christina Lupton, "On Lecturing and Being Beautiful: Zadie Smith, Elaine Scarry, and the Liberal Aesthetic," *ESC: English Studies in Canada* 39, no. 2 (2013): 124, https://doi.org/10.1353/esc.2013.0032; Hale, "On Beauty as Beautiful?" 836.
48 Smith, *On Beauty*, 250.
49 Smith, *On Beauty*, 250, 255.
50 Smith, *On Beauty*, 145.
51 Smith, *On Beauty*, 392.
52 Smith, *On Beauty*, 29.
53 Rita Felski, *The Limits of Critique* (Chicago: University of Chicago Press, 2015), 1; emphasis added.
54 Smith, *Changing My Mind*, 43.
55 Smith, *Changing My Mind*, 55.
56 Smith, *Changing My Mind*, 55.
57 See Philip Sayers, "Unhooking Oneself: Zadie Smith and Psychoanalysis" (Northeast Modern Language Association, Toronto, 2015). For Smith's allusions to *Beyond the Pleasure Principle*, see Zadie Smith, *White Teeth* (London: Hamish Hamilton, 2000), 140, 211.
58 Smith, *On Beauty*, 223, 226.
59 Smith, *On Beauty*, 226. Renata Salecl, for example, argues that from a Lacanian standpoint, despite the fact that one speaks more and differently than one intends, "the subject cannot escape responsibility, even if this responsibility accounts for no more than the mere fact that he or she is a subject"; see Renata Salecl, *(Per)Versions of Love and Hate* (London: Verso, 1998), 124. And Mari Ruti argues that my opacity to myself is not "a get-out-of-jail-free card" but "an invitation to a radical form of self-responsibility"; see *Between Levinas and Lacan*, 60.
60 Smith, *On Beauty*, 368–9.
61 Shoshana Felman, *The Scandal of the Speaking Body: Don Juan with J.L. Austin, or Seduction in Two Languages* (Stanford, CA: Stanford University Press, 1983), 67.

62 Judith Butler, *Excitable Speech: A Politics of the Performative* (New York: Routledge, 1997), 10; emphasis added.
63 Felman, *Scandal*, 132n23, 67.
64 Smith, *On Beauty*, 47.
65 Butler, *Excitable Speech*, 11.
66 Smith, *On Beauty*, 291.
67 Smith, *On Beauty*, 223–4.
68 Smith, *On Beauty*, 331.
69 Smith, *On Beauty*, 208.
70 Smith, *On Beauty*, 29, 145.
71 Jonathan P. A. Sell, "Experimental Ethics: Autonomy and Contingency in the Novels of Zadie Smith," in *The Ethical Component in Experimental British Fiction since the 1960's*, ed. Susan Onega and Jean-Michel Ganteau (Newcastle, UK: Cambridge Scholars Publishing, 2007), 151. Criticism on the Smith-Forster connection is cited above. On the connection between Smith and the "liberal humanist tradition of novel studies," see Hale, "On Beauty as Beautiful?" 833–5; on Smith's conditional endorsement of the "liberal realist mode of novel writing," see Bently, Hubble, and Wilson, eds., *The 2000s*, 174–98, 185; on Smith's liberalism in relation to the tradition of liberal lecturing, see Dick and Lupton, "On Lecturing"; and on *On Beauty* as part of a revival of "liberal-humanist concepts such as truth, beauty, or reality," see Pankratz, "Nothing That Is Worth Knowing," 20.
72 See also Konstantinou, *Cool Characters*, 3: Konstantinou suggests that "it would be a mistake to describe Zadie Smith as a literary-critical reactionary."
73 On the connections between Smith and Scarry, see Fiona Tolan, "Identifying the Precious in Zadie Smith's *On Beauty*" in Rod Mengham and Philip Tew, eds., *British Fiction Today* (London: Continuum, 2006), 128–38; Wall, "Ethics, Knowledge"; Philip Tew, "Zadie Smith's On Beauty: Art and Transatlantic Antagonisms in the Anglo-American Academy," *Symbiosis* 15, no. 2 (2011): 219–36.
74 Scarry, *On Beauty*, 57.
75 See Felski, *Limits of Critique*, 115–16.
76 Latour, "Why Has Critique," 226–7.
77 On post-critical reading, see Felski, *The Limits of Critique*, 190. On "just reading," see Sharon Marcus, *Between Women: Friendship, Desire, and Marriage in Victorian England* (Princeton, NJ: Princeton University Press, 2007), 75. On "reading with the grain," see Timothy Bewes, "Reading with the Grain: A New World in Literary Criticism," *Differences* 21, no. 3 (January 1, 2010): 1–33, https://doi.org/10.1215/10407391-2010-007. On "denotative reading," see Cannon Schmitt, "Tidal Conrad (Literally)," *Victorian Studies* 55, no. 1 (2012): 15. On "the descriptive turn," see Heather Love, "Close but Not Deep: Literary Ethics and the Descriptive Turn," *New Literary History* 41, no. 2 (2010): 371–91, https://doi.org/10.1353/nlh.2010.0007.
78 Felski, *Limits of Critique*, 55; Schmitt, "Tidal Conrad," 12–15.
79 Ngai is referring here to Edward Said's classic argument in *Culture and Imperialism* (New York: Vintage Books, 1993), 80–96. She made this point in a 2016 graduate workshop at the University of Toronto titled *Our Aesthetic Categories*.
80 See Peter Childs and James Green, *Aesthetics and Ethics in Twenty-First Century British Novels: Zadie Smith, Nadeem Aslam, Hari Kunzru and David Mitchell*

(London: Bloomsbury Academic, 2013), 54; Tolan, "Identifying the Precious," 137; Wall, "Ethics, Knowledge," 786. Hale, on the other hand, departs from this consensus, arguing that Smith "values her title for the difference it seeks to draw between the philosopher's treatment of beauty and the novelist's, between Scarry's phenomenological project and the novelistic aesthetics of alterity that Smith pursues"; see "On Beauty as Beautiful?" 814–15.

81 Smith, *On Beauty*, 442.
82 Smith, *On Beauty*, 443.
83 Smith, *On Beauty*, 443.
84 Smith, *On Beauty*, 442.
85 John Su, "Beauty and the Beastly Prime Minister," *ELH* 81, no. 3 (2014): 1098, https://doi.org/10.1353/elh.2014.0028. See also Tolan, "Forsterian Ethics," 137; Wall, "Ethics, Knowledge," 774.
86 Tolan, "Identifying the Precious," 137.
87 Love, "Close but Not Deep," 280.
88 Susan Sontag, *Essays of the 1960s & 70s* (New York: The Library of America, 2013), 14. The fact that Smith, describing a series of self-portraits that appear in Howard's slideshow, repeats "and the artist himself. And the artist himself. And the artist himself" suggests precisely this—that, contra Howard's planned book *Against Rembrandt*, this is a moment of Rembrandt reasserting himself against Howard. And in the final paragraph, when Howard's audience look at Hendrickje, "awaiting elucidation," the woman in the painting "for her part, look[s] away, coyly": here is the revenge of the painting itself against its interpreters. See Smith, *On Beauty*, 442.
89 Sontag, *Essays*, 303.
90 Sontag, *Essays*, 306.
91 Sontag, *Essays*, 315. This last theory, notably, is one that Sontag, who (unlike Scarry) thinks that "aesthetics is crippled by its dependence" on the "essentially vacant concept" of beauty, finds "not very interesting"; see Sontag, *Essays*, 315–16.
92 On critique's running out of steam within contemporary fiction, see Elliott, "Return of the Referent," 349–54, https://doi.org/10.1215/00295132-2009-026; Huehls, *After Critique*.
93 Smith, *On Beauty*, 252.
94 On critique as a "bad habit," see Ruti, "The Bad Habits of Critical Theory."
95 Smith, *On Beauty*, 141.
96 Smith, *On Beauty*, 442.
97 Smith, *On Beauty*, 443; emphasis added.
98 Butler, *Precarious Life*, 128–9.
99 Butler, *Precarious Life*, 129.
100 Smith, *On Beauty*, 252.
101 Butler, *Precarious Life*, 129.
102 Butler, *Precarious Life*, 129.
103 Butler, *Precarious Life*, 129.
104 Butler, *Precarious Life*, 129; emphasis added.
105 Judith Butler, *Gender Trouble: Feminism and the Subversion of Identity* (New York: Routledge Classics, 2006), 187.
106 Butler, *Excitable Speech*, 15–16; emphasis added.
107 Butler, *Precarious Life*, 129.

108 Butler, *Precarious Life*, 129.
109 See Judith Butler and Athena Athanasiou, *Dispossession: The Performative in the Political* (Cambridge: Polity Press, 2013); Judith Butler, *Notes Toward a Performative Theory of Assembly* (Cambridge, MA: Harvard University Press, 2015).
110 See Ahmed, *Willful Subjects*; bell hooks, *Talking Back: Thinking Feminist, Thinking Black* (Boston, MA: South End Press, 1989); Lauren Berlant, *Cruel Optimism* (Durham, NC: Duke University Press, 2011).
111 Butler, *Precarious Life*, 129; emphasis added.
112 hooks, *Talking Back*.
113 Ahmed, *Willful Subjects*, 16.
114 Smith, *On Beauty*, 326; emphasis added.
115 Smith, *On Beauty*, 326.
116 Smith, *On Beauty*, 326.
117 Smith, *On Beauty*, 326; emphasis added.
118 Smith, *On Beauty*, 327.
119 Smith, *On Beauty*, 252.
120 Smith, *On Beauty*, 328.
121 Smith, *On Beauty*, 328.
122 Butler, *Precarious Life*, 129.
123 Butler, *Precarious Life*, 129.
124 Butler, *Excitable Speech*, 50, 67.
125 Butler, *Excitable Speech*, 16.
126 Butler, *Excitable Speech*, 160.
127 Butler, *Excitable Speech*, 34.
128 Smith, *On Beauty*, 328.
129 Butler, *Excitable Speech*, 23.
130 For a response to Butler that shifts the focus on to the one who utters hate speech, see Salecl, "See No Evil, Speak No Evil: Hate Speech and Human Rights," in *(Per)versions of Love and Hate* (London: Verso, 1998), 118–40.
131 *On Beauty* approaches the topic of campus anti-Semitism during Howard's debate with Monty. In an effort to provide precedent for his request to regulate Monty's speech, Howard cites an incident the previous year, when "members of this university lobbied successfully to ban a philosopher who had been invited to read here, but who, it was decided by these members, could not have a platform because he expressed, in his printed work, what were deemed to be 'Anti-Israeli' views and arguments that were offensive to members of our community" (325). In its implicit critique of the elision of the difference between criticism of Israel and anti-Semitism, this passage could easily be read alongside Butler's work on the same topic in "The Charge of Anti-Semitism" or "Is Judaism Zionism?" in Judith Butler et al., *The Power of Religion in the Public Sphere* (New York: Columbia University Press, 2011), 70–91.
132 Butler, *Precarious Life*, 101.
133 Butler, *Precarious Life*, xvi.
134 Butler, *Precarious Life*, 104; emphasis added.
135 Butler, *Precarious Life*, 104–5.
136 Butler, *Precarious Life*, 105.
137 Butler, *Precarious Life*, 106.
138 Butler, *Precarious Life*, 106.

139 See Butler, *Excitable Speech*, 32.
140 Butler, *Precarious Life*, 110–11.
141 Smith, *Changing My Mind*, xi.
142 Barthes, *Preparation of the Novel*, 267.
143 Barthes, *Preparation of the Novel*, 267.
144 In his foreword to *A Lover's Discourse*, Wayne Koestenbaum draws an extended comparison between Barthes and Benjamin, drawing particular attention to their departure from Marxist orthodoxy and their uneasy, belated relationship with "academic legitimacy"; see Roland Barthes, *A Lover's Discourse: Fragments*, trans. Richard Howard (New York: Hill and Wang, 2010), xiv.
145 Barthes, *Neutral*, 11. This passage is also quoted by Nelson in *Art of Cruelty*, 13.
146 On inconsistency as a quality of novelistic thinking, see an alternative version of this chapter in Philip Sayers, "Zadie Smith's and Judith Butler's Novelistic Inconsistencies," *Continental Thought & Theory* 2, no. 3 (2019): 108–33.
147 In this sense, my argument comes close to the argument made by Susan Fischer, who quotes the same line from the foreword to *Changing My Mind* and argues that *On Beauty* attempts to move beyond the dogmatisms of both Howard and Monty; see Tew, ed., *Reading Zadie Smith*, 95; see also 134.
148 Barthes, *Roland Barthes*, 71.

Chapter 3

Epigraph: Ben Lerner, *10:04* (New York: Faber and Faber, 2014), 117.

1   Rebecca Solnit, *Men Explain Things to Me* (Chicago: Haymarket Books, 2014), 1–2.
2   Solnit, *Men Explain*, 2.
3   Solnit, *Men Explain*, 2.
4   Solnit, *Men Explain*, 3.
5   Solnit, *Men Explain*, 2.
6   Barthes, *Image Music Text*, 146.
7   Solnit, *Men Explain*, 3.
8   Solnit, *Men Explain*, 11.
9   Solnit, *Men Explain*, 13.
10 Autofiction is historically a French genre: the term was coined by Serge Doubrovsky to describe his 1977 novel *Fils*. The prominence of Anglophone autofiction is more recent: for an analysis of its popularity during the Obama years, see Christian Lorentzen, "Considering the Novel in the Age of Obama," *Vulture*, November 1, 2017, http://www.vulture.com/2017/01/considering-the-novel-in-the-age-of-obama.html. Lorentzen reads the autofiction of Ben Lerner, Sheila Heti, Teju Cole, Tao Lin, and Jenny Offill as the product of a broader cultural interest in the problem of authenticity, which he links to Obama's "aura of authenticity" and his opponents' attacks on that aura.
11 Lerner, *10:04*, 117.
12 Smith, *Changing My Mind*, 87. This line is taken from Smith's essay "Two Directions for the Novel," in her reading of race in Tom McCarthy's *Remainder*. She suggests that contemporary writers like McCarthy, having realized that

changes in the canon have afforded authenticity "to women, to those of colour, to people of different sexualities and to people from far off, war-torn places" at the seeming expense of straight white men, might be making a point of trying to "destroy the myth of cultural authenticity" altogether. The prominent "dead black man" in McCarthy's novel, Smith suggests, is proof that McCarthy is more interested in pulverizing subjectivity than in extending it to people previously excluded from that category; see Smith, *Changing My Mind*, 87–8.

13 Solnit, *Men Explain*, 6.
14 Chris Kraus, *I Love Dick*, Semiotext(e) Native Agents (Los Angeles: Semiotext(e), 2006), 191.
15 Sheila Heti, *How Should a Person Be?* (Toronto: House of Anansi Press, 2012), 224.
16 Lerner, *10:04*, 117.
17 Lucy O'Meara, *Roland Barthes at the Collège de France* (Liverpool: Liverpool University Press, 2012), 6. In his foreword to *How to Live Together*, editor Éric Marty writes: "The first principle of this edition—which is almost an axiom—is that Barthes's lecture courses at the Collège de France could not be and should not be *books*"; see Roland Barthes, *How to Live Together: Novelistic Simulations of Some Everyday Spaces: Notes for a Lecture Course and Seminar at the Collège de France (1976–1977)*, ed. Claude Coste, trans. Kate Briggs (New York: Columbia University Press, 2013), ix. Whereas some of Barthes's most famous books, such as *A Lover's Discourse*, *S/Z* and *Roland Barthes by Roland Barthes*, were based in part on lectures and seminars that Barthes gave at the École pratique des hautes études, it seems as if Barthes did not intend for his Collège courses to become books. In the first session of "The Neutral," he writes: "People tell me: 'You'll make a book with this course on the Neutral?' All other problems put aside (particularly problems of performance), my answer: No, the Neutral is the unmarketable... We'll have to hold on to the unsustainable for thirteen weeks: after that, it will fade"; see Barthes, *Neutral*, 13. He goes into more detail on "the decision not (or at least not for the moment) to publish the course on the Neutral" in *The Preparation of the Novel*; see Barthes, *The Preparation of the Novel*, 7; see also Jürgen Pieters and Kris Pint, "Introduction: An Unexpected Return. Barthes Lecture Courses at the Collège de France," *Paragraph* 31, no. 1 (2008): 1–2; O'Meara, *Collège de France*, 5–6.
18 Roland Barthes, "Lecture in Inauguration of the Chair of Literary Semiology, Collège de France, January 7, 1977," trans. Richard Howard, *October* 8 (1979): 5.
19 *The Preparation of the Novel* also includes notes for the introductory and closing sessions of the 1978–9 seminar, "The Metaphor of the Labyrinth," and, for a seminar on "Proust and Photography" that was never given due to the accident that eventually led to Barthes's death, a selection of "biographical notes on some of the key figures in Proust's circle, photographed by Paul Nadar"; see *Preparation of the Novel*, 305. Although the "Labyrinth" seminar notes contain important material on Barthes's relationships with other French thinkers of the period, especially Deleuze, and the "Proust" material provides a useful complement to *Camera Lucida* (written around the same period), they are less relevant to the concerns of this chapter.
20 Kraus, *I Love Dick*, 19.
21 Kraus, *I Love Dick*, 270.

22 Denise Frimer, "Chris Kraus in Conversation with Denise Frimer," *The Brooklyn Rail*, April 10, 2006, http://brooklynrail.org/2006/04/art/chris-kraus-in-conversation-with-denise-frimer.
23 Giovanni Intra, "A Fusion of Gossip and Theory," *artnet*, November 13, 1997, http://www.artnet.com/magazine_pre2000/index/intra/intra11-13-97.asp.
24 Anna Watkins Fisher, "Manic Impositions: The Parasitical Art of Chris Kraus and Sophie Calle," *WSQ: Women's Studies Quarterly* 40, no. 1 (2012): 228, https://doi.org/10.1353/wsq.2012.0029.
25 See Nicholas Dames, "The New Fiction of Solitude," *The Atlantic*, April 2016, https://www.theatlantic.com/magazine/archive/2016/04/the-new-fiction-of-solitude/471474/; Lorentzen, "Age of Obama"; Joanna Walsh, "I Love Dick by Chris Kraus Review—a Cult Feminist Classic Makes Its UK Debut," *The Guardian*, November 11, 2015, https://www.theguardian.com/books/2015/nov/11/i-love-dick-chris-kraus-review.
26 Frimer, "Chris Kraus." See also Timothy Bewes, "Recent Experiments in American Fiction," *Novel: A Forum on Fiction* 50, no. 3 (2017): 354–6, https://doi.org/10.1215/00295132-4194936.
27 Chris Kraus, "Chris Kraus: 'I Love Dick Happened in Real Life, but It's Not a Memoir,'" *The Guardian*, May 17, 2016, http://www.theguardian.com/books/2016/may/17/chris-kraus-i-love-dick-happened-in-real-life-but-its-not-a-memoir; Anna Poletti, "The Anthropology of the Setup: A Conversation with Chris Kraus," *Contemporary Women's Writing* 10, no. 1 (2016): 134, https://doi.org/10.1093/cww/vpv030.
28 Chris Kraus, "The New Universal," *Sydney Review of Books*, October 17, 2014, http://sydneyreviewofbooks.com/new-universal/.
29 Henry Schwarz and Anne Balsamo, "Under the Sign of Semiotext(e): The Story According to Sylvere Lotringer and Chris Kraus," *Critique: Studies in Contemporary Fiction* 37, no. 3 (1996): 214, https://doi.org/10.1080/00111619.1996.9936493.
30 Schwarz and Balsamo, "Under the Sign," 212.
31 Poletti, "Anthropology of the Setup," 134.
32 Kraus, "The New Universal."
33 Kraus, *I Love Dick*, 191.
34 McKenzie Wark, "I Love Dick," *Public Seminar*, August 25, 2016, http://www.publicseminar.org/2016/08/ild/. Joan Hawkins makes a similar argument in her afterword to *I Love Dick*: "'Who gets to speak and why…' Kraus writes, 'is the only question' (191). I would modify that as follows: who gets to speak, who gets to speak about **what**, and **why** are the only questions"; see Kraus, *I Love Dick*, 264; emphasis in original.
35 Wark, "I Love Dick."
36 Wark, "I Love Dick."
37 Kraus, *I Love Dick*, 193–4.
38 Kraus, *I Love Dick*, 194.
39 Kraus, *I Love Dick*, 194.
40 Walter Benjamin, *Illuminations*, ed. Hannah Arendt, trans. Harry Zohn (New York: Schocken Books, 1968), 257–8. Lerner's *10:04* also quotes this passage from Benjamin: the novel contains a full-page reproduction of Klee's painting, with the caption: "'The storm irresistibly propels him into the future to which

his back is turned.'—Walter Benjamin"; see Lerner, *10:04*, 25. Lerner does not explicitly engage with the line, though it connects to his concern with futurity and temporality, as well as with the literal storms that he describes.

41 Kraus, *I Love Dick*, 194.
42 Kraus, *I Love Dick*, 195.
43 Benjamin, *Illuminations*, 257.
44 Sam Cooper, "The Unreturnable Situationist International: Berfrois Interviews McKenzie Wark," *Berfrois*, September 2, 2011, http://www.berfrois.com/2011/09/berfrois-interviews-mckenzie-wark/.
45 Udi Greenberg, "The Politics of the Walter Benjamin Industry," *Theory, Culture & Society* 25, no. 3 (2008): 53–70, https://doi.org/10.1177/0263276408090657.
46 Elaine Blair writes in *The New Yorker*: "Last year, Lena Dunham gave a copy to the singer-songwriter Lorde, who Instagrammed its distinctive white cover"; see Elaine Blair, "Chris Kraus, Female Antihero," *The New Yorker*, November 21, 2016, http://www.newyorker.com/magazine/2016/11/21/chris-kraus-female-antihero.
47 Sheila Heti, "Interview with Chris Kraus," *The Believer*, September 1, 2013, http://www.believermag.com/issues/201309/?read=interview_kraus.
48 Michelle Dean, "Listening to Women," *Slate*, June 29, 2012, http://www.slate.com/articles/arts/books/2012/06/sheila_heti_s_how_should_a_person_be_reviewed_.html.
49 Chris Kraus, "What Women Say to One Another: Sheila Heti's 'How Should a Person Be?'" *Los Angeles Review of Books*, June 18, 2012, https://lareviewofbooks.org/article/what-women-say-to-one-another-sheila-hetis-how-should-a-person-be/.
50 Walsh, "I Love Dick."
51 Solnit, *Men Explain*, 2–3.
52 Heti, *How Should a Person Be*, 54.
53 Heti, *How Should a Person Be*, 122.
54 Heti, *How Should a Person Be*, 17.
55 Heti, *How Should a Person Be*, 224.
56 Heti, *How Should a Person Be*, 228.
57 Heti, *How Should a Person Be*, 228. For a more extensive analysis of Sheila's "philosophical confusion" over the question of authority and submission, see Christopher Fenwick, "How Should a Person Be?" *The Point Magazine*, April 7, 2014, https://thepointmag.com/2014/criticism/how-should-a-person-be.
58 Heti, *How Should a Person Be*, 227.
59 Heti, *How Should a Person Be*, 228.
60 Heti, *How Should a Person Be*, 301.
61 Heti, *How Should a Person Be*, 302; emphasis added.
62 Rachel Sagner Buurma and Laura Heffernan, "Notation after 'The Reality Effect': Remaking Reference with Roland Barthes and Sheila Heti," *Representations* 125, no. 1 (2014): 87–8.
63 Lerner, *10:04*, 3–4.
64 Lerner, *10:04*, 4.
65 Kate Zambreno, *Heroines* (Los Angeles: Semiotext(e), 2012), 260. *Heroines* was published as part of Semiotext(e)'s politically inclined Active Agents series of nonfiction books. Zambreno is another writer influenced by Kraus, writing in the Acknowledgments: "I feel lucky to have as an editor such a radical writer who has

revolutionized my own conceptions of the urgency of not erasing the self in our criticism"; see Zambreno, *Heroines*, 309. *Heroines*, like *I Love Dick*, is an analysis of the conditions of female authorship, focusing on female modernist writers and artists whose creative work has tended to be viewed as secondary to their relationships with male writers.

66   This is a similar tactic to one previously used by Dave Eggers, who, after the success of his memoir *A Heartbreaking Work of Staggering Genius* (2000), turned to the genre of oral history in order to tell other people's stories, in *What Is the What?* (2006) and *Zeitoun* (2009).
67   Lerner, *10:04*, 116.
68   Lerner, *10:04*, 117; emphasis added.
69   This passage from *10:04* echoes even more strongly another section in Solnit's essay, in which she describes going to dinner after a talk with a "male writer and translator" who insists (incorrectly) that Solnit has her history wrong; Solnit refers to him as "Mr. Very Important II"; see Solnit, *Men Explain*, 8.
70   Lerner, *10:04*, 117.
71   Lerner, *10:04*, 117.
72   For a discussion of Lerner's third novel *The Topeka School* and how it takes up these same ideas in its interrogation of masculinity, see Philip Sayers, "When Male Writers Confront Toxic Masculinity," *The Walrus*, January 23, 2020, https://thewalrus.ca/when-male-writers-confront-toxic-masculinity/.
73   Solnit, *Men Explain*, 13.
74   For more on how "What Is It to Hold Forth?" fails to address gender politics, see Philip Sayers, "Roland Barthes and the Urgency of Nuance," *Los Angeles Review of Books*, November 4, 2018, https://lareviewofbooks.org/article/roland-barthes-and-the-urgency-of-nuance/.
75   Barthes, *How to Live Together*, 155.
76   Barthes, *How to Live Together*, xxix.
77   Barthes, *How to Live Together*, xxx. Most importantly, the second year of the seminar on "le discours amoureux" (1975–6) included a second "restricted" seminar devoted to presentations by Barthes's students, titled "Les intimidations de langage"; see Roland Barthes, *Le Discours amoureux: Séminaire à l'École Pratique des Hautes Études 1974–1976, suivi de fragments d'un discours amoureux (pages inédites)*, ed. Claude Coste (Paris: Éditions du Seuil, 2007), 606. Barthes refers to this small seminar at the beginning of "What Is It to Hold Forth?" describing the 1977 seminar as a continuation of the earlier exploration; see *How to Live Together*, 141. Unfortunately, there is no published material on this seminar beyond a brief description in the (untranslated) edition of *Le Discours amoureux* seminars; see Barthes, *Le Discours amoureux*, 606.
78   Barthes, *How to Live Together*, 144.
79   Barthes, *How to Live Together*, 146.
80   Barthes, *How to Live Together*, 142.
81   Barthes, "Lecture," 5. For more on Barthes's remarks about the "fascism" of language, see De Villiers, "Great Pedagogy of Nuance." De Villiers suggests that it "comes from the individual position of someone aware of what language *compels you to say* (rather than censors), such as the confessional discourse which defines the situation of homosexuality." In *Opacity and the Closet*, de Villiers goes into further detail, suggesting that critics frequently fail to understand "the gay

specificity of this generalized suspicion" of the function of language; see Nicholas De Villiers, *Opacity and the Closet: Queer Tactics in Foucault, Barthes, and Warhol* (Minneapolis: University of Minnesota Press, 2012), 73. In his book on Barthes for the University of Chicago Press's Critical Lives series, Andy Stafford also highlights the fact that this claim is often "quoted out of context," suggesting that it is better understood as part of Barthes's frequent strategy of oscillating between two seemingly opposite views—here, radical suspicion of language and deep fascination with it; see Andy Stafford, *Roland Barthes*, Critical Lives (London: Reaktion Books, 2015), 124–5.
82 Barthes, "Lecture," 4.
83 Barthes, *How to Live Together*, 147.
84 Barthes, *How to Live Together*, xxi.
85 Kraus, *I Love Dick*, 194; Heti, *How Should a Person Be*, 76; Barthes, *How to Live Together*, 142.
86 Barthes, *How to Live Together*, 150; Kraus, *I Love Dick*, 193.
87 Heti, *How Should a Person Be*, 17; Lerner, *10:04*, 117. In fact, Barthes begins "What Is It to Hold Forth?" by using his own teaching as an example: he suggests that, just as an analysand is "forever holding forth on the same topic," so he as a teacher is "following on from what I was saying" the previous year, in the École pratique des hautes études seminar on "The Intimidations of Language"; see Barthes, *How to Live Together*, 141. For more on the connection between the teacher and the analysand in Barthes's work and on the way Barthes tries to undercut his pedagogical authority, see Helen Vendler, *The Music of What Happens: Poems, Poets, Critics* (Cambridge, MA: Harvard University Press, 1988), 71–2.
88 Barthes, *How to Live Together*, 148–9. Barthes explains that his description of holding forth as "invested speech" alludes to the way in which Jean Laplanche and Jean-Bertrand Pontalis understand Freud's concept of *Besetzung* (commonly rendered in English as "cathexis") as referring to the way in which psychic energy is *invested*, in explicitly economic terms, in an idea. Hence to hold forth is, psychoanalytically, to be cathected to (and to be invested in) what one is saying.
89 Lerner, *10:04*, 117; Solnit, *Men Explain*, 1.
90 Barthes, *How to Live Together*, 147; Solnit, *Men Explain*, 2.
91 Barthes, *How to Live Together*, 141; emphasis added.
92 Barthes, *How to Live Together*, 141.
93 Barthes, *How to Live Together*, 141; for the French version of this passage, see Roland Barthes, *Comment Vivre Ensemble: Simulations Romanesques de Quelques Espaces Quotidiens: Notes de Cours et de Séminaires Au Collège de France, 1976–1977*, ed. Claude Coste (Paris: Éditions du Seuil, 2002), 187.
94 Barthes, *How to Live Together*, 141.
95 Barthes, *How to Live Together*, 141.
96 Barthes, *How to Live Together*, 146.
97 Barthes, *How to Live Together*, 146.
98 Solnit, *Men Explain*, 3.
99 Barthes, *How to Live Together*, 150.
100 Barthes, *How to Live Together*, 150; Daniel Defoe, *Robinson Crusoe*, ed. Thomas Keymer (Oxford: Oxford University Press, 2007), 6–7.
101 Barthes, *How to Live Together*, 151.

102 Barthes, *How to Live Together*, 151.
103 Barthes, *How to Live Together*, 151.
104 For more on this term, which saw especially wide use in 2015, see Emma G. Fitzsimmons, "'Manspreading' on New York Subways Is Target of New M.T.A. Campaign," *The New York Times*, December 20, 2014, https://www.nytimes.com/2014/12/21/nyregion/MTA-targets-manspreading-on-new-york-city-subways.html. Fitzsimmons defines manspreading as "the lay-it-all-out sitting style that more than a few men see as their inalienable underground right."
105 For more on this term, see Jessica Bennett, "Hillary Clinton Will Not Be Manterrupted," *The New York Times*, September 27, 2016, https://www.nytimes.com/2016/09/28/opinion/campaign-stops/hillary-clinton-will-not-be-manterrupted.html. Bennett links "manterrupting" to "mansplaining": both, she writes, are "linguistic trademarks" of Donald Trump.
106 See Jamie Utt, "From Manspreading to Mansplaining—6 Ways Men Dominate the Spaces around Them," *Everyday Feminism*, September 1, 2015, http://everydayfeminism.com/2015/09/6-ways-men-dominate-space/. Utt discusses the ways in which men are socialized to feel entitlement to physical space (e.g., manspreading), intellectual space (e.g., mansplaining), professional space, social space (e.g., manterrupting), political space, and intimate space.
107 Solnit, *Men Explain*, 13.
108 See Maisha Z. Johnson, "6 Ways Well-Intentioned People Whitesplain Racism (And Why They Need to Stop)," *Everyday Feminism*, February 7, 2016, http://everydayfeminism.com/2016/02/how-people-whitesplain-racism/; Rich Juzwiak, "A Field Guide to Straightsplaining," *Gawker*, July 2, 2014, http://gawker.com/a-field-guide-to-straightsplaining-1516723100. Solnit expresses a degree of reservation about the term *mansplain*: "I have doubts about the word and don't use it myself much; it seems to go a little heavy on the idea that men are inherently flawed this way, rather than that some men explain things they shouldn't and don't hear things they should"; see Solnit, *Men Explain*, 13.
109 Annette Lavers, *Roland Barthes: Structuralism and After* (Cambridge, MA: Harvard University Press, 1982), 207.
110 Roland Barthes, "*The 'Scandal' of Marxism" and Other Writings on Politics*, trans. Chris Turner (London: Seagull Books, 2015), 104.
111 Nelson, *Argonauts*, 81–2.
112 Nelson, *Argonauts*, 112.
113 Nelson, *Argonauts*, 112.
114 Nelson, *Argonauts*, 112.
115 D. A. Miller, *Bringing Out Roland Barthes* (Berkeley: University of California Press, 1992), 14.
116 Miller, *Bringing Out*, 23.
117 Miller, *Bringing Out*, 24.
118 Miller, *Bringing Out*, 25.
119 Hervé Guibert, *Ghost Image*, trans. Robert Bononno (Chicago: University of Chicago Press, 2014), 83.
120 Ralph Sarkonak, *Angelic Echoes: Hervé Guibert and Company* (Toronto: University of Toronto Press, 2000), 51.
121 Miller, *Bringing Out*, 16.
122 Barthes, *Roland Barthes*, 63–4.

123 Barthes, *Neutral*, 69.
124 See Roland Barthes, *A Barthes Reader*, ed. Susan Sontag (New York: Hill and Wang, 1982), 481; De Villiers, *Opacity and the Closet*, 70.
125 For a related argument, see Andreas Bjørnerud, "Outing Barthes: Barthes and the Quest(Ion) of (a Gay) Identity Politics," *New Formations*, no. 18 (1992): 122–41. Bjørnerud assesses the question of why Barthes avoids explicit discussion of his sexuality in terms to the tension between the logic of "coming out" and the logic of the Neutral.
126 George Haggerty, ed., *Encyclopedia of Gay Histories and Cultures* (New York: Garland, 2000), 100. Barbara Johnson, in her response to D. A. Miller's book, makes a similar argument, suggesting that Barthes is engaged in a project of theorizing sexuality not so much as "a type of identity but a type of loss of identity"; see Barbara Johnson, *The Barbara Johnson Reader: The Surprise of Otherness*, ed. Melissa Feuerstein et al. (Durham, NC: Duke University Press, 2014), 152.
127 De Villiers, *Opacity and the Closet*, 64.
128 De Villiers, *Opacity and the Closet*, 65.
129 Roland Barthes, *The Rustle of Language*, trans. Richard Howard (Oxford: Basil Blackwell, 1986), 291; emphasis added.
130 For an overview of this current of queer theory, see Mari Ruti, *The Ethics of Opting Out: Queer Theory's Defiant Subjects* (New York: Columbia University Press, 2017), 13–27.
131 Edmund White, "From Albert Camus to Roland Barthes," *The New York Times*, December 9, 1982.
132 Brian Blanchfield, *Proxies: Essays Near Knowing* (New York: Nightboat Books, 2016), 90, 97–108.
133 *Empire of Signs* and "So, How Was China?" are the most widely discussed of Barthes's writings on China; see also Roland Barthes, *Travels in China*, ed. Anne Herschberg Pierrot, trans. Andrew Brown (Cambridge: Polity Press, 2012); Roland Barthes, "Compte Rendu Du Voyage En Chine," in *Le Lexique de l'auteur: Séminaire à l'Ecole Pratique Des Hautes Études, 1973–1974*, ed. Anne Herschberg Pierrot (Paris: Seuil, 2010), 227–45; Andy Stafford, "Roland Barthes's Travels in China: Writing a Diary of Dissidence within Dissidence?" *Textual Practice* 30, no. 2 (2016): 287–304, http://dx.doi.org/10.1080/0950236X.2016.1129730.
134 Lisa Lowe, *Critical Terrains: French and British Orientalisms* (Ithaca, NY: Cornell University Press, 1991), 21.
135 Barthes, *"Scandal" of Marxism*, 104. For defenses of Barthes, see Trinh T. Minh-Ha, "The Plural Void: Barthes and Asia," trans. Stanley Gray, *SubStance* 11, no. 3 (1982): 41–50, https://doi.org/10.2307/3684313; O'Meara, *Collège de France*, 119. O'Meara points out that Barthes's constructions of Japan and China are "shaped, above all, by a sardonic awareness of what Westerners *expect* to find in these countries, and by a concomitant rejection of these expectations."
136 Lowe, *Critical Terrains*, 184–5.
137 Barthes's persistent interest in figures of utopia, which Knight's book foregrounds, also provides another potential point of resonance between Barthes and queer theory (though one that is as yet unexplored): for more on the question of utopia in queer theoretical thinking, see Lee Edelman, *No Future: Queer Theory and the Death Drive* (Durham, NC: Duke University Press, 2004); José Esteban Muñoz,

Cruising Utopia: The Then and There of Queer Futurity (New York: New York University Press, 2009).
138 Diana Knight, *Barthes and Utopia: Space, Travel, Writing* (Oxford: Clarendon Press, 1997), 2; emphasis added.
139 Knight, *Barthes and Utopia*, 3.
140 See also Rudolphus Teeuwen, "'The Dream of a Minimal Sociality': Roland Barthes' Skeptic Intensity," *Theory, Culture & Society*, Special Section: Neutral Life: Reflections on Roland Barthes' Late Works (2016): 1–16, https://doi.org/10.1177/0263276416659695. Teeuwen makes a case for the ethical and political import of Barthes's utopian project in *How to Live Together*.
141 Barthes, *"Scandal" of Marxism*, 107.
142 Barthes, *"Scandal" of Marxism*, 107.
143 For the original French, see Roland Barthes, *Œuvres complètes*, ed. Éric Marty, vol. IV: 1972–1976 (Paris: Éditions du Seuil, 2002), 532.
144 Roland Barthes, *The Grain of the Voice: Interviews 1962–1980*, trans. Linda Coverdale (Evanston, IL: Northwestern University Press, 2009), 218; *Œuvres complètes*, vol. IV, 862.
145 Notably, Chris Kraus takes a position opposed to Barthes's (and closer to Lisa Lowe's), expressing frustration with the kinds of theories that value the sphere of the political over the everyday struggles of politics; see Heti, "Interview with Chris Kraus." For her, the emphasis on the political—what Barthes would call *le politique*—has made concrete political engagement (which she locates in the sphere of politics: *la politique*) seem "banal":

> As soon as we're concerned with "*the* political" as opposed to "politics," we're dealing with an abstraction. Politics is topical—it's what's happening now, and we can either respond in the present or avoid it. I felt terrible writing for these magazines that had an "engagement with the political" but said nothing about the arrest, under the PATRIOT Act, of contemporary artists. It was considered *so* uncool, so obvious, and so kind of gross to talk about what was happening in front of our faces.

146 Bruno Bosteels, "Politics, Infrapolitics, and the Impolitical: Notes on the Thought of Roberto Esposito and Alberto Moreiras," *CR: The New Centennial Review* 10, no. 2 (2011): 221, https://doi.org/10.1353/ncr.2010.0027.
147 See Burke, *Death and Return*, 28; Gallop, *Deaths of the Author*, 31; Stafford, *Roland Barthes*, 26–7.
148 Barthes, *Image Music Text*, 142.
149 Barthes, *Image Music Text*, 142.
150 Toril Moi, *Sexual/Textual Politics: Feminist Literary Theory* (London: Routledge, 1985), 62–3.
151 Moi, *Sexual/Textual Politics*, 63.
152 Peggy Kamuf, "Replacing Feminist Criticism," *Diacritics* 12, no. 2 (1982): 45, https://doi.org/10.2307/464678.
153 Rita Felski, *Literature after Feminism* (Chicago: University of Chicago Press, 2003), 58.
154 Nancy K. Miller, *Subject to Change: Reading Feminist Writing* (New York: Columbia University Press, 1988), 106.
155 Kamuf, "Replacing Feminist Criticism"; Nancy K. Miller, "The Text's Heroine: A Feminist Critic and Her Fictions," *Diacritics* 12, no. 2 (1982): 48–53, https://

doi.org/10.2307/464679. See also Toril Moi, "'I Am Not a Woman Writer': About Women, Literature and Feminist Theory Today," *Feminist Theory* 9, no. 3 (2008): 261–4, https://doi.org/10.1177/1464700108095850; Felski, *Literature after Feminism*, 58–9; Jay Clayton and Eric Rothstein, eds., *Influence and Intertextuality in Literary History* (Madison: University of Wisconsin Press, 1991), 157.

156 Kraus, *I Love Dick*, 191.
157 Miller, *Subject to Change*, 104.
158 Miller, *Getting Personal*, 9.
159 Miller, *Getting Personal*, 9.
160 Zambreno, *Heroines*, 309.
161 Cheryl Walker, "Feminist Literary Criticism and the Author," *Critical Inquiry* 16, no. 3 (1990): 571.
162 Sara Ahmed, *Differences That Matter: Feminist Theory and Postmodernism* (Cambridge: Cambridge University Press, 1998), 123.
163 Ahmed, *Differences That Matter*, 123.
164 Ahmed, *Differences That Matter*, 137, 135.
165 Gallop, *Deaths of the Author*, 37–49.
166 Barthes, *Pleasure of the Text*, 27.
167 Heti, *How Should a Person Be*, 17.
168 Barthes, *Preparation of the Novel*, 209.
169 Barthes, *Preparation of the Novel*, 81.
170 Jonathan Culler, "Preparing the Novel: Spiraling Back," *Paragraph* 31, no. 1 (2008): 118.
171 O'Meara, *Collège de France*, 28.
172 O'Meara, *Collège de France*, 28.
173 Barthes, "Lecture," 4.
174 Stafford, *Roland Barthes*, 138.
175 Barthes, "Lecture," 15; for the French original, see Roland Barthes, *Œuvres complètes*, ed. Éric Marty, vol. V: 1977–1980 (Paris: Éditions du Seuil, 2002), 444.
176 Barthes, *How to Live Together*, 172. We can draw another parallel between teaching and holding forth: just as Barthes understands holding forth as a form of repetition, so he asks in a 1974 article titled "To the Seminar": "Is not to teach, invariably, to repeat?"; see *Rustle of Language*, 340. It is worth noting here that Barthes did not repeat any of his teaching at the Collège de France.
177 Barthes, *Neutral*, 12.
178 Diana Leca, "Roland Barthes and Literary Minimalism," *Barthes Studies* 1 (2015): 113.
179 O'Meara, *Collège de France*, 7; Barthes, *How to Live Together*, 24.
180 Barthes, *How to Live Together*, 133.
181 Barthes, *How to Live Together*, 134.
182 Barthes, *How to Live Together*, 133–4.
183 Jacques Rancière, *The Ignorant Schoolmaster: Five Lessons in Intellectual Emancipation*, trans. Kristin Ross (Stanford, CA: Stanford University Press, 1991).
184 hooks, *Talking Back*, 100.
185 Barthes, *The "Scandal" of Marxism*, 104.
186 The way that Barthes takes steps to share his pedagogical authority, ceding the stage to other voices, recalls Lerner's strategy for mitigating his privilege by acting as a voice for other people's stories.

187 Barthes, *Preparation of the Novel*, 127.
188 Barthes, *Preparation of the Novel*, 129; emphasis added.
189 Barthes, *Preparation of the Novel*, 18; *Roland Barthes*, 149.
190 Barbara Christian, "The Race for Theory," *Cultural Critique*, no. 6 (1987): 56, 60, https://doi.org/10.2307/1354255.
191 Sara Ahmed makes a similar point: "While we may question any assumption that there is an author of postmodernism, we can nevertheless recognise that postmodernism may become (ironically) authorised through the narrativisation of the author's death"; see Ahmed, *Differences that Matter*, 119. See also Longolius, *Performing Authorship*, 26; Burke, *Death and Return*, 99. Longolius writes, "Barthes performed his own *becoming an author* in ['The Death of the Author'] by genealogically positioning and staging his author persona as the *enfant terrible* of literary criticism." Relatedly, Seán Burke points out in his discussion of Foucault—though the point arguably applies as much to Barthes—that "the subject who announces the disappearance of subjectivity does so only at the risk of becoming—inferentially at least—the sole subject, the Last and Absolute Subject."
192 Barthes, Preparation of the Novel, 208. On the cut passage, see Kris Pint, *The Perverse Art of Reading: On the Phantasmatic Semiology in Roland Barthes' Cours Au Collège de France*, trans. Christopher M. Gemerchak (Amsterdam: Rodopi, 2010), 229–30. Pint writes, "because there had been problems with the microphone in the previous lecture, Barthes was obliged to skip a portion of his notes," including this section.
193 Barthes, *Preparation of the Novel*, 208.
194 Barthes, *Preparation of the Novel*, 172. Barthes refers here to Iranian Leader Ayatollah Khomeini (who was later to declare a fatwa against Salman Rushdie), US President Jimmy Carter, 1981 presidential candidate for the French Communist Party Georges Marchais, and French President Valéry Giscard d'Estaing.
195 On the history of the National Endowment for the Arts, see Donna M. Binkiewicz, *Federalizing the Muse United States Arts Policy and the National Endowment for the Arts, 1965–1980* (Chapel Hill: University of North Carolina Press, 2004), 218. Binkiewicz argues that Reagan's move toward privatization "opened the door for the federal government to step back and eventually remove itself from the arena of arts and humanities funding."
196 Sopan Deb, "Trump Proposes Eliminating the Arts and Humanities Endowments," *The New York Times*, March 15, 2017, https://www.nytimes.com/2017/03/15/arts/nea-neh-endowments-trump.html.

Chapter 4

Epigraph: Roland Barthes, *The Preparation of the Novel: Lecture Courses and Seminars at the Collège de France (1978–1979 and 1979–1980)*, ed. Nathalie Léger, trans. Kate Briggs (New York: Columbia University Press, 2011), 248–9.

1 Butler, *Precarious Life*, 129.
2 Barthes, *Image Music Text*, 146; "Lecture in Inauguration of the Chair of Literary Semiology, Collège de France, January 7, 1977," 4.
3 Barthes, *Preparation of the Novel*, 211.

4   Barthes, *Image Music Text*, 144–5.
5   Barthes, *Preparation of the Novel*, 249.
6   Barthes, *Preparation of the Novel*, 245.
7   Barthes, *Preparation of the Novel*, 245.
8   Barthes, *Preparation of the Novel*, 248–9.
9   Here I draw on the distinction Jasper Bernes draws between the quantitative critique and the qualitative critique in the domain of labor reform—his reorientation of the distinction that Luc Boltanski and Ève Chiapello draw in *The New Spirit of Capitalism* (1999) between the social critique and the artistic critique; Jasper Bernes, *The Work of Art in the Age of Deindustrialization* (Stanford, CA: Stanford University Press, 2017), 9.
10 Benjamin, *Arcades Project*, 670.
11 David Hering, *David Foster Wallace: Fiction and Form* (New York: Bloomsbury Academic, 2016), 125.
12 Barthes, *Preparation of the Novel*, 245.
13 Sianne Ngai, *Our Aesthetic Categories: Zany, Cute, Interesting* (Cambridge, MA: Harvard University Press, 2012), 156.
14 In his widely cited interview with Larry McCaffery, Wallace expands on his relationship with "The Death of the Author": "This is the way Barthian and Derridean post-structuralism's helped me the most as a fiction writer: once I'm done with the thing, I'm basically dead, and probably the text's dead; it becomes simply language, and language lives not just in but *through* the reader. The reader becomes God, for all textual purposes"; see Larry McCaffery, "An Interview with David Foster Wallace," *Review of Contemporary Fiction* 13, no. 2 (1993): 141. For more on Wallace's reading of "The Death of the Author," see Marshall Boswell, ed., *David Foster Wallace and "The Long Thing": New Essays on the Novels* (New York: Bloomsbury Academic, 2014), 35, 99.
15 David Foster Wallace, *A Supposedly Fun Thing I'll Never Do Again: Essays and Arguments* (New York: Back Bay Books, 1998), 144.
16 Hering, *Fiction and Form*, 7–8.
17 Hering, *Fiction and Form*, 9.
18 Amy Hungerford, *Making Literature Now* (Stanford, CA: Stanford University Press, 2016), 4.
19 Hungerford, *Making Literature Now*, 3–4.
20 Hungerford also published an abbreviated version of the piece in *The Chronicle of Higher Education*; see Amy Hungerford, "On Not Reading," *The Chronicle of Higher Education*, September 11, 2016, https://www.chronicle.com/article/On-Refusing-to-Read/237717.
21 Hungerford, *Making Literature Now*, 142.
22 Franco Moretti, *Distant Reading* (London: Verso, 2013), 65–6.
23 Margaret Cohen, *The Sentimental Education of the Novel* (Princeton, NJ: Princeton University Press, 1999), 23.
24 Moretti, *Distant Reading*, 67.
25 Hungerford, *Making Literature Now*, 4.
26 Hungerford, *Making Literature Now*, 162.
27 Hungerford, *Making Literature Now*, 156.
28 Hungerford, *Making Literature Now*, 152.
29 Hungerford, *Making Literature Now*, 150.

30 Jeffrey Severs, *David Foster Wallace's Balancing Books: Fictions of Value* (New York: Columbia University Press, 2017), 66.
31 David Hering, "Thinking about David Foster Wallace, Misogyny and Scholarship," *Bloomsbury Literary Studies Blog*, February 19, 2018, http://bloomsburyliterarystudiesblog.com/continuum-literary-studie/2018/02/thinking-david-foster-wallace-misogyny-scholarship.html.
32 This claim—that literary scholarship and the writing of literature both depend on the same kind of activity—carries an implication that is one of this study's central refrains: that both novels and critical or theoretical texts can *do the same kind of work* and can answer the same kinds of questions. This claim is fleshed out in Section 3.3.
33 David Foster Wallace, *The Pale King: An Unfinished Novel* (New York: Back Bay Books, 2012), 18.
34 Wallace, *Pale King*, 9.
35 Ben Lerner, *10:04* (New York: Faber and Faber, 2014), 19. For another example, see Ling Ma's 2018 novel *Severance*, in which the protagonist, who works at a book production firm, picks up a copy of a Bible she had overseen the manufacture of and describes the transnational supply chain that brought it from its printer in China to its eventual buyer in the United States; see Ling Ma, *Severance* (New York: Picador, 2018), 66–8.
36 Bruno Latour, *Reassembling the Social: An Introduction to Actor-Network-Theory*, Clarendon Lectures in Management Studies (Oxford: Oxford University Press, 2005), 255. On literature's capacity for Latourian sociology, see David J. Alworth, "Melville in the Asylum: Literature, Sociology, Reading," *American Literary History* 26, no. 2 (2014): 234–61, https://doi.org/10.1093/alh/aju019.
37 Hungerford, *Making Literature Now*, 4.
38 Latour, *Reassembling the Social*, 115. Wallace's papers from the accounting classes he took can be found in David Foster Wallace, "The Pale King: An Unfinished Novel" (Draft Materials, Harry Ransom Humanities Research Center, University of Texas at Austin), Boxes 26.2–4, David Foster Wallace Papers.
39 Wallace, *Pale King*, 547.
40 Boswell, ed., *Long Thing*, 171, 176.
41 Boswell, ed., *Long Thing*, 149–68.
42 Tor Nørretranders, *The User Illusion: Cutting Consciousness Down to Size*, trans. Jonathan Sydenham (New York: Penguin, 1999), 31.
43 Severs, *Balancing Books*, 242; Wallace, *Pale King*, 343–4. For more on the way that Wallace draws on *The User Illusion* in *The Pale King*, see Toon Staes, "Work in Process: A Genesis for The Pale King," *English Studies* 95, no. 1 (2014): 76–7.
44 Severs, *Balancing Books*, 242.
45 Severs, *Balancing Books*, 203.
46 Cole, *Known and Strange Things*, 231.
47 David Foster Wallace, ed., *The Best American Essays 2007* (Boston, MA: Houghton Mifflin, 2007), xiv; emphasis added.
48 Wallace, ed., *Best American Essays* 2007, xxi.
49 Cole, *Known and Strange Things*, 230–1.
50 Rosalind Krauss, "Notes on the Index: Seventies Art in America. Part 2," *October* 4 (1977): 65; emphasis added, https://doi.org/10.2307/778437. Jasper Bernes quotes this same passage as part of his argument about the increasing importance of "symbol-based work, which … asks workers to treat written signs as a kind of

51. Barthes, *Image Music Text*, 146.
52. On *The Pale King*'s relative conventionality, see also Timothy Bewes, "Recent Experiments in American Fiction," *Novel: A Forum on Fiction* 50, no. 3 (2017): 351–9, https://doi.org/10.1215/00295132-4194936.
53. Barthes, *Preparation of the Novel*, 208.
54. Barthes, *Preparation of the Novel*, 299, 301.
55. Barthes, *Image Music Text*, 146.
56. Hering, *Fiction and Form*, 136; Wallace, ed., *Best American Essays 2007*, xiv.
57. Barthes, *Preparation of the Novel*, 245; Wallace, Box 39.1, David Foster Wallace Papers.
58. Wallace, Box 39.1, David Foster Wallace Papers.
59. Staes, "Work in Process," 83.
60. There is some evidence in the archive of Wallace's own thinking about how the various pieces of *The Pale King* should be ordered: for example, he labels a draft of the piece that became §1 as "Opening to something longer"; see Box 38.7, David Foster Wallace Papers. For more on the way Wallace and Pietsch collaborated on the ordering of pieces in Wallace's work, we can turn to their correspondence regarding the contents of *Oblivion*. One tonally representative sentence from a letter from Wallace to Pietsch dated October 7, 2003: "Let me hit you with my concerns (comparatively few) about your proposed order here, and then maybe we can noodle about them together at lunch a week from Friday"; see Box 3.5, Little, Brown and Company Collection of David Foster Wallace.
61. Wallace, ed., *Best American Essays 2007*, xiv.
62. Severs, *Balancing Books*, 171–3.
63. Boswell, ed., *Long Thing*, 75.
64. Ngai, *Our Aesthetic Categories*, 156.
65. Ngai, *Our Aesthetic Categories*, 140.
66. Sianne Ngai, "Merely Interesting," *Critical Inquiry* 34, no. 4 (2008): 777–817. *Infinite Jest* in fact alludes to a specific piece of art that Ngai analyzes as a key example of the interesting: Ed Ruscha's *Various Small Fires and Milk* (1964); see Ngai, *Our Aesthetic Categories*, 147–8. *Jest*'s James O. Incandenza makes a film called *Various Small Flames*, the release of which is blocked due to a copyright claim by Ruscha; see David Foster Wallace, *Infinite Jest* (London: Abacus, 2009), 988.
67. Wallace, *Pale King*, xiii.
68. Ngai, *Our Aesthetic Categories*, 140.
69. Wallace, *Pale King*, ix; emphasis added.
70. This is a point that Jeffrey Severs also makes, suggesting that §1's long list of different types of grass indicates that, as far as "the question of how many details to include" goes, "the novel's sympathies" lie on the side of encyclopedic profusion rather than stark minimalism; see Severs, *Balancing Books*, 240.
71. Ngai, *Our Aesthetic Categories*, 152.
72. Wallace, *Pale King*, 548.
73. Wallace, *Pale King*, 548; David Hering dates this outline to November 1999; see Hering, *Fiction and Form*, 130; Wallace, Box 38.8, David Foster Wallace Papers.

74 Mark McGurl, "The Institution of Nothing: David Foster Wallace in the Program," *boundary 2* 41, no. 3 (2014): 47.
75 Wallace, *Pale King*, 312.
76 Wallace, *Pale King*, 315.
77 Wallace, *Pale King*, 314. For an overview of Wallace's history with this line, see D. T. Max, *Every Love Story Is a Ghost Story: A Life of David Foster Wallace* (New York: Penguin, 2013), 310n7.
78 Wallace, *Pale King*, 387; Ngai, *Our Aesthetic Categories*, 25.
79 Wallace, Box 26.2, David Foster Wallace Collection.
80 Wallace, *Pale King*, 230–5.
81 Wallace, *Pale King*, 156, 234, 235.
82 Wallace, *Pale King*, 261.
83 Wallace, Box 37.1, David Foster Wallace Collection.
84 Liam Connell, *Precarious Labour and the Contemporary Novel* (Cham, Switzerland: Palgrave Macmillan, 2017), 139, 140.
85 Boswell, ed., Long Thing, 223; Clare Hayes-Brady, *The Unspeakable Failures of David Foster Wallace: Language, Identity, and Resistance* (New York: Bloomsbury Academic, 2017), 11.
86 Richard Sennett, *The Craftsman* (New Haven, CT: Yale University Press, 2008), 9; Wallace, *Pale King*, 233.
87 Sennett, *Craftsman*, 286, 23.
88 Angela McRobbie, *Be Creative: Making a Living in the New Culture Industries* (Cambridge: Polity Press, 2016), 160.
89 McRobbie, *Be Creative*, 147.
90 Wallace, *Pale King*, 219.
91 Wallace, *Pale King*, 219, 228. For more on Wallace's "investment in the symbolic value of ordinary whiteness," see McGurl, "Institution of Nothing," 49.
92 Sennett, *Craftsman*, 10.
93 Sennett, *Craftsman*, 80.
94 Wallace, *Pale King*, 229. Fogle later realizes that the substitute professor is in fact probably a high-ranking IRS employee, filling in for the regular professor for the last two weeks of class. It seems to be at least in part his IRS employment background that gives him his sense of authority.
95 Wallace, *Pale King*, 229.
96 McGurl, "Institution of Nothing," 49.
97 McGurl, "Institution of Nothing," 49, 52.
98 McGurl, "Institution of Nothing," 50.
99 Wallace, *Pale King*, 234.
100 Wallace, *Pale King*, 235.
101 Daniel Worden, *Masculine Style: The American West and Literary Modernism* (New York: Palgrave Macmillan, 2011), 1.
102 Eve Kosofsky Sedgwick and Adam Frank, eds., *Shame and Its Sisters: A Silvan Tomkins Reader* (Durham, NC: Duke University Press, 1995), 5.
103 Worden, *Masculine Style*, 10; Blake Allmendinger, *The Cowboy: Representations of Labor in an American Work Culture* (New York: Oxford University Press, 1992), 5.
104 Wallace, *Pale King*, 149.
105 Wallace, *Pale King*, 150.
106 Wallace, *Supposedly Fun Thing*, 81.

107 Boswell, ed., *Long Thing*, 216–17.
108 Wallace, *Pale King*, 235; emphasis added.
109 Allmendinger, *Cowboy*, 8.
110 Allmendinger, *Cowboy*, 9.
111 Allmendinger, *Cowboy*, 6.
112 Wallace, *Pale King*, 106.
113 Allmendinger, *Cowboy*, 6; Wallace, *Pale King*, 106.
114 Wallace, *Pale King*, 461; emphasis added.
115 McRobbie, *Be Creative*, 76.
116 McRobbie, *Be Creative*, 14.
117 McRobbie, *Be Creative*, 71.
118 McRobbie, *Be Creative*, 67.
119 Wallace, *Pale King*, 547.
120 Boswell, ed., *Long Thing*, 218.
121 Stephen Shapiro, "From Capitalist to Communist Abstraction: The Pale King's Cultural Fix," *Textual Practice* 28, no. 7 (2014): 1250; David Hering, "David and Dutch: Wallace, Reagan and the 1980s" (OzWallace, RMIT University, Melbourne, Australia, 2017); Connell, *Precarious Labour*, 93–144.
122 On the latter point, see Connell, *Precarious Labour*, 112: "the Reagan administration ... employed an anti-tax rhetoric while seeking to use the power of the state to produce and guarantee a market society."
123 Wendy Brown, "Booked #3: What Exactly Is Neoliberalism?" *Dissent Magazine*, April 2, 2015, https://www.dissentmagazine.org/blog/booked-3-what-exactly-is-neoliberalism-wendy-brown-undoing-the-demos.
124 Wendy Brown, *Undoing the Demos: Neoliberalism's Stealth Revolution* (New York: Zone Books, 2015), 9.
125 Wallace, *Pale King*, 116.
126 Bernes, *Age of Deindustrialization*, 1–2; Richard Godden and Michael Szalay, "The Bodies in the Bubble: David Foster Wallace's *The Pale King*," *Textual Practice* 28, no. 7 (2014): 1273–322.
127 McKenzie Wark, *General Intellects: Twenty-One Thinkers for the Twenty-First Century* (New York: Verso, 2017), 179; emphasis added.
128 See Paul Gilroy, *The Black Atlantic: Modernity and Double-Consciousness* (Cambridge, MA: Harvard University Press, 1993), 42.
129 McKenzie Wark, *A Hacker Manifesto* (Cambridge, MA: Harvard University Press, 2004), section 313.
130 Wark, *Hacker Manifesto*, section 205.
131 Wark, *Hacker Manifesto*, sections 083, 085. On the quasi-material status of information, see also Bernes, *Age of Deindustrialization*, 21: "The name for this partly materialized and partly dematerialized object is ... information. Information is a sign that behaves like matter, or is treated like one, as in the case of binary code, which maps exactly (rather than merely approximately, as in the case of the written mark) to the physical arrangement of transistors in a chip."
132 Wark, *General Intellects*, 241.
133 Bernes, *Age of Deindustrialization*, 19.
134 Bernes, *Age of Deindustrialization*, 23.
135 Bernes, *Age of Deindustrialization*, 21.

136 Bernes, *Age of Deindustrialization*, 23.
137 Bernes, *Age of Deindustrialization*, 9, 16.
138 Bernes, *Age of Deindustrialization*, 17; Luc Boltanski and Ève Chiapello, *The New Spirit of Capitalism*, trans. Gregory Elliott (London: Verso, 2005).
139 Bernes, *Age of Deindustrialization*, 17.
140 Bernes, *Age of Deindustrialization*, 19.
141 Ngai, *Our Aesthetic Categories*, 156.
142 Ngai, *Our Aesthetic Categories*, 1.
143 Ngai, *Our Aesthetic Categories*, 146.
144 Bernes, *Age of Deindustrialization*, 30.
145 Marc Redfield, *Theory at Yale: The Strange Case of Deconstruction in America* (New York: Fordham University Press, 2016), 6; Moten, *In the Break*, 90.
146 Stuart Hall, "Gramsci's Relevance for the Study of Race and Ethnicity," *Journal of Communication Inquiry* 10, no. 2 (1986): 6.
147 J. Jack Halberstam, *The Queer Art of Failure* (Durham, NC: Duke University Press, 2011), 16.
148 McKenzie Wark, "Preoccupying: McKenzie Wark," *The Occupied Times*, August 2, 2012, https://theoccupiedtimes.org/?p=6451; Halberstam, *Queer Art of Failure*, 16.
149 Halberstam, *Queer Art of Failure*, 16, 21.
150 Halberstam, *Queer Art of Failure*, 19; Wark, *General Intellects*, 219.
151 Sara Ahmed, *Living a Feminist Life* (Durham, NC: Duke University Press, 2017), 8.
152 Wark, *General Intellects*, 144, 142.
153 Wark, *General Intellects*, 142.
154 Adam Phillips, *Darwin's Worms: On Life Stories and Death Stories* (New York: Basic Books, 2000), 74.
155 Wark, *General Intellects*, 144.
156 Michael Hardt and Antonio Negri, *Multitude: War and Democracy in the Age of Empire* (New York: Penguin, 2005), 107.
157 Hardt and Negri, *Multitude*, 106.
158 Preciado, *Testo Junkie*, 40.
159 Wark, *Hacker Manifesto*; *Gamer Theory* (Cambridge, MA: Harvard University Press, 2007); see also *General Intellects*, 116.
160 Wallace, *Pale King*, viii.
161 Wallace, *Pale King*, 69.
162 Wallace, *Pale King*, vii, 69; Boswell, ed., *Long Thing*, 185; Severs, *Balancing Books*, 199. See also Bewes, "Recent Experiments."

Conclusion

1 For a discussion of the way that a notion of sovereign authorship persists in the work of anti-authorial high theorists, see Burke, *Death and Return*. For more on low theory as a collective rather than an individualist project, see Wark, *General Intellects*, 219–20.
2 Smith, *NW*, 3.
3 Stefano Harney and Fred Moten, *The Undercommons: Fugitive Planning & Black Study* (Wivenhoe, UK: Minor Compositions, 2013), 110.

4 Harney and Moten, *Undercommons*, 112.
5 Harney and Moten, *Undercommons*, 109.
6 Heti, *How Should a Person Be*, 17.
7 Harney and Moten, *Undercommons*, 112.
8 Robin D. G. Kelley, *Freedom Dreams: The Black Radical Imagination* (Boston, MA: Beacon Press, 2002), 9. Study therefore has a deeply critical and revolutionary orientation. This is perhaps especially visible in the Black Studies tradition of Kelley, Moten, and Robinson. In a widely quoted passage, Robinson describes Black Studies as follows: "Black Studies is revolutionary in its political and historical origins and intellectual impulses. To paraphrase C.L.R. James, who insisted that Black Studies was the study of Western Civilization, Black Studies is a critique of Western Civilization"; see Cedric Robinson and Chuck Morse, "Capitalism, Marxism, and the Black Radical Tradition: An Interview with Cedric Robinson," *Perspectives on Anarchist Theory* 3, no. 1 (1999): 1, 6–8. Note how Robinson paraphrases "study" as "critique." Moten, however, insists that study cannot be entirely reduced to critique; see Harney and Moten, *Undercommons*, 120–1.
9 Ahmed, *Living a Feminist Life*, 10.
10 Ahmed, *Living a Feminist Life*, 10. See also Hartman, *Lose Your Mother*, 7; Sharpe, *In the Wake*, 8.
11 Ahmed, *Living a Feminist Life*, 11; emphasis added.
12 Ahmed, *Living a Feminist Life*, 10, 11.
13 Harney and Moten, *Undercommons*, 110.
14 Moten, *In the Break*, xi–xii. One of the scholars whose work Moten acknowledges here is Nahum Chandler. Chandler's work in *X—The Problem of the Negro as a Problem for Thought* (2014) is especially relevant here for the argument it makes that W. E. B. Du Bois ought to be understood as a theorist; see Nahum Dimitri Chandler, *X—The Problem of the Negro as a Problem for Thought* (New York: Fordham University Press, 2014), 81, 133–4. Chandler also makes a similar claim with regard to Moten's own work, in *In the Break* and in his poetry collection *B Jenkins*: "I would propose to recognize the work of Fred Moten as fully and equally generative as both poetry and theory, not only poetical theory (as if could ever be only that), but of such capaciousness that it is now also theoretical poetry"; Chandler, *X*, 247n10.
15 For an analysis of academic acknowledgments sections as a form of queer family-making, see Branden Buehler and Roxanne Samer, "Queer Acknowledgments," in *Mapping Queer* Space(s) *of Praxis and Pedagogy*, ed. Elizabeth McNeil, James E. Wermers, and Joshua O. Lunn (Cham, Switzerland: Palgrave Macmillan, 2017), 21–38.
16 Nelson, *Argonauts*, 57–8, 105.
17 Zambreno, *Heroines*, 14. Zambreno quotes Hélène Cixous in "Coming to Writing": "I found my counterparts in poetry (there were some), I entered into alliances with my paper soulmates, I had brothers, equivalents, substitutes"; see Hélène Cixous, *"Coming to Writing" and Other Essays*, ed. Deborah Jenson, trans. Sarah Cornell et al. (Cambridge, MA: Harvard University Press, 1991), 29.
18 Harney and Moten, *Undercommons*, 11.
19 Wark, *General Intellects*, 220.

20 Kraus, *I Love Dick*, 181.
21 Robin D. G. Kelley, "Black Study, Black Struggle," *Boston Review*, March 7, 2016, http://bostonreview.net/forum/robin-d-g-kelley-black-study-black-struggle.
22 Harney and Moten, *Undercommons*, 110.
23 Alastair Minnis, *Medieval Theory of Authorship: Scholastic Literary Attitudes in the Later Middle Ages*, Second Edition (Philadelphia: University of Pennsylvania Press, 2010); Rachel Sagner Buurma, "Anonymity, Corporate Authority, and the Archive: The Production of Authorship in Late-Victorian England," *Victorian Studies* 50, no. 1 (2007): 15–42; Jo-Ann (Q'um Q'um Xiiem) Archibald, *Indigenous Storywork: Educating the Heart, Mind, Body, and Spirit* (Vancouver: UBC Press, 2008).

BIBLIOGRAPHY

Ahmed, Sara. "Against Students." *The New Inquiry*, June 29, 2015. http://thenewinquiry.com/essays/against-students/.

Ahmed, Sara. *Differences That Matter: Feminist Theory and Postmodernism*. Cambridge: Cambridge University Press, 1998.

Ahmed, Sara. *Living a Feminist Life*. Durham, NC: Duke University Press, 2017.

Ahmed, Sara. *Willful Subjects*. Durham, NC: Duke University Press, 2014.

Allmendinger, Blake. *The Cowboy: Representations of Labor in an American Work Culture*. New York: Oxford University Press, 1992.

Althusser, Louis. *Lenin and Philosophy and Other Essays*. Translated by Ben Brewster. New York: Monthly Review Press, 2001.

Altman, Janet Gurkin. *Epistolarity: Approaches to a Form*. Columbus, OH: Ohio State University Press, 1982.

Alworth, David J. "Melville in the Asylum: Literature, Sociology, Reading." *American Literary History* 26, no. 2 (2014): 234–61. https://doi.org/10.1093/alh/aju019.

Aravamudan, Srinivas. "In the Wake of the Novel: The Oriental Tale as National Allegory." *Novel* 33, no. 1 (1999): 5–31. https://doi.org/10.2307/1346025.

Archibald, Jo-Ann (Q'um Q'um Xiiem). *Indigenous Storywork: Educating the Heart, Mind, Body, and Spirit*. Vancouver: UBC Press, 2008.

Arnett, James. "Neoliberalism and False Consciousness before and after Brexit in Zadie Smith's NW." *The Explicator* 76, no. 1 (2018): 1–7. https://doi.org/10.1080/00144940.2017.1416329.

Asad, Talal, Wendy Brown, Judith Butler, and Saba Mahmood. *Is Critique Secular? Blasphemy, Injury, and Free Speech*. New York: Fordham University Press, 2013.

Barthes, Roland. *A Barthes Reader*. Edited by Susan Sontag. New York: Hill and Wang, 1982.

Barthes, Roland. *A Lover's Discourse: Fragments*. Translated by Richard Howard. New York: Hill and Wang, 2010.

Barthes, Roland. *Camera Lucida: Reflections on Photography*. Translated by Richard Howard. New York: Hill and Wang, 2010.

Barthes, Roland. *Comment Vivre Ensemble: Simulations Romanesques de Quelques Espaces Quotidiens: Notes de Cours et de Séminaires Au Collège de France, 1976–1977*. Edited by Claude Coste. Paris: Éditions du Seuil, 2002.

Barthes, Roland. "Compte Rendu Du Voyage En Chine." In *Le Lexique de l'auteur: Séminaire à l'Ecole Pratique Des Hautes Études, 1973–1974*, edited by Anne Herschberg Pierrot, 227–45. Paris: Seuil, 2010.

Barthes, Roland. *Empire of Signs*. Translated by Richard Howard. London: Jonathan Cape, 1982.

Barthes, Roland. *The Grain of the Voice: Interviews 1962–1980*. Translated by Linda Coverdale. Evanston, IL: Northwestern University Press, 2009.

Barthes, Roland. *How to Live Together: Novelistic Simulations of Some Everyday Spaces: Notes for a Lecture Course and Seminar at the Collège de France (1976–1977)*. Edited

by Claude Coste. Translated by Kate Briggs. New York: Columbia University Press, 2013.
Barthes, Roland. *Image Music Text*. Translated by Stephen Heath. London: Fontana Press, 1977.
Barthes, Roland. *Le Discours Amoureux: Séminaire à l'École Pratique Des Hautes Études 1974–1976, Suivi de Fragments d'un Discours Amoureux (Pages Inédites)*. Edited by Claude Coste. Paris: Éditions du Seuil, 2007.
Barthes, Roland. "Lecture in Inauguration of the Chair of Literary Semiology, Collège de France, January 7, 1977." Translated by Richard Howard. *October* 8 (1979): 3–16.
Barthes, Roland. *Mourning Diary*. Translated by Richard Howard. New York: Hill and Wang, 2010.
Barthes, Roland. *Mythologies: The Complete Edition, in a New Translation*. Translated by Annette Lavers and Richard Howard. New York: Hill and Wang, 2012.
Barthes, Roland. *The Neutral: Lecture Course at the Collège de France (1977–1978)*. Edited by Thomas Clerc and Éric Marty. Translated by Rosalind E. Krauss and Denis Hollier. New York: Columbia University Press, 2005.
Barthes, Roland. *The Pleasure of the Text*. Translated by Richard Miller. New York: Hill and Wang, 1975.
Barthes, Roland. *The Preparation of the Novel: Lecture Courses and Seminars at the Collège de France (1978–1979 and 1979–1980)*. Edited by Nathalie Léger. Translated by Kate Briggs. New York: Columbia University Press, 2011.
Barthes, Roland. *Œuvres Complètes*. Edited by Éric Marty. Vol. IV: 1972–1976. Paris: Éditions du Seuil, 2002.
Barthes, Roland. *Œuvres Complètes*. Edited by Éric Marty. Vol. V: 1977–1980. Paris: Éditions du Seuil, 2002.
Barthes, Roland. *Roland Barthes by Roland Barthes*. Translated by Richard Howard. New York: Hill and Wang, 2010.
Barthes, Roland. *The Rustle of Language*. Translated by Richard Howard. Oxford: Basil Blackwell, 1986.
Barthes, Roland. *Sade, Fourier, Loyola*. Translated by Richard Miller. New York: Hill and Wang, 1976.
Barthes, Roland. *"The 'Scandal' of Marxism" and Other Writings on Politics*. Translated by Chris Turner. London: Seagull Books, 2015.
Barthes, Roland. *S/Z*. Translated by Richard Miller. New York: Hill and Wang, 1974.
Barthes, Roland. *Travels in China*. Edited by Anne Herschberg Pierrot. Translated by Andrew Brown. Cambridge: Polity Press, 2012.
Barton, David, and Nigel Hall. *Letter Writing as a Social Practice*. Philadelphia: John Benjamin, 1999.
Beer, Gillian. "The Reader as Author." *Authorship* 3, no. 1 (2014): 1–9.
Benjamin, Walter. *The Arcades Project*. Edited by Rolf Tiedemann. Translated by Howard Eiland and Kevin McLaughlin. Cambridge, MA: Belknap Press, 2002.
Benjamin, Walter. *Illuminations*. Edited by Hannah Arendt. Translated by Harry Zohn. New York: Schocken Books, 1968.
Bennett, Andrew. *The Author*. London: Routledge, 2005.
Bentley, Nick, Nick Hubble, and Leigh Wilson, eds. *The 2000s: A Decade of Contemporary British Fiction*. London: Bloomsbury Academic, 2015.
Berlant, Lauren. *Cruel Optimism*. Durham, NC: Duke University Press, 2011.

Bernes, Jasper. *The Work of Art in the Age of Deindustrialization*. Stanford, CA: Stanford University Press, 2017.
Best, Stephen, and Sharon Marcus. "Surface Reading: An Introduction." *Representations*, no. 108 (2009): 1–21.
Bewes, Timothy. "Reading with the Grain: A New World in Literary Criticism." *Differences* 21, no. 3 (January 1, 2010): 1–33. https://doi.org/10.1215/10407391-2010-007.
Bewes, Timothy. "Recent Experiments in American Fiction." *Novel: A Forum on Fiction* 50, no. 3 (2017): 351–9. https://doi.org/10.1215/00295132-4194936.
Binkiewicz, Donna M. *Federalizing the Muse United States Arts Policy and the National Endowment for the Arts, 1965–1980*. Chapel Hill: University of North Carolina Press, 2004.
Bjørnerud, Andreas. "Outing Barthes: Barthes and the Quest(Ion) of (a Gay) Identity Politics." *New Formations*, no. 18 (1992): 122–41.
Blanchfield, Brian. *Proxies: Essays Near Knowing*. New York: Nightboat Books, 2016.
Boltanski, Luc, and Ève Chiapello. *The New Spirit of Capitalism*. Translated by Gregory Elliott. London: Verso, 2005.
Bosteels, Bruno. "Politics, Infrapolitics, and the Impolitical: Notes on the Thought of Roberto Esposito and Alberto Moreiras." *CR: The New Centennial Review* 10, no. 2 (2011): 205–38. https://doi.org/10.1353/ncr.2010.0027.
Boswell, Marshall, ed. *David Foster Wallace and "The Long Thing": New Essays on the Novels*. New York: Bloomsbury Academic, 2014.
Boswell, Marshall, ed. *Understanding David Foster Wallace*. Columbia: University of South Carolina Press, 2003. http://www.loc.gov/catdir/toc/ecip047/2003016596.html.
Brand, Dionne. *A Map to the Door of No Return: Notes to Belonging*. Toronto: Vintage Canada, 2001.
Breton, André. *Mad Love*. Translated by Mary Ann Caws. Lincoln: University of Nebraska Press, 1987.
Brown, Wendy. "Booked #3: What Exactly Is Neoliberalism?" *Dissent Magazine*, April 2, 2015. https://www.dissentmagazine.org/blog/booked-3-what-exactly-is-neoliberalism-wendy-brown-undoing-the-demos.
Brown, Wendy. *Undoing the Demos: Neoliberalism's Stealth Revolution*. New York: Zone Books, 2015.
Buehler, Branden, and Roxanne Samer. "Queer Acknowledgments." In *Mapping Queer Space(s) of Praxis and Pedagogy*, edited by Elizabeth McNeil, James E. Wermers, and Joshua O. Lunn, 21–38. Cham, Switzerland: Palgrave Macmillan, 2017.
Burke, Seán, ed. *Authorship: From Plato to the Postmodern: A Reader*. Edinburgh: Edinburgh University Press, 1995.
Burke, Seán, ed. *The Death and Return of the Author: Criticism and Subjectivity in Barthes, Foucault and Derrida*. 3rd ed. Edinburgh: Edinburgh University Press, 2008.
Burn, Stephen J. *Jonathan Franzen at the End of Postmodernism*. London: Bloomsbury Academic, 2008.
Butler, Judith. *Excitable Speech: A Politics of the Performative*. New York: Routledge, 1997.
Butler, Judith. *Frames of War: When Is Life Grievable?* London: Verso, 2009.

Butler, Judith. *Gender Trouble: Feminism and the Subversion of Identity*. New York: Routledge Classics, 2006.
Butler, Judith. *Notes toward a Performative Theory of Assembly*. Cambridge, MA: Harvard University Press, 2015.
Butler, Judith. "'Philosophy Has Become Worldly': Marx on Ruthless Critique." *PMLA* 131, no. 2 (2016): 460–8. https://doi.org/10.1632/pmla.2016.131.2.460.
Butler, Judith. *Precarious Life: The Powers of Mourning and Violence*. London: Verso, 2004.
Butler, Judith. *The Psychic Life of Power: Theories in Subjection*. Stanford, CA: Stanford University Press, 1997.
Butler, Judith. *Senses of the Subject*. New York: Fordham University Press, 2015.
Butler, Judith, and Athena Athanasiou. *Dispossession: The Performative in the Political*. Cambridge: Polity Press, 2013.
Butler, Judith, Jurgen Habermas, Charles Taylor, and Cornel West. *The Power of Religion in the Public Sphere*. New York: Columbia University Press, 2011.
Buurma, Rachel Sagner. "Anonymity, Corporate Authority, and the Archive: The Production of Authorship in Late-Victorian England." *Victorian Studies* 50, no. 1 (2007): 15–42.
Buurma, Rachel Sagner, and Laura Heffernan. "Notation after 'The Reality Effect': Remaking Reference with Roland Barthes and Sheila Heti." *Representations* 125, no. 1 (2014): 80–102.
Caldwell, Chloe. "Author Maggie Nelson on Fielding Nosy Questions about Queer Families: 'You Have to Be Tough and Foxy.'" *Salon*, May 8, 2015. http://www.salon.com/2015/05/08/author_maggie_nelson_on_fielding_nosy_questions_about_queer_families_you_have_to_be_tough_and_foxy%e2%80%9d/.
Chandler, Nahum Dimitri. *X—The Problem of the Negro as a Problem for Thought*. New York: Fordham University Press, 2014.
Childs, Peter, and James Green. *Aesthetics and Ethics in Twenty-First Century British Novels: Zadie Smith, Nadeem Aslam, Hari Kunzru and David Mitchell*. London: Bloomsbury Academic, 2013.
Christian, Barbara. "The Race for Theory." *Cultural Critique*, no. 6 (1987): 51–63. https://doi.org/10.2307/1354255.
Cixous, Hélène. *"Coming to Writing" and Other Essays*. Edited by Deborah Jenson. Translated by Sarah Cornell, Deborah Jenson, Ann Liddle, and Susan Sellers. Cambridge, MA: Harvard University Press, 1991.
Clayton, Jay, and Eric Rothstein, eds. *Influence and Intertextuality in Literary History*. Madison: University of Wisconsin Press, 1991.
Coates, Ta-Nehisi. *Between the World and Me*. New York: Spiegel & Grau, 2015.
Cohen, Margaret. *The Sentimental Education of the Novel*. Princeton, NJ: Princeton University Press, 1999.
Cole, Teju. *Every Day Is for the Thief*. New York: Random House, 2014.
Cole, Teju. *Known and Strange Things: Essays*. New York: Random House, 2016.
Cole, Teju. *Open City*. New York: Random House, 2011.
Cole, Teju. "Teju Cole—Open City (Excerpt)." *Genius*. Accessed August 17, 2016. http://genius.com/Teju-cole-open-city-excerpt-annotated.
Collins, Katie. "The Morbidity of Maternity: Radical Receptivity in Maggie Nelson's The Argonauts." *Criticism* 6, no. 3 (2019): 311–34. https://doi.org/10.13110/criticism.61.3.0311.

Connell, Liam. *Precarious Labour and the Contemporary Novel*. Cham, Switzerland: Palgrave Macmillan, 2017.

Cooper, Lydia R. *Masculinities in Literature of the American West*. New York: Palgrave Macmillan, 2017.

Cooper, Sam. "The Unreturnable Situationist International: Berfrois Interviews McKenzie Wark." *Berfrois*, September 2, 2011. http://www.berfrois.com/2011/09/berfrois-interviews-mckenzie-wark/.

Culler, Jonathan. "Preparing the Novel: Spiraling Back." *Paragraph* 31, no. 1 (2008): 109–20.

Dames, Nicholas. "The New Fiction of Solitude." *The Atlantic*, April 2016. https://www.theatlantic.com/magazine/archive/2016/04/the-new-fiction-of-solitude/471474/.

Dames, Nicholas. "The Theory Generation." *n+1*, Summer 2012.

Davis, Colin. *After Poststructuralism: Reading, Stories, Theory*. London: Routledge, 2004.

De Villiers, Nicholas. "A Great Pedagogy of Nuance: Roland Barthes's The Neutral." *Theory & Event* 8, no. 4 (2005).

De Villiers, Nicholas. *Opacity and the Closet: Queer Tactics in Foucault, Barthes, and Warhol*. Minneapolis: University of Minnesota Press, 2012.

Dean, Michelle. "Listening to Women." *Slate*, June 29, 2012. http://www.slate.com/articles/arts/books/2012/06/sheila_heti_s_how_should_a_person_be_reviewed_.html.

Deb, Sopan. "Trump Proposes Eliminating the Arts and Humanities Endowments." *The New York Times*, March 15, 2017. https://www.nytimes.com/2017/03/15/arts/nea-neh-endowments-trump.html.

Decker, William Merrill. *Epistolary Practices: Letter Writing in America before Telecommunications*. Chapel Hill: University of North Carolina Press, 1998.

Defoe, Daniel. *Robinson Crusoe*. Edited by Thomas Keymer. Oxford: Oxford University Press, 2007.

Deleuze, Gilles, and Claire Parnet. *Dialogues II*. Translated by Hugh Tomlinson and Barbara Habberjam. New York: Columbia University Press, 2007.

Derrida, Jacques. *The Post Card: From Socrates to Freud and Beyond*. Translated by Alan Bass. Chicago: University of Chicago Press, 1987.

Derrida, Jacques. *Specters of Marx: The State of the Debt, the Work of Mourning and the New International*. Translated by Peggy Kamuf. New York: Routledge, 1994.

Dick, Alexander, and Christina Lupton. "On Lecturing and Being Beautiful: Zadie Smith, Elaine Scarry, and the Liberal Aesthetic." *ESC: English Studies in Canada* 39, no. 2 (2013): 115–37. https://doi.org/10.1353/esc.2013.0032.

Donoghue, Denis. *Speaking of Beauty*. New Haven, CT: Yale University Press, 2003.

Driscoll, Lawrence. *Evading Class in Contemporary British Literature*. New York: Palgrave Macmillan, 2009.

DuBois, Andrew. *Ashbery's Forms of Attention*. Tuscaloosa: The University of Alabama Press, 2006.

Eagleton, Terry. *After Theory*. London: Penguin, 2004.

Edelman, Lee. *No Future: Queer Theory and the Death Drive*. Durham, NC: Duke University Press, 2004.

Eggers, Dave. *A Heartbreaking Work of Staggering Genius*. New York: Simon & Schuster, 2000.

Eggers, Dave. *What Is the What: The Autobiography of Valentino Achak Deng*. San Francisco: McSweeney's, 2006.

Eggers, Dave. *Zeitoun*. San Francisco: McSweeney's, 2009.
Eliot, T. S. "Tradition and the Individual Talent." In *The Sacred Wood: Essays on Poetry and Criticism*, 42–53. London: Methuen, 1920.
Elliott, Jane. "The Return of the Referent in Recent North American Fiction: Neoliberalism and Narratives of Extreme Oppression." *Novel: A Forum on Fiction* 42, no. 2 (2009): 349–54. https://doi.org/10.1215/00295132-2009-026.
Elliott, Jane, and Derek Attridge, eds. *Theory after "Theory."* London: Routledge, 2011.
Engelmann, Paul. *Letters from Ludwig Wittgenstein with a Memoir*. Edited by B. F. McGuinness. Translated by L. Furtmüller. Oxford: Basil Blackwell, 1967.
Esposito, Roberto. *Categories of the Impolitical*. Translated by Connal Parsley. New York: Fordham University Press, 2015.
Felman, Shoshana. *The Scandal of the Speaking Body: Don Juan with J.L. Austin, or Seduction in Two Languages*. Stanford, CA: Stanford University Press, 1983.
Felski, Rita. *The Limits of Critique*. Chicago: University of Chicago Press, 2015.
Felski, Rita. *Literature after Feminism*. Chicago: University of Chicago Press, 2003.
Fenwick, Christopher. "How Should a Person Be?" *The Point Magazine*, April 7, 2014. https://thepointmag.com/2014/criticism/how-should-a-person-be.
Fisher, Anna Watkins. "Manic Impositions: The Parasitical Art of Chris Kraus and Sophie Calle." *WSQ: Women's Studies Quarterly* 40, no. 1 (2012): 223–35. https://doi.org/10.1353/wsq.2012.0029.
Fitzgerald, F. Scott. *The Great Gatsby*. Edited by Ruth Prigozy. Oxford: Oxford University Press, 1998.
Forster, E. M. *Howards End*. New York: Penguin Classics, 2000.
Foucault, Michel. *The Birth of Biopolitics: Lectures at the Collège de France, 1978–1979*. Edited by Michel Senellart. Translated by Graham Burchell. Palgrave Macmillan, n.d.
Foucault, Michel. "What Is an Author?" In *The Foucault Reader*, edited by Paul Rabinow, translated by Josué V. Harari, 101–20. New York: Vintage Books, 2010.
Freeman, Elizabeth. *Time Binds: Queer Temporalities, Queer Histories*. Durham, NC: Duke University Press, 2010.
Freud, Sigmund. *Beyond the Pleasure Principle*. Translated by James Strachey. New York: W. W. Norton, 1961.
Frimer, Denise. "Chris Kraus in Conversation with Denise Frimer." *The Brooklyn Rail*, April 10, 2006. http://brooklynrail.org/2006/04/art/chris-kraus-in-conversation-with-denise-frimer.
Funk, Wolfgang. *The Literature of Reconstruction: Authentic Fiction in the New Millennium*. London: Bloomsbury Academic, 2015.
Gallop, Jane. *The Deaths of the Author: Reading and Writing in Time*. Durham, NC: Duke University Press, 2004.
Gang, Joshua. "'No Symbols Where None Intended.'" *PMLA* 130, no. 3 (2015): 679–83. https://doi.org/10.1632/pmla.2015.130.3.679.
Gilroy, Paul. *The Black Atlantic: Modernity and Double-Consciousness*. Cambridge, MA: Harvard University Press, 1993.
Godden, Richard, and Michael Szalay. "The Bodies in the Bubble: David Foster Wallace's The Pale King." *Textual Practice* 28, no. 7 (2014): 1273–1322.
Goldsmith, Elizabeth. *Writing the Female Voice: Essays on Epistolary Literature*. Boston, MA: Northeastern University Press, 1989.
Greenberg, Udi. "The Politics of the Walter Benjamin Industry." *Theory, Culture & Society* 25, no. 3 (2008): 53–70. https://doi.org/10.1177/0263276408090657.

Grossman, Vasily. *Life and Fate*. Translated by Robert Chandler. New York: New York Review of Books, 1985.
Guibert, Hervé. *Ghost Image*. Translated by Robert Bononno. Chicago: University of Chicago Press, 2014.
Guillory, John. *Cultural Capital: The Problem of Literary Canon Formation*. Chicago: University of Chicago Press, 1993.
Gupta, Akhil. *Red Tape: Bureaucracy, Structural Violence, and Poverty in India*. Durham, NC: Duke University Press, 2012.
Haggerty, George, ed. *Encyclopedia of Gay Histories and Cultures*. New York: Garland, 2000.
Halberstam, J. Jack. *The Queer Art of Failure*. Durham, NC: Duke University Press, 2011.
Hale, Dorothy J. "On Beauty as Beautiful? The Problem of Novelistic Aesthetics by Way of Zadie Smith." *Contemporary Literature* 53, no. 4 (2012): 814–44.
Hall, Stuart. "Gramsci's Relevance for the Study of Race and Ethnicity." *Journal of Communication Inquiry* 10, no. 2 (1986): 5–27.
Halley, Janet, and Andrew Parker, eds. *After Sex? On Writing since Queer Theory*. Durham, NC: Duke University Press, 2011.
Harbach, Chad, ed. *MFA vs NYC: The Two Cultures of American Fiction*. New York: n+1/Faber and Faber, 2014.
Hardt, Michael, and Antonio Negri. *Multitude: War and Democracy in the Age of Empire*. New York: Penguin, 2005.
Harney, Stefano, and Fred Moten. *The Undercommons: Fugitive Planning & Black Study*. Wivenhoe, UK: Minor Compositions, 2013.
Hartman, Saidiya. *Lose Your Mother: A Journey along the Atlantic Slave Route*. New York: Farrar, Straus and Giroux, 2007.
Hayes-Brady, Clare. *The Unspeakable Failures of David Foster Wallace: Language, Identity, and Resistance*. New York: Bloomsbury Academic, 2017.
Hering, David. "David and Dutch: Wallace, Reagan and the 1980s." RMIT University, Melbourne, Australia, 2017.
Hering, David. *David Foster Wallace: Fiction and Form*. New York: Bloomsbury Academic, 2016.
Hering, David. "Thinking about David Foster Wallace, Misogyny and Scholarship." *Bloomsbury Literary Studies Blog*, February 19, 2018. http://bloomsburyliterarystudiesblog.com/continuum-literary-studie/2018/02/thinking-david-foster-wallace-misogyny-scholarship.html.
Heti, Sheila. *How Should a Person Be?* Toronto: House of Anansi Press, 2012.
Heti, Sheila. "Interview with Chris Kraus." *The Believer*, September 1, 2013. http://www.believermag.com/issues/201309/?read=interview_kraus.
Hirsch, E. D., Jr. *Validity in Interpretation*. New Haven, CT: Yale University Press, 1967.
Hix, H. L. *Morte d'Author: An Autopsy*. The Arts and Their Philosophies. Philadelphia, PA: Temple University Press, 1990.
Holland, Mary K. *Succeeding Postmodernism: Language and Humanism in Contemporary American Literature*. New York: Bloomsbury Academic, 2013.
Hooks, Bell. *Talking Back: Thinking Feminist, Thinking Black*. Boston, MA: South End Press, 1989.
Houser, Tammy Amiel. "Zadie Smith's NW: Unsettling the Promise of Empathy." *Contemporary Literature* 58, no. 1 (2017): 116–48.

Howard, Rebecca Moore. "Foreword." In *Authorship Contested: Cultural Challenges to the Authentic, Autonomous Author*, edited by Amy E. Robillard and Ron Fortune, ix–xii. New York: Routledge, 2016.

Huehls, Mitchum. *After Critique: Twenty-First-Century Fiction in a Neoliberal Age*. New York: Oxford University Press, 2016.

Huehls, Mitchum. "The Post-Theory Theory Novel." *Contemporary Literature* 56, no. 2 (2015): 280–310. https://doi.org/10.3368/cl.56.2.280.

Hungerford, Amy. *Making Literature Now*. Stanford, CA: Stanford University Press, 2016.

Hungerford, Amy. "On Not Reading." *The Chronicle of Higher Education*, September 11, 2016. https://www.chronicle.com/article/On-Refusing-to-Read/237717.

Intra, Giovanni. "A Fusion of Gossip and Theory." *artnet*, November 13, 1997. http://www.artnet.com/magazine_pre2000/index/intra/intra11-13-97.asp.

Irigaray, Luce. *To Be Two*. Translated by Monique M. Rhodes and Marco F. Cocito-Monoc. New York: Routledge, 2001.

Jameson, Fredric. *Postmodernism, or, the Cultural Logic of Late Capitalism*. London: Verso, 1991.

Jardine, Lisa. *Still Harping on Daughters: Women and Drama in the Age of Shakespeare*. Brighton, UK: The Harvester Press, 1983.

Johnson, Barbara. *The Barbara Johnson Reader: The Surprise of Otherness*. Edited by Melissa Feuerstein, Bill Johnson González, Lili Porten, and Keja Valens. Durham, NC: Duke University Press, 2014.

Johnson, Barbara. *The Wake of Deconstruction*. Oxford: Blackwell, 1994.

Jolly, Margaretta. *In Love and Struggle*. New York: Columbia University Press, 2008.

Joughin, John J., and Simon Malpas, eds. *The New Aestheticism*. Manchester: Manchester University Press, 2003.

Kamuf, Peggy. "Replacing Feminist Criticism." *Diacritics* 12, no. 2 (1982): 42–7. https://doi.org/10.2307/464678.

Kauffman, Linda S. *Special Delivery: Epistolary Modes in Modern Fiction*. Chicago: University of Chicago Press, 1992.

Kelley, Robin D. G. "Black Study, Black Struggle." *Boston Review*, March 7, 2016. http://bostonreview.net/forum/robin-d-g-kelley-black-study-black-struggle.

Kelley, Robin D. G. *Freedom Dreams: The Black Radical Imagination*. Boston, MA: Beacon Press, 2002.

Kelly, Adam. *American Fiction in Transition: Observer-Hero Narrative, the 1990s, and Postmodernism*. New York: Bloomsbury Academic, 2013.

Kelly, Adam. "David Foster Wallace: The Death of the Author and the Birth of a Discipline." *Irish Journal of American Studies*, no. 2 (2010): 47–59.

Kermode, Frank. "Here She Is." *London Review of Books*, October 6, 2005.

Kervick, Mollie Ann. "Embracing Maternal Eroticism: Queer Experiences of Pleasure in Maggie Nelson's The Argonauts." *Feminist Encounters: A Journal of Critical Studies in Culture and Politics* 3, no. 1–2 (2019): 1–10. https://doi.org/10.20897/femenc/5914.

Kitaj, R. B. *The Autumn of Central Paris (After Walter Benjamin)*. 73 1972. Oil on canvas. Collection of Mrs. Susan Lloyd, New York.

Knapp, Steven, and Walter Benn Michaels. "Against Theory." *Critical Inquiry* 8, no. 4 (1982): 723–42.

Knight, Diana. *Barthes and Utopia: Space, Travel, Writing*. Oxford: Clarendon Press, 1997.
Knight, Diana., ed. *Critical Essays on Roland Barthes*. New York: G. K. Hall, 2000.
Konstantinou, Lee. *Cool Characters: Irony and American Fiction*. Cambridge, MA: Harvard University Press, 2016.
Kornbluh, Anna. "We Have Never Been Critical: Toward the Novel as Critique." *Novel: A Forum on Fiction* 50, no. 3 (2017): 397–408. https://doi.org/10.1215/00295132-4195016.
Kraus, Chris. "Chris Kraus: 'I Love Dick Happened in Real Life, but It's Not a Memoir.'" *The Guardian*, May 17, 2016. http://www.theguardian.com/books/2016/may/17/chris-kraus-i-love-dick-happened-in-real-life-but-its-not-a-memoir.
Kraus, Chris. *I Love Dick*. Semiotext(e) Native Agents. Los Angeles: Semiotext(e), 2006.
Kraus, Chris. "The New Universal." *Sydney Review of Books*, October 17, 2014. http://sydneyreviewofbooks.com/new-universal/.
Kraus, Chris. "What Women Say to One Another: Sheila Heti's 'How Should a Person Be?'" *Los Angeles Review of Books*, June 18, 2012. https://lareviewofbooks.org/article/what-women-say-to-one-another-sheila-hetis-how-should-a-person-be/.
Krauss, Rosalind. "Notes on the Index: Seventies Art in America. Part 2." *October* 4 (1977): 58–67. https://doi.org/10.2307/778437.
Kushner, Tony. *Angels in America: A Gay Fantasia on National Themes*. New York: Theatre Communications Group, 2013.
Lacoue-Labarthe, Philippe, and Jean-Luc Nancy. *Retreating the Political*. Edited by Simon Sparks. London: Routledge, 1997.
Latour, Bruno. *Reassembling the Social: An Introduction to Actor-Network-Theory*. Clarendon Lectures in Management Studies. Oxford: Oxford University Press, 2005.
Latour, Bruno. *We Have Never Been Modern*. Translated by Catherine Porter. Cambridge, MA: Harvard University Press, 1993.
Latour, Bruno. "Why Has Critique Run out of Steam? From Matters of Fact to Matters of Concern." *Critical Inquiry* 30, no. 2 (2004): 225–48.
Lavers, Annette. *Roland Barthes: Structuralism and After*. Cambridge, MA: Harvard University Press, 1982.
Leca, Diana. "Roland Barthes and Literary Minimalism." *Barthes Studies* 1 (2015): 100–22.
Lerner, Ben. *Leaving the Atocha Station*. Minneapolis, MN: Coffee House Press, 2011.
Lerner, Ben. *10:04*. New York: Faber and Faber, 2014.
Lerner, Ben. *The Topeka School*. New York: Farrar, Straus and Giroux, 2019.
Levinas, Emmanuel. *Entre Nous: On Thinking-of-the-Other*. Translated by Michael B. Smith and Barbara Harshav. New York: Columbia University Press, 1998.
Lévi-Strauss, Claude. *Structural Anthropology*. Translated by Claire Jacobson and Brooke Grundfest Schoepf. New York: Basic Books, 1963.
Lewiton, Ariel. "Inflections Forever New." *Guernica*, March 16, 2015. https://www.guernicamag.com/interviews/inflections-forever-new/.
Longolius, Sonja. *Performing Authorship: Strategies of "Becoming an Author" in the Works of Paul Auster, Candice Breitz, Sophie Calle, and Jonathan Safran Foer*. Bielefeld, Germany: Transcript, 2016.

Lopez, Gemma. "After Theory: Academia and the Death of Aesthetic Relish In." *Critique: Studies in Contemporary Fiction* 51, no. 4 (2010): 350–65. https://doi.org/10.1080/00111610903380030.
Lorentzen, Christian. "Considering the Novel in the Age of Obama." *Vulture*, November 1, 2017. http://www.vulture.com/2017/01/considering-the-novel-in-the-age-of-obama.html.
Love, Heather. "Close but Not Deep: Literary Ethics and the Descriptive Turn." *New Literary History* 41, no. 2 (2010): 371–91. https://doi.org/10.1353/nlh.2010.0007.
Love, Heather. *Feeling Backward: Loss and the Politics of Queer History*. Cambridge, MA: Harvard University Press, 2009.
Lowe, Lisa. *Critical Terrains: French and British Orientalisms*. Ithaca, NY: Cornell University Press, 1991.
Luckyj, Christina. *"A Moving Rhetoricke": Gender and Silence in Early Modern England*. Manchester: Manchester University Press, 2002.
Ma, Ling. *Severance*. New York: Picador, 2018.
MacKinnon, Catharine A. *Only Words*. Cambridge, MA: Harvard University Press, 1993.
Marcus, David. "Post-Hysterics: Zadie Smith and the Fiction of Austerity." *Dissent* 60, no. 2 (2013): 67–73. https://doi.org/10.1353/dss.2013.0035.
Marcus, Sharon. *Between Women: Friendship, Desire, and Marriage in Victorian England*. Princeton, NJ: Princeton University Press, 2007.
Markson, David. *Wittgenstein's Mistress*. Chicago: Dalkey Archive Press, 1988.
Martin, Theodore. "Contemporary, Inc." *Representations* 142, no. 1 (2018): 124–44. https://doi.org/10.1525/rep.2018.142.1.124.
Max, D. T. *Every Love Story Is a Ghost Story: A Life of David Foster Wallace*. New York: Penguin, 2013.
McCaffery, Larry. "An Interview with David Foster Wallace." *Review of Contemporary Fiction* 13, no. 2 (1993): 127–50.
McGurl, Mark. "The Institution of Nothing: David Foster Wallace in the Program." *boundary 2* 41, no. 3 (2014): 27–54.
McGurl, Mark. *The Program Era: Postwar Fiction and the Rise of Creative Writing*. Cambridge, MA: Harvard University Press, 2009.
McLuhan, Marshall. *Media Research: Technology, Art and Communication*. Edited by Michel Moos. New York: Routledge, 2013.
McRobbie, Angela. *Be Creative: Making a Living in the New Culture Industries*. Cambridge: Polity Press, 2016.
Mengham, Rod, and Philip Tew, eds. *British Fiction Today*. London: Continuum, 2006.
Michaels, Walter Benn. *The Beauty of a Social Problem: Photography, Autonomy, Economy*. Chicago: University of Chicago Press, 2015.
Miller, D. A. *Bringing Out Roland Barthes*. Berkeley: University of California Press, 1992.
Miller, Nancy K. *Getting Personal: Feminist Occasions and Other Autobiographical Acts*. New York: Routledge, 1991.
Miller, Nancy K. *Subject to Change: Reading Feminist Writing*. New York: Columbia University Press, 1988.
Miller, Nancy K. "The Text's Heroine: A Feminist Critic and Her Fictions." *Diacritics* 12, no. 2 (1982): 48–53. https://doi.org/10.2307/464679.

Minh-Ha, Trinh T. "The Plural Void: Barthes and Asia." Translated by Stanley Gray. *SubStance* 11, no. 3 (1982): 41–50. https://doi.org/10.2307/3684313.
Minnis, Alastair. *Medieval Theory of Authorship: Scholastic Literary Attitudes in the Later Middle Ages*. Second Edition. Philadelphia: University of Pennsylvania Press, 2010.
Mitchell, Kaye. *Intention and Text: Towards an Intentionality of Literary Form*. London: Continuum, 2008.
Moi, Toril. "'I Am Not a Woman Writer': About Women, Literature and Feminist Theory Today." *Feminist Theory* 9, no. 3 (2008): 259–71. https://doi.org/10.1177/1464700108095850.
Moi, Toril. *Sexual/Textual Politics: Feminist Literary Theory*. London: Routledge, 1985.
Moretti, Franco. *Distant Reading*. London: Verso, 2013.
Moten, Fred. *In the Break: The Aesthetics of the Black Radical Tradition*. Minneapolis: University of Minnesota Press, 2003.
Muñoz, José Esteban. *Cruising Utopia: The Then and There of Queer Futurity*. New York: New York University Press, 2009.
Muth, Katie R. "Postmodern Fiction as Poststructuralist Theory: Kathy Acker's Blood and Guts in High School." *Narrative* 19, no. 1 (2011): 86–110. https://doi.org/10.1353/nar.2011.0000.
Nealon, Jeffrey T. *Post-Postmodernism: Or, the Cultural Logic of Just-in-Time Capitalism*. Stanford, CA: Stanford University Press, 2012.
Nealon, Jeffrey T. "Realisms Redux; or, against Affective Capitalism." In *Neoliberalism and Contemporary Literary Culture*, edited by Mitchum Huehls and Rachel Greenwald Smith, 70–85. Baltimore: Johns Hopkins University Press, 2017.
Nehamas, Alexander. *Only a Promise of Happiness: The Place of Beauty in a World of Art*. Princeton, NJ: Princeton University Press, 2007.
Nelson, Maggie. *The Argonauts*. Minneapolis, MN: Graywolf Press, 2015.
Nelson, Maggie. *The Art of Cruelty: A Reckoning*. New York: W. W. Norton, 2011.
Nelson, Maggie. *Bluets*. Seattle, WA: Wave Books, 2009.
Nelson, Maggie. "Bookforum Talks with Maggie Nelson." Interview by Sarah Nicole Prickett. *Bookforum*, May 29, 2015. http://www.bookforum.com/interview/14663.
Nelson, Maggie. "CS671: Wild Theory." CalArts School of Critical Studies Course Catalog, Fall 2013. https://catalog.calarts.edu/Documents/School%20of%20Critical%20Studies%20-%20Fall%202013.pdf.
Nelson, Maggie. "Riding the Blinds." Interview by Micah McCrary. *Los Angeles Review of Books*, April 26, 2015. https://lareviewofbooks.org/interview/riding-the-blinds/.
Nelson, Maggie. "Slipping the Surly Bonds of Earth: On Ben Lerner's Latest." *Los Angeles Review of Books*, August 24, 2014. https://lareviewofbooks.org/article/95063/.
Nelson, Maggie. *Women, the New York School, and Other True Abstractions*. Iowa City: University of Iowa Press, 2007.
Ngai, Sianne. "Merely Interesting." *Critical Inquiry* 34, no. 4 (2008): 777–817.
Ngai, Sianne. *Our Aesthetic Categories: Zany, Cute, Interesting*. Cambridge, MA: Harvard University Press, 2012.
Nordmann, Alfred. *Wittgenstein's Tractatus: An Introduction*. Cambridge: Cambridge University Press, 2005.
Nørretranders, Tor. *The User Illusion: Cutting Consciousness Down to Size*. Translated by Jonathan Sydenham. New York: Penguin, 1999.

Novick, Miriam Hannah. "Impostures: Subjectivity, Memory, and Untruth in the Contemporary Memoir." PhD dissertation, University of Toronto, 2015.
O'Meara, Lucy. *Roland Barthes at the Collège de France*. Liverpool: Liverpool University Press, 2012.
Pankratz, Anette. "'Nothing That Is Worth Knowing Can Be Taught': Artists and Academia in Novels by A.S. Byatt, David Lodge and Zadie Smith." In *Portraits of the Artists as a Young Thing in British, Irish and Canadian Fiction after 1945*, edited by Anette Pankratz and Barbara Puschmann-Nalenz, 259–81. Heidelberg, Germany: Universitätsverlag Winter, 2012.
Perloff, Marjorie. *Wittgenstein's Ladder: Poetic Language and the Strangeness of the Ordinary*. Chicago: University of Chicago Press, 1999.
Phillips, Adam. *Darwin's Worms: On Life Stories and Death Stories*. New York: Basic Books, 2000.
Phillips, Adam. *Missing Out: In Praise of the Unlived Life*. New York: Picador, 2012.
Phillips, Adam. *Terrors and Experts*. Cambridge, MA: Harvard University Press, 1995.
Phillips, Adam. *Winnicott*. London: Penguin, 2007.
Pieters, Jürgen, and Kris Pint. "Introduction: An Unexpected Return. Barthes Lecture Courses at the Collège de France." *Paragraph* 31, no. 1 (2008): 1–8.
Pint, Kris. *The Perverse Art of Reading: On the Phantasmatic Semiology in Roland Barthes' Cours Au Collège de France*. Translated by Christopher M. Gemerchak. Amsterdam: Rodopi, 2010.
Poletti, Anna. "The Anthropology of the Setup: A Conversation with Chris Kraus." *Contemporary Women's Writing* 10, no. 1 (2016): 123–35. https://doi.org/10.1093/cww/vpv030.
Potts, Jason, and Daniel Stout, eds. *Theory Aside*. Durham, NC: Duke University Press, 2014.
Preciado, Paul B. *Testo Junkie: Sex, Drugs, and Biopolitics in the Pharmacopornographic Era*. Translated by Bruce Benderson. New York: The Feminist Press, 2013.
Purdy, Jedediah. *After Nature: A Politics for the Anthropocene*. Cambridge, MA: Harvard University Press, 2015.
Purdy, Jedediah. "Maybe Connect." *The Los Angeles Review of Books*, October 4, 2015. https://lareviewofbooks.org/essay/maybe-connect/.
Quayson, Ato. *Postcolonialism: Theory, Practice or Process?* Cambridge: Polity Press, 2000.
Rancière, Jacques. *The Ignorant Schoolmaster: Five Lessons in Intellectual Emancipation*. Translated by Kristin Ross. Stanford, CA: Stanford University Press, 1991.
Redfield, Marc. *Theory at Yale: The Strange Case of Deconstruction in America*. New York: Fordham University Press, 2016.
Ricoeur, Paul. *Freud and Philosophy: An Essay on Interpretation*. Translated by Denis Savage. New Haven, CT: Yale University Press, 1970.
Robinson, Cedric, and Chuck Morse. "Capitalism, Marxism, and the Black Radical Tradition: An Interview with Cedric Robinson." *Perspectives on Anarchist Theory* 3, no. 1 (1999): 1, 6–8.
Rose, Mark. *Authors and Owners: The Invention of Copyright*. Cambridge, MA: Harvard University Press, 1993.
Ruti, Mari. "The Bad Habits of Critical Theory." *The Comparatist*, no. 40 (2016): 5–27.
Ruti, Mari. *Between Levinas and Lacan: Self, Other, Ethics*. New York: Bloomsbury Academic, 2015.

Ruti, Mari. *The Ethics of Opting Out: Queer Theory's Defiant Subjects*. New York: Columbia University Press, 2017.
Ruti, Mari. *Penis Envy and Other Bad Feelings: The Emotional Costs of Everyday Life*. New York: Columbia University Press, 2018.
Ryan, Judith. *The Novel after Theory*. New York: Columbia University Press, 2012.
Said, Edward W. *Culture and Imperialism*. New York: Vintage Books, 1993.
Salecl, Renata. *(Per)Versions of Love and Hate*. London: Verso, 1998.
Sarkonak, Ralph. *Angelic Echoes: Hervé Guibert and Company*. Toronto: University of Toronto Press, 2000.
Sayers, Philip. "Roland Barthes and the Urgency of Nuance." *Los Angeles Review of Books*, November 4, 2018. https://lareviewofbooks.org/article/roland-barthes-and-the-urgency-of-nuance/.
Sayers, Philip. "When Male Writers Confront Toxic Masculinity." *The Walrus*, January 23, 2020. https://thewalrus.ca/when-male-writers-confront-toxic-masculinity/.
Sayers, Philip. "Zadie Smith's and Judith Butler's Novelistic Inconsistencies." *Continental Thought & Theory* 2, no. 3 (2019): 108–33.
Scarry, Elaine. *On Beauty and Being Just*. Princeton, NJ: Princeton University Press, 1999.
Schmitt, Cannon. "Tidal Conrad (Literally)." *Victorian Studies* 55, no. 1 (2012): 7–29.
Schwarz, Henry, and Anne Balsamo. "Under the Sign of Semiotext(e): The Story According to Sylvere Lotringer and Chris Kraus." *Critique: Studies in Contemporary Fiction* 37, no. 3 (1996): 205–20. https://doi.org/10.1080/00111619.1996.9936493.
Sedgwick, Eve Kosofsky. *Touching Feeling: Affect, Pedagogy, Performativity*. Durham, NC: Duke University Press, 2003.
Sedgwick, Eve Kosofsky, and Adam Frank, eds. *Shame and Its Sisters: A Silvan Tomkins Reader*. Durham, NC: Duke University Press, 1995.
Segal, Ben. "The Fragment as a Unit of Prose Composition: An Introduction." *Continent* 1, no. 3 (2011): 158–70.
Sell, Jonathan P. A. "Experimental Ethics: Autonomy and Contingency in the Novels of Zadie Smith." In *The Ethical Component in Experimental British Fiction since the 1960's*, edited by Susan Onega and Jean-Michel Ganteau, 150–70. Newcastle, UK: Cambridge Scholars Publishing, 2007.
Sennett, Richard. *The Craftsman*. New Haven, CT: Yale University Press, 2008.
Severs, Jeffrey. *David Foster Wallace's Balancing Books: Fictions of Value*. New York: Columbia University Press, 2017.
Shakespeare, William. "The Tragedy of King Lear: The Folio Text." In *The Norton Shakespeare Based on the Oxford Edition*, edited by Stephen Greenblatt, Walter Cohen, Jean E. Howard, and Katherine Eisaman Maus, 2319–478. New York: W. W. Norton, 1997.
Shapiro, Stephen. "From Capitalist to Communist Abstraction: The Pale King's Cultural Fix." *Textual Practice* 28, no. 7 (2014): 1249–71.
Sharpe, Christina. *In the Wake: On Blackness and Being*. Durham, NC: Duke University Press, 2016.
Silverblatt, Michael. "Maggie Nelson: The Argonauts." KCRW's Bookworm, n.d.
Smith, Zadie. *Changing My Mind: Occasional Essays*. London: Penguin, 2009.
Smith, Zadie. *Feel Free: Essays*. New York: Hamish Hamilton, 2018.
Smith, Zadie. *NW*. Toronto: Penguin, 2012.

Smith, Zadie. *On Beauty*. Toronto: Penguin Canada, 2005.
Smith, Zadie. *White Teeth*. London: Hamish Hamilton, 2000.
Snediker, Michael D. *Queer Optimism: Lyric Personhood and Other Felicitous Persuasions*. Minneapolis: University of Minnesota Press, 2009.
Solnit, Rebecca. *Men Explain Things to Me*. Chicago: Haymarket Books, 2014.
Sontag, Susan. *Essays of the 1960s & 70s*. New York: The Library of America, 2013.
Staes, Toon. "Work in Process: A Genesis for The Pale King." *English Studies* 95, no. 1 (2014): 70–84.
Stafford, Andy. *Roland Barthes*. Critical Lives. London: Reaktion Books, 2015.
Stafford, Andy. "Roland Barthes's Travels in China: Writing a Diary of Dissidence Within Dissidence?" *Textual Practice* 30, no. 2 (2016): 287–304. http://dx.doi.org/10.1080/0950236X.2016.1129730.
Stanley, Liz. "The Epistolary Gift, the Editorial Third-Party, Counter-Epistolaria: Rethinking the Epistolarium." *Life Writing* 8, no. 2 (2011): 135–52.
Stein, Jordan Alexander. "Jordan Alexander Stein in Conversation with Jordy Rosenberg." *Social Text Online*, July 3, 2018. https://socialtextjournal.org/jordan-alexander-stein-in-conversation-with-jordy-rosenberg/.
Su, John. "Beauty and the Beastly Prime Minister." *ELH* 81, no. 3 (2014): 1083–110. https://doi.org/10.1353/elh.2014.0028.
Summers, Lawrence. "Speech: Address at Morning Prayers, 9/17/02." *Harvard.edu*, September 17, 2002. http://www.harvard.edu/president/speeches/summers_2002/morningprayers.php.
Teeuwen, Rudolphus. "'The Dream of a Minimal Sociality': Roland Barthes' Skeptic Intensity." *Theory, Culture & Society*. Special Section: Neutral Life: Reflections on Roland Barthes' Late Works (2016): 1–16. https://doi.org/10.1177/0263276416659695.
Tew, Philip, ed. *Reading Zadie Smith: The First Decade and Beyond*. London: Bloomsbury Academic, 2013.
Tew, Philip, ed. "Zadie Smith's On Beauty: Art and Transatlantic Antagonisms in the Anglo-American Academy." *Symbiosis* 15, no. 2 (2011): 219–36.
Tolan, Fiona. "Zadie Smith's Forsterian Ethics: White Teeth, The Autograph Man, On Beauty." *Critique: Studies in Contemporary Fiction* 54, no. 2 (2013): 135–46. https://doi.org/10.1080/00111619.2010.550340.
Tompkins, Jane. *West of Everything: The Inner Life of Westerns*. New York: Oxford University Press, 1993.
Vendler, Helen. *The Music of What Happens: Poems, Poets, Critics*. Cambridge, MA: Harvard University Press, 1988.
Wachtel, Eleanor. "25th Anniversary Panel Interview." *Writers & Company*. Toronto: CBC Radio, August 11, 2015.
Walker, Cheryl. "Feminist Literary Criticism and the Author." *Critical Inquiry* 16, no. 3 (1990): 551–71.
Wall, Kathleen. "Ethics, Knowledge, and the Need for Beauty: Zadie Smith's On Beauty and Ian McEwan's Saturday." *University of Toronto Quarterly* 77, no. 2 (2008): 757–88. https://doi.org/10.1353/utq.0.0281.
Wallace, David Foster, ed. *The Best American Essays 2007*. Boston, MA: Houghton Mifflin, 2007.
Wallace, David Foster. *The Broom of the System*. New York: Viking, 1987.

Wallace, David Foster. *Infinite Jest*. London: Abacus, 2009.
Wallace, David Foster. "Oblivion: Stories." Draft Materials. Harry Ransom Humanities Research Center, University of Texas at Austin, Boxes 3.5–3.6. Little, Brown and Company Collection of David Foster Wallace.
Wallace, David Foster. "The Pale King: An Unfinished Novel." Draft Materials. Harry Ransom Humanities Research Center, University of Texas at Austin, Boxes 26.1–26.8 and 36.1–41.9. David Foster Wallace Papers.
Wallace, David Foster. *The Pale King: An Unfinished Novel*. New York: Back Bay Books, 2012.
Wallace, David Foster. *A Supposedly Fun Thing I'll Never Do Again: Essays and Arguments*. New York: Back Bay Books, 1998.
Walsh, Joanna. "I Love Dick by Chris Kraus Review—a Cult Feminist Classic Makes Its UK Debut." *The Guardian*, November 11, 2015, sec. Books. https://www.theguardian.com/books/2015/nov/11/i-love-dick-chris-kraus-review.
Wark, McKenzie. *Gamer Theory*. Cambridge, MA: Harvard University Press, 2007.
Wark, McKenzie. *General Intellects: Twenty-One Thinkers for the Twenty-First Century*. New York: Verso, 2017.
Wark, McKenzie. *A Hacker Manifesto*. Cambridge, MA: Harvard University Press, 2004.
Wark, McKenzie. "I Love Dick." *Public Seminar*, August 25, 2016. http://www.publicseminar.org/2016/08/ild/.
Wark, McKenzie. "Preoccupying: McKenzie Wark." *The Occupied Times*, August 2, 2012. https://theoccupiedtimes.org/?p=6451.
White, Edmund. "From Albert Camus to Roland Barthes." *The New York Times*, December 9, 1982.
Widiss, Benjamin. *Obscure Invitations: The Persistence of the Author in Twentieth-Century American Literature*. Stanford, CA: Stanford University Press, 2011.
Wiegman, Robyn. "In the Margins with The Argonauts." *Angelaki* 23, no. 1 (2018): 209–13. https://doi.org/10.1080/0969725X.2018.1435403.
Wilson, Timothy D. *Strangers to Ourselves: Discovering the Adaptive Unconscious*. Cambridge, MA: Belknap Press, 2002.
Wimsatt, W. K., Jr., and Monroe C. Beardsley. "The Intentional Fallacy." In *The Verbal Icon: Studies in the Meaning of Poetry*, 3–20. Lexington: University of Kentucky Press, 1954.
Wittgenstein, Ludwig. "Tractatus Logico-Philosophicus." In *Major Works: Selected Philosophical Writings*, translated by C. K. Ogden, 1–83. New York: Harper Perennial, 2009.
Woodmansee, Martha. *The Author, Art, and the Market: Rereading the History of Aesthetics*. New York: Columbia University Press, 1994.
Worden, Daniel. *Masculine Style: The American West and Literary Modernism*. New York: Palgrave Macmillan, 2011.
Zambreno, Kate. *Heroines*. Los Angeles: Semiotext(e), 2012.
Zemer, Lior. *The Idea of Authorship in Copyright*. Abingdon, UK: Routledge, 2016.
Žižek, Slavoj. *The Parallax View*. Cambridge, MA: MIT Press, 2006.

INDEX

afterness 9–15, 163 n.59
agency 16–17, 76, 77–116, 117, 138–9, 153
   in Judith Butler 67, 71, 74
   in Zadie Smith 51, 55
Ahmed, Sara 149, 154–6
   critique of postmodernism 99, 108, 110–11, 187 n.191
   Willful Subjects 28, 68, 167 n.57
Althusser, Louis 26–7, 73, 167 n.51
autofiction 17, 79–80, 177 n.10
autotheory 15, 16, 23, 42, 148, 163 n.64.
   See also low theory; Nelson, Maggie; Preciado, Paul B.

Barthes, Roland. *See also* nuance
   Camera Lucida 7, 102, 178 n.19
   Collège de France 6, 7, 17, 82–3, 108, 111–16, 117, 153
   "The Death of the Author" 3–4, 6–7, 9, 11–16, 19–23, 33–4, 49–55, 57, 65, 78–81, 83, 94, 107–10, 114–16, 117–19, 122, 131, 153, 156, 188 n.14
   doxa 64, 75–6, 100, 116
   Empire of Signs 104
   fascism of language 26–9, 94
   gender 81–2, 92–3, 97–9, 107–11
   How to Live Together 7, 82–3, 93, 103, 105–6, 111, 115
   A Lover's Discourse 93, 102, 103
   Mythologies 55
   The Neutral 7, 27, 37, 76, 83, 102, 115, 178 n.17
   orientalism 104–5
   The Pleasure of the Text 7, 53, 98, 111
   The Preparation of the Novel 7, 51, 83, 108, 112, 114–16, 117–20, 131, 178 n.19
   Roland Barthes by Roland Barthes 43, 102, 113

S/Z 53, 93, 172 n.34
Sade Fourier Loyola 7, 108
sexuality 100–3, 181 n.81
"So, How Was China?" 99, 103–5
"What Is It to Hold Forth?" 17, 81–3, 92–8, 108, 113–14, *see also* holding forth
Benjamin, Walter 6, 76
   The Arcades Project 86–7, 120, 127
   in *I Love Dick* 82, 85–7, 89, 91, 94
   "Theses on the Philosophy of History" 10, 86
Bernes, Jasper 121–2, 145–8, 188 n.9, 189 n.50, 192 n.131
Black Studies 10, 154–55, 194 n.8.
   See also Moten, Fred; Sharpe, Christina
Breton, André 25–7, 45
Brown, Wendy 122, 145, 148, 150
Burke, Seán 49–50, 187 n.191
Butler, Judith 103, 111
   Excitable Speech 67, 70–6
   Frames of War 38
   Gender Trouble 67, 70–1
   Precarious Life 6, 17, 50, 64–8, 70–6, 153
   subjectivity 27, 50, 67–8, 117–18, 164 n.11

canonicity 61, 124
   critical theory 6, 8–9, 12–15, 84–7
   gender 65, 67, 78, 80, 90, 107–9, 178 n.12
capitalism 11–13, 126–7, 144–50, 161 n.33
Christian, Barbara 108, 115–16
Coetzee, J. M. 4, 8, 47
Cole, Teju 4, 47–9, 54, 129–32
communication 16, 19–45, 111–12, 113, 153

cowboys 18, 121, 135–43, 150
critique 51, 56–7, 60–4, 67–8, 84. *See also* postcritique

Dames, Nicholas 4–5, 159 n.22
de Villiers, Nicholas 102–3, 107–8, 181 n.81
deconstruction 4, 11, 14
Derrida, Jacques 10, 22, 41–2, 149
Dodge, Harry 20, 25, 41, 45, 99–100. *See also* Nelson, Maggie
Du Bois, W. E. B. 6, 194 n.14

Eggers, Dave 4, 181 n.66
Elliott, Jane 10, 11–12, 162 n.46
epistolarity 21–7

Felman, Shoshana 58–9
Felski, Rita 50, 61–2, 76, 109
feminism 17, 22, 50, 68, 97, 138. *See also* Ahmed, Sara; mansplaining
    female authorship 78–81, 87–8, 90–2
    personal criticism 23, 149, 155, 166 n.32
    poststructuralism 107–11
Forster, E. M. 55, 60–1, 68, 172 n.41
Foucault, Michel 6–7, 9, 71, 145–6, 149, 187 n.191
fragmentation 11
    David Foster Wallace 120, 131, 133
    Maggie Nelson 20, 42–4, 113
    Roland Barthes 37, 43, 113–15
Frankfurt School 11, 86, 120, 138. *See also* Benjamin, Walter
Freud, Sigmund 10, 41–2, 102, 117, 182 n.88
    hermeneutics of suspicion 50, 61, 67
    in *On Beauty* (Smith) 57–9, 60
    "useful fictions" (Phillips) 33–4, 150

Gallop, Jane 107–10
The Great Gatsby (Fitzgerald) 47–9
Guibert, Hervé 101–3, 104–5

Halberstam, Jack 155
Hartman, Saidiya 15, 155

Hering, David 120, 122–3, 125, 131–2, 144
Heti, Sheila 17, 112, 153
    How Should a Person Be? 79–82, 87–94, 111, 154
holding forth 17–18, 78–83, 111, 123, 138, 153. *See also* Barthes, Roland
    in *How Should a Person Be?* 88
    in *I Love Dick* 85–6
    Roland Barthes 92–8, 113–16
    in *10:04* 91–2
hooks, bell 68, 114, 149, 155
Huehls, Mitchum 4, 11–12
Hungerford, Amy 121, 123–5, 127, 156

information 120–2, 124–9, 132, 134–5, 139, 143–8, 192 n.131
intention 11, 15–17, 22, 34, 44–5, 47–76, 94, 111–12, 153
    "The Intentional Fallacy" (Wimsatt and Beardsley) 48–9, 55, 69
Irigaray, Luce 6, 16, 20, 108
    To Be Two 38–9

Jameson, Frederic 11, 50
Johnson, Barbara 14–15, 184 n.126

King Lear (Shakespeare) 27–9, 30, 41–2
Knight, Diana 99, 104–7, 108, 111
Koestenbaum, Wayne 41–2, 44, 103, 177 n.144
Kraus, Chris 54, 90, 153, 185 n.145
    I Love Dick 6, 17, 79–82, 83–7, 88–9, 93–4, 109–11, 155

labor 7, 9, 16, 18, 117–51, 153
Lacan, Jacques 11, 58–9, 89, 155, 173 n.59
Latour, Bruno 61, 124, 127, 156, 161 n.42, 189 n.36
Lerner, Ben 4, 123, 153
    Leaving the Atocha Station 88, 90, 169 n.116
    10:04 17, 79–82, 88, 90–5, 111, 126–7, 179 n.40

low theory 85, 87, 121–2, 148–51, 153–4. *See also* autotheory; Wark, McKenzie
Lowe, Lisa 99, 104–5, 107–8, 185 n.145

Ma, Ling 189 n.35
mansplaining 9, 77–9, 81, 92, 97, 183 n.108
Marx, Karl 10, 50, 51, 61, 67, 102, 150
Marxism 13, 50, 114, 120, 127, 148, 177 n.144
maternity 20, 28, 34, 44–5, 59, 155–6
McGurl, Mark 5, 134, 138, 156
McRobbie, Angela 137, 142, 156
Michaels, Walter Benn 50, 53–4, 57, 60, 171 n.19
Miller, D. A. 99, 101–5, 107–8
Miller, Nancy K. 23, 108–10, 165 n.18
minimalism 42, 113, 133, 190 n.70
Moten, Fred 10, 44, 149, 154–5, 194 n.8, 194 n.14

Nabokov, Vladimir 11, 19, 57. *See also* Smith, Zadie
Nealon, Jeffrey 11–12, 162 n.46, 162 n.48
neoliberalism 3, 8, 18, 54, 84, 121–22, 142–8, 150. *See also* Reagan, Ronald; Thatcher, Margaret
Nelson, Maggie 7, 15, 19, 54, 76, 91, 111. *See also* autotheory; Dodge, Harry
  The Argonauts 6, 16, 20, 23–33, 40–5, 81, 99–100, 103, 113, 148, 155–6, 163 n.59
  The Art of Cruelty 36–7, 40, 41
  Bluets 21–4, 43
  wild theory 6, 15, 23, 44
New Criticism 15, 49, 52
Ngai, Sianne 62, 121–2, 132–5, 145, 147–8, 190 n.66
Nietzsche, Friedrich 6, 50, 61, 67
nuance 17, 23, 52, 70, 71, 139
  Barthes, Roland 7, 76, 82, 100, 160 n.31

originality 4, 7–8, 16, 96

pedagogy 35, 51, 55–6, 88–90, 111–16, 154, 186 n.186
Phillips, Adam 16, 20, 40, 150
  Winnicott 33–4. *See also* Winnicott, Donald
Pietsch, Michael 120, 132–3, 136, 190 n.60
Plato 15, 24, 119
postcolonial studies 9–10, 62, 107, 161 n.42
  orientalism 81, 98, 104–7
postcritique 12, 50, 60–4. *See also* critique
postmodernism 10–13, 55, 61, 109, 140, 162 n.44, 162 n.48, 187 n.191. *See also* Smith, Zadie
poststructuralism 149
  anti-authorialism 3, 5, 12, 80–1, 107–8
  in *On Beauty* (Smith) 17, 56, 60, 69
Preciado, Paul B. 15, 23, 149–50, 155, 163 n.64. *See also* autotheory
psychoanalysis 7, 10, 13, 17, 50, 95, 182 n.88. *See also* Freud, Sigmund; Lacan, Jacques; Phillips, Adam; trauma
  in *On Beauty* (Smith) 57–60
  repetition compulsion 57, 95–6

queer theory 10, 13, 23, 50, 68, 103, 184 n.137

Reagan, Ronald 116, 140, 143–4
Ruti, Mari 51, 171 n.21
Ryan, Judith 4–5, 7, 8, 10

Scarry, Elaine 50–2, 61–2
Sedgwick, Eve 20, 139, 166 n.32
  "Paranoid Reading and Reparative Reading" 28–9
Sennett, Richard 137–8, 142
seriality 42, 121, 133–5
Severs, Jeffrey 128, 132, 145, 190 n.70
Sharpe, Christina 14–15, 155
silence 27–30, 63–4, 102, 129–30, 132, 134

Smith, Zadie 6, 18, 80, 111, 153
  On Beauty 4, 16–17, 50, 55–64, 68–70, 176 n.131
  Changing My Mind 75–6
  NW 1–3, 5, 8
  postmodernism 51, 52, 55, 60–1, 65, 161 n.33
  "Rereading Barthes and Nabokov" 19–20, 36, 39, 51, 52–6, 122
  "sole author" 1–3, 4, 5, 8, 14, 15, 154, 156, *see also* study
Solnit, Rebecca 17, 77–81, 85, 88–9, 91–6, 111
Sontag, Susan 61, 63
study (Moten and Harney) 154–6, 194 n.8

Thatcher, Margaret 2, 3, 8, 161 n.35
trauma 10, 15, 57–8

wake 13–16, 18, 82, 104, 107, 148, 154, 156, 163 n.59

Wallace, David Foster 11, 54, 168 n.92, 188 n.14
  "Deciderization 2007: A Special Report" 129–32
  "Greatly Exaggerated" 122, 131
  Infinite Jest 133, 135, 190 n.66
  The Pale King 6, 18, 119–22, 124–46, 148, 150–1, 153
  papers at Harry Ransom Center 18, 120, 123, 132, 134, 135, 156, 190 n.60
Wark, McKenzie 85–7, 121–2, 145–50, 153, 155. *See also* low theory
Widiss, Benjamin 4–5, 7, 8
Winnicott, Donald 16, 20, 30, 33, 41–2. *See also* Phillips, Adam
Wittgenstein, Ludwig 16, 19–21, 30–7, 39, 42–3, 168 n.92
  Letter to Paul Engelmann 30–2, 35
  Tractatus Logico-Philosophicus 30–5

Zambreno, Kate 90–1, 110, 155, 180 n.65

www.ingramcontent.com/pod-product-compliance
Lightning Source LLC
Chambersburg PA
CBHW072234290426
44111CB00012B/2089